JAPANESE CONSUMER BEHAVIOR
From Worker Bees to Wary Shoppers

ConsumAsiaN Book Series
edited by
Brian Moeran and Lise Skov
The Curzon Press and The University of Hawai'i Press

Women, Media and Consumption in Japan
Edited by Lise Skov and Brian Moeran
Published 1995

A Japanese Advertising Agency
An Anthropology of Media and Markets
Brian Moeran
Published 1996

Contemporary Japan and Popular Culture
Edited by John Whittier Treat
Published 1996

Packaged Japaneseness
Weddings, Business and Brides
Ofra Goldstein-Gidoni
Published 1997

Australia and Asia
Cultural Transactions
Edited by Maryanne Dever
Published 1997

Staging Hong Kong
Gender and Performance in Transition
Rozanna Lilley
Published 1998

Asian Department Stores
Edited by Kerrie L. MacPherson
Published 1998

Consuming Ethnicity and Nationalism
Edited by Kosaku Yoshino
Published 1999

The Commercialized Crafts of Thailand
Hill Tribes and Lowland Villages
Erik Cohen
Published 1999

Japanese Consumer Behavior
From Worker Bees To Wary Shoppers
John L. McCreery
Published 2000

JAPANESE CONSUMER BEHAVIOR

From Worker Bees to Wary Shoppers

An anthropologist reads research
by the Hakuhodo Institute of Life and Living

John L. McCreery

UNIVERSITY OF HAWAI'I PRESS
HONOLULU

© 2000 John L. McCreery

Published in North America by
University of Hawai'i Press
2840 Kolowalu Street
Honolulu, Hawai'i 96822

First published in the United Kingdom
by Curzon Press
Richmond, Surrey
England

Printed in Great Britain

Library of Congress Cataloging-in-Publication Data

McCreery, John Linwood, 1944-
    Japanese consumer behaviour : from worker bees to wary shoppers / John McCreery.
      p. cm. – (ConsumAsiaN book series)
    Includes bibliographical references and index.
    ISBN 0–8248–2315–X (cloth : alk. paper) – ISBN 0–8248–2316–8 (pbk. : alk. paper)
    1. Consumer behavior–Japan. I. Title.

HF5415.33.J3 M38 1999
381.3'0952'09045–dc21   99-049175

CONTENTS

ACKNOWLEDGEMENTS

This book is dedicated to the memories of three men: Victor Turner, Tio Se-lian, and Kimoto Kazuhiko.

The first was an anthropologist whose teaching is inscribed in the shape of this book. He taught me that an anthropologist works with three kinds of data, things observed (here the *Lifestyle Times*, the internal newsletter produced by the Hakuhodo Institute of Life and Living that provides much of this book's content), the native exegesis (represented here by the conversations with HILL researchers interleaved between the chapters), and the economic and demographic background that cultural analysis neglects at its peril.

The second was a Grand Master of Daoist Magic who allowed a fledgling fieldworker to become his disciple and, by trotting him the length and breadth of Taiwan, made it perfectly clear how much goes on in modern, urban Asian societies that escapes the boundaries of the villages and neighborhoods in which anthropologists usually work.

The third was a Senior Creative Director who hired a hapless scholar and turned him, with much labor, into a copywriter unable to tolerate stereotypes of the kind this book attacks.

Looking back what I see in all three is a willingness to listen, a passion for detail, a flair for the dramatic, and a breadth of humanity that transcends the places and moments in which we met. I am proud to call them my mentors and to try, however poorly, to follow their example.

No words can express the debt of gratitude I feel to my wife, business partner, and editor, Ruth South McCreery. Talk of unwavering support pales beside the reality of thirty years of shared trials and adventures.

To my daughter Kathryn McCreery I owe the inspiration to consider the military origins of the forms of organization characteristic of corporations.

Many others have been involved in bringing this book about. Onodera Kenji and Oyama Satoshi are Hakuhodo marketing planners. Their invitations to join them in presentations to multinational clients and to MBA tour groups visiting Hakuhodo were, in a very real sense, the starting point for the interests that led to my writing the book. It was Fujiwara Mariko who first remarked to me on one of these occasions that Japan's Greying Corporate Warriors had suffered a great deal but also had one thing that later generations of Japanese salarymen have lacked, the passionate commitment to overtaking the West that made their work deeply meaningful to them.

Mike Lieber at the University of Illinois Chicago Circle, Dave Jacobson at Brandeis University, James Ennis at Tufts University, and Peter Palij at the University of South Carolina all extended invitations to speak at their institutions that became opportunities to think more about the kinds of issues the book raises. Richard Katz, senior editor of *The Oriental Economist Report*, and Ken Okamura, a former student who is presently a financial strategist at Dresdner Kleinwort Benson, pointed me to the work of Nakamura Takafusa and Tsuru Shigeto on Japanese economic history and were always ready to answer a non-economist's questions about economic issues. James Farrer of Sophia University made several useful suggestions concerning the way that the book is structured.

It hardly needs saying that the book owes much to the generous support of Lise Skov and Brian Moeran, the editors of the ConsumAsian Series.

But most of all, my deepest thanks must go to Sekizawa Hidehiko, the director of HILL, and to all the members of the HILL team whose research provides most of its content: Hayashi Hikaru, Hiraku Kazutoshi, Masuko Miki, Nanbu Tetsuhiro, Ogisako Ichirō, Ōta Masakazu, Satō Keiko, Shimamoto Tatsushi, Shindō Kazuma, Yamada Mariko, and Yamamoto Takayo. Readers should be aware that the work covered here only scratches the surface of a very large and constantly growing body of research that deserves the closest attention.

Finally, very special thanks must go to Kobayashi Yoshiko, Director of Hakuhodo CAPCO, Incorporated, and to Shōji Takashi, President and Chief Executive Officer, Hakuhodo Incorporated, who were both among the founders of HILL and who graciously agreed to be interviewed for this book.

BIOGRAPHICAL NOTE

John McCreery is an anthropologist who has lived and worked in Japan since 1980. For thirteen of those years, he worked as a copywriter and creative director for Hakuhodo Incorporated, Japan's second largest advertising agency. In 1984, he and his wife and business partner Ruth McCreery founded The Word Works, a supplier of translation, copywriting and presentation services. While earning his living as vice-president and managing director of The Word Works, McCreery is also a lecturer in the Graduate Program in Comparative Culture at Sophia University in Tokyo. There he teaches seminars on 'The Making and Meaning of Advertising' and 'Marketing in Japan'. When asked, 'How did an anthropologist get into advertising?' he replies, 'In Taiwan I studied magicians. In Japan I joined the guild'.

INTRODUCTION

An argument erupts. The subject is Japan.

On one side are those who are firmly convinced that they know the essential Japan, a vertical society of group-oriented people whose lives are closely regulated. As pre-school children, they enjoy a bit of indulgence. That, it turns out, is a snare, a way to encourage dependence on mother. Once school begins, the discipline is overt. Now each day begins in quasi-military formation, lined up to hear the principal's morning exhortation. In junior and senior high school, the military image stiffens. Mandatory uniforms recall Prussian originals; seniority is rigidly enforced. Strong us-versus-them attitudes promote close identification with the unit – class or club – to which the student belongs.

School is training in ferocious competition, preparation for examinations that determine which young Japanese will go on to better schools and jobs and which will fall by the wayside. To survive the 'examination hell' requires exhausting labor and immense feats of memorization. In contrast, universities provide a few short years of relaxation. Then, however, their graduates go on to jobs in factories and offices, employed by companies as neatly ranked as the schools from which they hire. A chosen few, the *crème de la crème*, will join the government ministries that administer the whole system. At all levels of corporate and political life, the identity that matters most is the group. For the sake of the company or ministry, or the section or group within it, men – and the women who choose, where they can, to pursue traditionally male careers – will work long, exhausting hours that leave little time for family or for friendship outside the workplace.

In this stereotype, the great divide is gender. For males, a meaningful life is lifetime employment. For most females – career women are exceptions – full-time employment is only a brief transition to marriage, family, and housework, with the option of part-time work outside the home to add to household income. With husbands commuting long distances to work and rarely returning until late at night, women are largely responsible for such community life as there is. In their role as 'education mamas', women's primary task, however, is seducing and pressuring new generations to work hard at school. It is they whose duty it is to indoctrinate their children with the docile, hardworking conformity that first the school and then 'the Japanese system' as a whole require. Thus, it is said, the essential Japan reproduces itself.

Opposed to this view are those like myself who cannot help asking the question, who, precisely, are we talking about when we talk about 'the Japanese'? Put aside differences in region, class and occupation. Attend, for a moment, only to the men who dominate the Kafkaesque image sketched above. One can still want to know, 'Are we talking about the corporate warriors who rebuilt postwar Japan, who directly experienced war, defeat, and poverty and were literally zealous in their efforts to catch up with and overcome the West? Are we talking about Baby Boomers, whose sheer numbers made them a glut on the labor market, encouraging self-effacement as a strategy for securing lifetime employment and the means to support an American-style, Ozzie and Harriet family? Are we talking about the New Breed, a smaller demographic cohort in a booming economy, for whom job-hopping was a realistic possibility and the sheer euphoria of Japan's apparent invincibility in world markets an encouragement to extravagant expectations? What about the Boomers' children, the Boomer Juniors? Or teens with dyed and ratted hair, a ring in one ear and a cellular phone in the other? Can we safely ignore the fact that while all these generations have grown up in a place called Japan, each has come (or is coming) of age in a radically different world?

We have only considered the men. What of the lives of the women who are, in demographic fact, the majority of Japan's population; 64 million vs. 61 million in 1996? The much-heralded 'Era of Women' has not yet brought equality in the male-dominated realms of work and politics (Fujimura-Fanselow 1995:xix). There is no denying, however, that rapid economic growth has transformed Japanese women into the world's most visible and highly regarded consumers.

As Skov and Moeran (1995) note, their faces and bodies are everywhere, held up in a glare of media attention that may leave us wondering what goes on behind those glossy images. Many now stay unmarried or marry late and have fewer children, a fact of ominous significance to those who fear the aging of Japan and the shrinking of the younger generations who will have to care for the burgeoning elderly. As untraditional mothers, they may, critics fear, undermine the vertical society's deepest foundations.

But these, too, are stereotypes. Complicating our models of Japanese society with generation and gender makes them more concrete. Still, however, we want to know more; whether marketers, scholars or journalists, what we need are details. It is only when our models are grounded in details and sufficiently rich to comprehend them that, instead of substituting simplistic understandings for complex realities, we are able instead to capture reality's complexities with a clarity equal to that which simplistic understandings seem to offer (Geertz 1973:33).

There is no end to this quest. One place to make some progress, however, is the work of native experts, who, because of their deep involvement in advertising and marketing, are constantly searching for what is changing in Japanese society.

In Search of the Japanese Consumer

This book explores changes in Japanese consumer behavior in the 1980s and 1990s as seen through the eyes of Japanese researchers, who are, as it were, guerrilla ethnographers. Their lightning raids into the nooks and crannies of their own culture show us what is going on, through Japanese eyes. In this book I will focus both on what they see and on how they see it: both on the changes in consumer behavior that catch their attention and the structures of thought and feeling that shape their interpretations.

A thesis implicit in the book is that marketers and anthropologists have much to say to each other. One inspiration is Mark Zimmerman, a former president of the American Chamber of Commerce in Japan, who writes,

> When I first arrived in Japan, like many other businessmen, I thought of culture as a mere cultivation of aesthetic sensibilities, and of sociology and anthropology as abstruse academic specialties of limited practical application.

> (Zimmerman 1985:4)

He changed his mind when he found himself in need of deeper understandings than his everyday interactions with Japanese businessmen provided. There is something to be said, it seems, for escaping the blinders that any particular job imposes and thinking about what is written by those privileged to explore widely and study whatever they wish.

Another inspiration is anthropologist John Sherry, who argues from the other side of the marketer-academic divide that to understand the world in which we live scholars should devote more attention to contemporary cultures of consumption (Sherry 1995). Sherry's motivation is to get beyond the culture-bound assumptions of the conventional social-psychological models used by market researchers.

Consumerism has also been of central concern in cultural studies, where its impact on self and society is much debated. (See, for example, for the case of Japan, Miyoshi and Harootunian 1989; Tobin 1992; Skov and Moeran 1995; Treat 1996; Clammer 1997.)

By far the most important inspiration, however, for putting together this book is the work of the researchers at HILL, the Hakuhodo Institute of Life and Living, whose studies provide the bulk of its content. Theirs are the eyes that have noticed what is going on in Japan. Theirs are the minds that have framed the understandings that the author attempts to interpret for his readers. Theirs are the voices that, within the limits of translation, allow us to listen in as they write for other Japanese about what they have seen and studied. As we listen to their voices and observe the images that accompany their words, we not only learn a good deal about contemporary Japan. We are also given the opportunity to explore the motivations that direct their attention to certain topics and to analyze the verbal and visual means by which they give form to what they discover.

First, however, the background: Why is it that we have this opportunity? And what am I going to do with it?

The Anthropologist Enters the Field

Through a long series of accidents of a type all too familiar to those who know the vagaries of the academic job market, the author, an anthropologist, came to Japan in 1980. I came tagging along after my wife, a student of modern Japanese literature. In 1983, I found a job as a copywriter at Hakuhodo Incorporated. Founded in 1895, Hakuhodo is Japan's second largest advertising agency. Second in size, in Japan, only to arch-rival Dentsu, it is one of the world's largest advertising agencies.

For the 13 years I worked for Hakuhodo, first as a writer of English-language advertising and then as an International Creative Director, I, like other Hakuhodo employees, found on my desk every few weeks the latest issue of the *Lifestyle Times* (*Seikatsu Shimbun*). That publication is the internal newsletter in which HILL gives agency staff a first look at the latest results of its research.

HILL was created by Hakuhodo in 1981 to serve as the agency's 'antenna'. It would be in effect an early warning system, alerting the agency and its clients to changes in Japanese society and culture as these affect the everyday lives of Japanese consumers. Hakuhodo promotional literature points to HILL research as a source of unique insights that add a special edge to the agency's marketing, creative and media strategies. The creation of HILL, whose research transcends the limitations of marketing studies devoted to particular brands, products or campaigns, is a point of pride for the agency. It represents a commitment to advertising and marketing based on a deep understanding of how Japanese consumers think, feel and act.

But What Strange Form of Knowledge Is This?

HILL produces several types of publications. To foreigners working in Japan, the institute is, perhaps, best known for a series of large-scale topical studies that have focused on particular market segments and, while published in Japanese, have also appeared in summary form in English. It also publishes the *Lifestyle Annual* (*Seikatsu Teiten*), an omnibus study of Japanese consumer attitudes, conducted once every two years since 1986.

In contrast to the major topical studies and the omnibus panel research reported in the *Lifestyle Annual*, the bulk of the research reported in the *Lifestyle Times* is composed of the smaller studies I have labeled guerrilla ethnography. Something seen in the street or on TV, in the popular press or in scholarly works, catches a HILL researcher's eye. A study is put together to examine the phenomenon. A few months later the results are reported in the *Lifestyle Times*. It is here that we find HILL's antenna function operating in its purest form. It is here, too, that we find a form of reporting research that, at first glance, seems to violate established academic conventions.

Visually, the *Lifestyle Times* is the very antithesis of the academic journals in which scholarly research is published. The academic journal imposes a uniform style. In typeface and layout each issue looks precisely like all of the others in the same series. Its form displays the accumulation of knowledge as the piling up of facts and logic. The tone is cool and distant; the passive voice predominates. The style is designed to demonstrate the scholarly researcher's objectivity.

Each issue of the *Lifestyle Times* is individually designed. Typeface, layout, the form of illustrations, and other conventions are all subject to radical change from one issue to the next. Where the academic journal accumulates knowledge, the *Lifestyle Times* delivers stimulation. Both images and language are playful and often frankly emotional. Like the advertising agency that sponsors its production, this form of 'being in the know' thrives on novelty. It speaks to the needs, not of a world in which facts and logic are scarce, but instead of a world in which information is superabundant and inspiration in short supply.

Where the academic journal seeks to capture and fix the forms of knowledge, the *Lifestyle Times* belongs to a world where 'meaning flows' (McCracken 1990), where marketers are more like surfers catching waves than engineers building dikes. In its playfulness with design and language, this in-house agency newsletter anticipates that most postmodern of media, the Internet Web page.

And Then, One Day

While talking with Sekizawa Hidehiko, the Director of HILL, I remarked that the research produced by the agency's marketing divisions is like boiled rice. It is solid and nutritious, but it needs spicing up. In presentations to multinational clients, I had often found the *Lifestyle Times* a useful source of *furikake*, the spicy toppings which, sprinkled on boiled rice, turn it into a tasty meal. 'You know', I said, 'HILL research is interesting; someone should write a book about it'.

'You', Sekizawa said, 'will write it'. There was the opportunity, but with it came the question, what kind of book to write?

To reduce the results reported in the *Lifestyle Times* to academic prose would not only remove the unique flavour of HILL's presentation. It would, at the same time, destroy the most interesting data of all, the visible forms of thought and feeling recast and reconfigured with each new issue published. How, then, to write a book that would, as far as possible, preserve the *Lifestyle Times*' playfulness, while at the same time exposing the anxieties that motivate HILL research? How to do both and remain true to the voices of the HILL researchers as they struggle to articulate their interpretations of what is going on in a culture driven by consumerism to seek constant change?

The answer I offer here is a book with multiple layers. The core is translations from a series of studies reported in the *Lifestyle Times*. Since 1981, when HILL was founded, it has published, on average, 15 issues of the *Lifestyle Times* per year. The issues from which material has been translated are, says Sekizawa, among the most interesting. We began with a set that he had selected. A few were then added to fill out the material on issues related to women. Some of the original set were removed because of space limitations, based on a joint decision that while they were, indeed, interesting, their topics diverged from those which emerged as central to the book. In reading the material presented here, the reader should bear in mind that it is only a sample of a body of work that already numbers nearly 300 individual studies.

The translations are divided into chapters that focus on themes that lie at the heart of HILL research and are also central to debates about what is going on in Japan. Each chapter ends with one or more conversations with HILL researchers. In these conversations, we discuss the theme of the chapter and what has been going on in Japan since the research translated was done.

The wrapping that surrounds both core and conversation is the anthropologist's reflections on what he has read and heard. Unlike Japanese packaging, which, it is said, can be more important than the substance it conceals (Hendry 1993), this layer is intended to complement – and by no means replace – the material it surrounds. It is deliberately one voice among many, speaking in counterpoint to the voices of HILL researchers. There are also other voices, those of subjects involved in HILL studies, who are often quoted verbatim in *Lifestyle Times* reports.

The result is not, in any sense, a definitive treatise on Japanese consumer behavior. HILL now has competitors. In 1987, Hakuhodo's arch-rival Dentsu founded the Dentsu Institute of Human Studies. ('It does not', says Sekizawa, 'do the same sorts of research as HILL'.) Surveys conducted by government agencies, newspapers, and magazines address topics similar to those examined by HILL researchers. There is also a specialized trade press that caters to the needs of advertisers and employees of the agencies that develop their marketing strategies and create their advertising.

Japanese consumer behavior also accounts for much of the news in TV and radio broadcasts, newspapers and magazines offered for public consumption. There are magazines entirely devoted to the latest trends in products, fads, and fashions. Given the superabundance of information readily available in Japanese sources, any claim to provide a definitive picture of what Japanese consumers are doing must be taken with a large pinch of salt.

How Have Japanese Consumers Changed?

In the studies translated and discussed in this book, readers will find a history of Japanese consumer behavior in the 1980s and 1990s, as Japan's Baby Boomers matured, married, had children, pursued careers, and then looked forward to retirement in the world's most rapidly aging society. These were also years in which women entered the work force in increasing numbers, and the growing prominence of women, both as consumers and in public life, led husbands and pundits as well as feminist theorists to reassess gender and the nature of family relationships.

During the 1980s, and especially the late 1980s, the years of the Bubble Economy, when, for a brief moment, it seemed that Japan was indeed No. 1, the New Breed (*shinjinrui*) came of age. Fewer in number than the Baby Boomers, they would find themselves in high demand by employers, able to change jobs and demand time off to pursue an active social life outside their companies. They would marry late or not at all. Producing fewer children, they would help to accelerate the aging of Japan's population. Their lavish spending habits made Japanese consumers seem spendthrifts, willing to pay absurd prices for globally famous brands. Their lifestyles seemed to some scholars to herald Japan's transformation into a fully postmodern, radically consumerist society.

The New Breed would be followed in the nineties by the children of the Baby Boomers, the Baby Boomer Juniors – Japan's Generation X. The largest generation since the Boomers themselves, the Boomer Juniors would enter an economy dampened by the Bubble's collapse. Watching their fathers' dreams of successful corporate careers shattered by corporate restructurings, they would lower their own expectations. Then, as this generation came of age and began to enter the workforce, a new generation of teens appeared. Described as cool and dry, avoiding the intrusive commitments of 'wet' (close and warm) relationships, they worry critics who fear both their small numbers (who will take care of the elderly and pay for their retirement? And provide new workers for Japanese industry?) and their attitudes (they lack the dreams and drive that made Japan an economic superpower! Their schooling, has stunted the creativity the nation now needs to excel in the global information economy!).

How Do HILL Researchers Think and Feel About These Changes?

What first attracted my attention to the *Lifestyle Times* was the playfulness of its language and layout, which seemed so flagrantly different from academic conventions. My initial impression was of having found a new, postmodern form of knowledge akin to the Web page. There is much to be said for this view, but several important points need making.

First, the playfulness that caught my attention is deeply rooted in Japanese culture. When reading the *Lifestyle Times*, I am constantly reminded of traditional forms of Japanese comedy, of *rakugo* and *manzai*, and the wordplay and banter of their modern successors in TV talk and variety shows.

It would be unfair, however, to see in the *Lifestyle Times* only the playful manipulation of language and imagery. HILL research is no mere pastiche in which seriousness of intent and deep feeling are missing. Wherever surveys are reported, there are careful descriptions of the research designs, samples, and methodologies used. Those searching for scholarly apparatus will find what they are looking for. Feeling is expressed in language that is often strongly emotional, and the imagery used to illustrate arguments frequently carries a strong punch.

Beneath the formal playfulness which first catches the eye, there are deep and anxiety-provoking questions. What is the meaning of a salaryman's life? How should men and women behave? What is happening to Japanese families? What will become of the children? What will become of Japan? How are we being manipulated? How can we make choices in an increasingly confusing world? Where, if at all, can we find relief from life's pressures, from feeling constantly pushed and squeezed by society's demands? The excitement and interest of reading the *Lifestyle Times* derives in large part from seeing how HILL researchers address concerns shared throughout the developed world.

A Note on Reading and Romanization

Chapters 2 through 8 are divided into three sections: An introduction written by myself provides some of the background information that HILL researchers can assume that Japanese readers bring to the *Lifestyle Times*. It also includes material taken from other Japanese sources or scholarly studies by Japanologists that point to issues raised by HILL's research. The bulk of these chapters is composed of the translations from the *Lifestyle Times*. Since, however, the visual imagery used in the *Lifestyle Times* is an integral part of its message and provides an opportunity to see how HILL researchers visualize the people whose lives they are talking about, each translation is preceded by 'The Art', a brief discussion of the cover art and, sometimes, the illustrations that appeared inside the issue in question. Also, where available, the type of research, dates, locations and sample sizes are summarized in 'The Research Design'. The final section of each chapter is composed of the interviews with HILL researchers mentioned above. Additional interviews appear at the end of the introductory and final chapters.

Japanese terms are in modified Hepburn romanization with macrons indicating double vowels, except for place names where standard conventions omit them. Tokyo, for example, is 'Tokyo', not 'Tōkyō.

Interview with Sekizawa Hidehiko, Director of HILL
February 1998

JLM: Why was HILL founded?

SH: HILL was founded in 1981. Hakuhodo felt a need to collect information by putting itself in the consumer's shoes. Historically speaking, advertising agencies started out as media brokers. In Japan, they acted as intermediaries selling space in, for example, the *Asahi* newspaper. They would act on behalf of the media and take a margin for providing this service. Later, they introduced the account executive system. Agencies then started to work on behalf of advertisers, helping to plan their marketing strategies. It was then that they began to be called advertising companies (*kōkoku kaisha*) instead of agencies (*kōkoku dairiten*). Hakuhodo was among the first to introduce this system.

JLM: When was that?

SH: It was during the 1960s that the idea that advertising companies should act on behalf of advertisers as well as the media took off. But theoretically speaking, there was also the possibility that agencies could represent consumers as well. Our problem was that agency clients already had lots of information about their customers. If an agency used the same methods and only collected similar kinds of information, the agency's role as a marketing partner would be too weak. We thought that we might be able to say that the agency brings the consumers' perspective to its clients. That was the reason we created HILL.

Hakuhodo's marketing divisions continue to act on behalf of clients, but HILL has a different position, speaking on behalf of consumers. Thus, for example, if consumers don't like the way a company is doing things, we can say that. In this respect our position is totally different from that of the marketing divisions. We can also present views that contradict the data that clients are constantly collecting through their POS (point of sale) systems.

That isn't, however, the only reason that HILL was founded. We don't look at consumers as just 'people who consume' *(shōhisha)*. We look at them as 'people with lives' *(seikatsusha)*. We see them, in other words, as people whose lives include far more than just consumption.

Look at it this way. Toyota, Nissan, Honda, Mazda ... they all produce cars; they all see consumers as people who buy cars. But cars are not the only thing that people care about. Suppose you have 500,000 yen. You could use it as a down payment on a car. You could also use it to buy a fur coat or to take a trip overseas. Products don't always compete with other products in the same category. They also compete with products in other categories. That is why marketers have to look beyond the purchase of particular products and see the consumer's life as a whole. We have to recognize that, besides being consumers, people are also voters, citizens, fathers, and mothers. Their lives include moments when they aren't thinking of buying anything. Our basic concept is that you first need to think about all that and only then think about your product.

JLM: Has HILL achieved its goals?

SH: Our goal is to see consumers from a different perspective than that of the agency's marketing divisions. In this respect we have been successful. HILL reports and the results of our surveys are often picked up and reported in the mass media.

We have been a success, I think, in increasing Hakuhodo's visibility. Consider our competitive situation. In Japan, Hakuhodo competes with Dentsu. Our share of media billings has risen steadily, but, still, we are only in second place. There is, however, no limit on how much press coverage we can get. From this perspective, HILL has been a great success for Hakuhodo.

We've also been able to get Hakuhodo employees to see consumers as more than consumers, as people, too. A growing number of advertisers see HILL as giving Hakuhodo a unique selling point. New graduates are eager to join Hakuhodo, not because they see us as number two and trying harder, but because they see us as doing the best and most interesting work. That's another tremendous success.

JLM: In my introduction I've written that HILL functions as Hakuhodo's antenna. What do you think about that?

SH: HILL is an antenna for the Hakuhodo employees who read our reports. In the *Lifestyle Times*, they learn about trends before they become hot topics in the media. In 1981, when HILL was founded, magazines that provided this kind of information were still rare.

Now, however, if we did nothing but be an antenna, we would be in trouble. There's *ACROS* and *Nikkei Trendy*, and *Dime*, all sorts of antenna magazines. Today's journalism picks up on what is going on very fast. While HILL is still an antenna, what our audience looks for now is judgement, new thinking, and what it all means. That's a major concern for us.

JLM: What is HILL's relationship to Hakuhodo in organizational and financial terms?

SH: HILL was set up as an independent organization. Compared to an agency, a research institute is neutral. That makes an important difference in how we are seen by scholars and ordinary consumers when we go to interview them.

Because we identify ourselves as a research institute, people are less defensive, more willing to talk openly. Also, our publications are of interest to a wider audience, to people in the president's office and the R&D divisions of companies and not just those in the advertising and marketing divisions.

HILL publishes many reports. We sell them to Hakuhodo and receive money in return. At present about 20 per cent of our income is derived from non-Hakuhodo sources, such as from sales of our books. Sales to Hakuhodo account for about 80 per cent of our funding. In this respect, we are different from other think tanks that not only receive funds from more than one company but also do research commissioned by more than one company. Hakuhodo is HILL's only client. We don't do research for other firms.

This was a difficult issue when we were founded. From a funding point of view, doing research for other clients was attractive. Our staff, however, is small. We were once asked, for example, to do research for the housing industry, but to focus in that direction would have limited our ability to pose new problems and serve as an antenna. Hakuhodo was not interested in setting up a think tank in direct competition with, say, the Nomura or Mitsubishi research institutes. Instead our role is to provide stimulation to Hakuhodo employees.

JLM: Where do HILL staff come from?

SH: With only two exceptions, our researchers are all seconded to us from Hakuhodo.

JLM: That is, they all come to HILL from Hakuhodo. And some return to Hakuhodo?

SH: Yes, it's a kind of rotation.

JLM: So those who are Hakuhodo employees remain Hakuhodo employees?

SH: That is the way the system works.

Most research institutes assemble researchers with advanced degrees, doctorates in economics or sociology. At HILL we don't do that. Why? The answer might be called sectionalism, or excessive professionalism. Experts tend to say, 'As an economist ...' or 'From a sociological perspective ...' Experts always speak as specialists, as if they were still at university and constrained by their disciplines.

We are, in the best sense of the term, amateurs. We're a group of amateurs just big enough to fit around one table. We think of ourselves as resembling members of the CIA or MI5. We are amateurs, but high-level amateurs.

The study of lifestyle is not a profession. That's why our being what we call 'high-amateurs' is best. Depending on the project, we do use professionals as consultants. We are always ready to learn. But, fundamentally, we want our people to be able to think freely. That has always been our policy.

JLM: How do you recruit these 'high amateurs'?

SH: Curiosity is the most important criterion. Next, they have to want to come to HILL. We don't insist that they have particular backgrounds. It's much more important that they have curiosity. There aren't any other strong criteria. As people who are happy working at an advertising agency, they are bound to have an interest in consumers, so other qualifications are not a problem.

Our people come to us from many sections: from marketing, but also from the creative divisions, personnel, computer systems. It doesn't matter what their original section was. At present there are two, no three, from creative divisions, five from marketing, one from systems.

JLM: How do you see the influence of the 'Sneaker Middles' on the way that HILL is run?

SH: HILL's founding members were Baby Boomers. So the way we see society is from a Baby Boomer's perspective. Now, however, HILL's perspective is changing. The Baby Boomers are aging and approaching retirement. Now it's the turn of the Boomer Juniors.

One point to remember, though, about Japan's Baby Boomers is the very short span of years in which we were born, 1947 to 1949. After that the birthrate declined sharply. That is why we've had such a high impact on society.

JLM: How would you describe the history of HILL? Have there been distinct periods?

SH: HILL was founded in 1981. That was a really exciting time The 1970s were an interesting period in which many new products and a segmented market appeared. It was also the period of the first oil shock, in 1973, and the second, in 1979. But in the 1980s, consumption became, how shall we say it, more symbolic, more meaningful, not just consuming but a way of constructing a personal identity. Advertising became a powerful sub-culture. It was an interesting period. In Tokyo new businesses were popping up all over the place. It was a great time for 'town-watching', just looking to see what was going on.

Then in the second half of the 1980s, the Bubble happened. It was a mistake on the part of the Bank of Japan. It was ... 1988, 89, 90, 91 ... when the Bubble expanded. During this time, Japan produced excellent automobiles and other excellent products. Advertising got better, too. But it was the logic of capital more than individuals' aspirations that shaped what happened. Land prices rose so high that individuals could no longer afford to start up interesting new businesses. In Tokyo, big companies were funding all the new construction. What we saw was a pattern. If a certain area seemed to be catching on, capital poured in, swamping individual efforts. From an analytical point of view, it wasn't very interesting. The broader issues involved in Japan's becoming richer and developing a new culture – those became more interesting.

Then the Bubble burst. Starting in 1992, consumption slowed down, the economy stagnated. In the 1980s, if a new place opened in Azabu or the Bay Area, everyone rushed to see it. In the 1990s, it was more relaxing to go to a neighborhood karaoke spot and sing. It was no longer necessary to be wearing the latest fashions. The assumption that consumers are constantly chasing the latest thing has become increasingly out of synch with reality. There are still some consumers like that, but even if something catches on with early adopters, it won't necessarily spread to others. So it is more important now to pay attention to people's ordinary feelings. Thanks to our studies in the eighties, we now have a baseline for tracing changes in how people feel at ten or twenty year intervals. So now instead of looking for new types of consumers, we are aiming at a more comprehensive perspective.

1

MATERIAL CONDITIONS

On January 1, 1997, the *Nihon Keizai Shimbun* (the *Nikkei*), Japan's equivalent of the *Wall Street Journal*, began publishing a front-page series grimly entitled 'Warning Bell from the Year 2020: Part 1, Japan disappears' (*2020 Nen Kara no Keishō: Nihon ga Kieru*). A year and a half later, on Friday, June 12, 1998, Japan's Economic Planning Agency announced that the nation's economy, stagnant since the 1991 collapse of the Bubble economy of the late 1980s, had slipped into recession. The 0.7 per cent decline in real GNP was greater than the 0.5 per cent decline in 1973, the year of the first Oil Shock. Domestic demand was down 2.2 per cent and housing starts down 21.1 per cent. Both, said the *Nikkei*, were the sharpest declines since the end of World War II.

For the first time since the end of the war, personal consumption had also declined, by 1.2 per cent. Public works spending, historically the government's preferred form of economic stimulus, was down by 7.2 per cent. A weak rise in consumer demand had been squashed by the April 1, 1997, rise in the consumption tax from 3 per cent to 5 per cent. Japan's financial system was tottering under a massive burden of bad debt resulting from excessive lending to real estate and stock speculators during the Bubble. Stories of graft and corruption involving officials of major banks and brokerages and officials of the Ministry of Finance filled the pages of daily papers and weekly magazines.

The events described above might be a shock to those whose image of Japan was formed in the high-growth period of the sixties and seventies when, roaring past its European rivals, Japan became the world's second largest economy. They must also be upsetting to those whose image was formed in the eighties, when Japan seemed destined to dominate global markets, Japanese shoppers were portrayed as the world's most avid consumers of local and global brands, and scholars saw Japanese culture becoming the very epitome of postmodern pastiche. They should be especially disturbing to those who have looked to traditional social systems and values to explain Japan's economic success.

How changed is Japan? HILL research provides some answers. To understand those answers, however, we need to know some history. Three key elements stand out.

The first is the story of Japan's recovery from World War II. The account offered here draws heavily on the work of economists Nakamura Takafusa (1995) and Tsuru Shigeto (1994). The periods into which they divide the history of Japan's economic development constitute a framework shared by a broad range of analysts, critics, and commentators – including HILL researchers. They are part of the shared memory by which Japanese interpret their nation's history since 1945.

The second is the changing composition of Japan's population. In Japan, the Baby Boom was brief. It lasted only from 1947 to 1949. Japan's birth rate has declined ever since. The falling birth rate, combined with what is now the world's longest average life span, makes Japan one of the world's most rapidly aging societies.

The third is the rapid concentration of Japan's population in cities, especially in Tokyo, where real estate prices in the central city drove people to live elsewhere and a well-organized mass transit system made commuting by train and subway a way of life. While rail and subway stations have become the cores of shopping, entertainment, and office districts, a house in the suburbs has become the middle-class dream.

Having laid out this basic framework, I will end this chapter by examining some recent attempts to explain the changes that have taken place in Japan's political economy since World War II. First is the thesis that the core institutions of Japanese government, finance, and industry were created during the 1930s and 1940s as Japan mobilized for war (Johnson 1995; Nakamura 1995; Noguchi 1995). This '1940s system' was, in effect, the continuation of efforts to achieve the Meiji ideal of rich country, strong army (*fukoku kyōhei*). While defeat in World War II removed a strong military from the nation's list of priorities, a core of centralized institutions continued to work to make Japan rich. Guided by these institutions, Japan rose from the ashes of defeat to become the world's second largest economy.

Next is the proposition that what Japan became during the 1950s and 1960s is the world's most perfect modern industrial society: a society superbly organized to maximize the output of factory assembly lines controlled by large, bureaucratic organizations. It is thus doomed, without radical change, to increasing impotence in global markets, says Sakaiya Taichi (1997, 1998) the author and critic appointed to head the Economic Planning Agency in the cabinet of Prime Minister Obuchi Keizō. Japan has become, in the words of Richard Katz (1998:3–26), an example of 'Mainframe Economics in a PC world'.

A third, more political take on what is happening in Japan is that of T. J. Pempel (1998). Pempel argues that Japanese politics are undergoing a regime shift brought on by fissures in the broad coalition of large and small business and agricultural interests that kept the Liberal Democratic Party (LDP) in power for the four decades following its founding in November, 1955.

A fourth perspective is that of Harada Yutaka (1998). A career bureaucrat in the Economic Planning Agency headed by Sakaiya Taichi, Harada is another of Japan's most prolific authors on the state of the Japanese economy. Born in 1950,

Harada is fifteen years younger than Sakaiya and belongs to the nameless generation born just after the end of Japan's Baby Boom in 1949. With Harada we come full circle from authors who stress Japan's uniqueness and point to the 1940s system as a source of competitive strength in global markets, at least during the fifties and sixties. Harada argues that the 1940s system was not only a failure in wartime; it also had little to do with Japan's postwar transformation into the world's second largest economy. It was, instead, Harada argues, the postwar freeing of Japanese industry from wartime restrictions that unleashed a surge of economic energy that was only damped in the 1970s, when a people and politicians satisfied with the growth already achieved and fearful of further change opted instead for stability.

From Postwar Poverty to High Growth

It has become a cliché of Japanese writing on the postwar period to begin by describing a defeated Japan as devastated. This cliché is rooted in fact. Nearly three million Japanese died in the war. Material losses totaled ¥64.3 billion. National wealth had shrunk to ¥188.9 billion, about what it had been in 1935. Food and energy resources were both in short supply. One fear, however, the threat of massive unemployment, did not materialize. Nakamura Takafusa (1995: 23) explains why.

> The conditions under which people lived left no leeway for such a thing as being unemployed. Unless they had sufficient savings to live on, the demobilized troops and those thrown out of work had to find some means or other of making a living. Even if they did this by setting up open-air stalls or by becoming petty black marketers or black market brokers, they were not 'unemployed'.

Some of those left jobless returned to the countryside.

> In 1947 rural communities also absorbed a labor force of 18 million, about 4 million more than before the war.

Thus, while official labor statistics did not show as many 'unemployed' as might have been expected, they concealed widespread underemployment.

> The problem of the low-income 'underemployed' persisted long afterwards in the form of a 'dual structure' within the [Japanese] economy.

Japan's future looked bleak, but the gloom concealed latent strengths. The chemical and heavy industries, which would lead Japan's growth during the rapid-growth period from the mid-1950s to the early 1970s, had ended the war with far more equipment and plant capacity than they had started with. Wartime bombing had damaged factories, but the nation's most valuable asset, the skills of its workers, remained intact. Machine gun factories turned to making sewing machines. Optical equipment manufacturers made cameras and binoculars for

16

civilian markets. The steel and chemicals once required for weapons were in high demand in global as well as domestic markets. Shipbuilders deprived of a navy would build freighters and tankers instead.

To skills we should add motivation and discipline. Those who returned from the battlefield or grew up during the war and joined the labor force during the immediate postwar years were driven by the shame of defeat to overcome their enemies on other battlefields. Being used to military discipline made them an ideal workforce for heavy industrial companies organized along military lines.

Even so, Japan's rise from postwar ashes to economic superpower would seem an 'economic miracle'. From 1954 to 1958, Japan's GNP grew at an average rate of 7.0 per cent per year. From 1959 to 1963, GNP growth accelerated to 10.8 per cent. From 1964 to 1968, the average was 10.9 per cent, and from 1969 to 1973 it was 9.6 per cent. Germans who lived in West Germany also had their miracle. It pales, however, by comparison with what the Japanese accomplished. In the first half of the 1950s, West Germany outpaced Japan, with GDP growing on average 9.3 per cent per year. Then, however, West Germany's growth decelerated to 6.6 per cent for 1955–60, 5.0 per cent for 1960–65, and 4.7 per cent for 1965–70 – years in which the norm for Japan was double-digit growth.

How to explain Japan's rapid growth is a problem much debated by economists and political scientists. We have already mentioned the skilled, motivated, and highly disciplined workforce that Japan had at the end of the war. Institutions created in the thirties and forties were also an important factor, providing a strong framework for national mobilization. A third critical element was a fast-growing global economy that created opportunities Japan was ready to seize.

According to UN statistics, from 1950 to the mid-1960s, global GDP expanded at a rate of around 5 per cent. This figure compared favorably with the 2.7 per cent growth rate of Europe and America from 1870 to 1913 and was much higher than the 1.3 per cent these regions posted between 1930 and 1950. World trade was increasing at an annual rate of 7.6 per cent. The time was right for an export-oriented economy with the capital, the labor, and the institutions to tap rising global demand.

Japan also enjoyed a special advantage. In 1949, the yen was pegged at ¥360 to the U.S. dollar, where it stayed until 1971. This was, says Tsuru Shigeto, like extending special treatment to a convalescent golfer until long after he is already well. 'The dynamically yen-cheap exchange rate must have greatly helped the expansion of Japan's exports' (Tsuru 1994:78). One additional factor should also be noted. A nation's investments in imported technology and raw materials are limited by the availability of foreign exchange. The Korean War required special procurements in Japan by the U.S. military that nearly doubled Japanese foreign currency reserves and provided a kick-start to an economy ready to take off (Nakamura 1995:60).

There is no denying, however, that, presented with these opportunities, Japan moved quickly and effectively to take advantage of them. Double-digit growth became a habit. The shocks of the early 1970s thus seemed all the more traumatic.

The Pivotal 1970s

The Tokyo Olympics in 1964 were heralded as Japan's reentry into the community of nations. The Osaka Expo in 1970 marked Japan's emergence as an economic great power. During the 1960s, the ambitious (some had said 'over-ambitious') 'Income-Doubling' plan announced by Prime Minister Ikeda Hayato as the decade began had, in fact, exceeded its targets.

Already, however, there were signs that all was not as well as GNP figures indicated. In 1968, students at Japanese universities had joined their peers in Europe and America in massive demonstrations against 'the system' that was blamed for the Vietnam War. The environmental impact of heavy and chemical industries had become so alarming that GNP could be read as 'Gross National Pollution' (Tsuru 1994:129). The year 1970 would be remembered as 'Pollution, Year One' (*Kōgai Gannen*).

In addition, the global economic environment so favorable to Japan's growth would soon undergo radical change. The 'Nixon shock' of 1971 would end the pegging of the yen at ¥360 to the U.S. dollar. Then, in 1973, Japan faced 'the first oil shock'. The fourfold increase in the price of oil between October 1973 and January 1974 was a harsh blow to a nation dependent on imports of fuels and raw materials. As panicked housewives scrambled to hoard toilet paper, they bought little else: consumer spending fell by 8.5 per cent. More ominously still, private investment in plant and equipment declined by 19.8 per cent.

Japan's recovery from the first oil shock and the second in 1979 would become the stuff of economic legend. In the 1970s and 1980s, Japanese industry's ability to reduce costs, lower energy and resource consumption, develop new products, and continue to expand exports in the face of a steadily strengthening yen would enhance the mystique of Japan Inc. By 1981, the year that HILL was founded, Japan was rich. Consumerism was flourishing. But a demographic clock was ticking – and serious problems remained to be addressed.

The Changing Structure of Japan's Population

To marketers, the most elementary facts about a market are its demographics, the distribution of potential consumers by age, sex, marital status, occupation, and income. The reason is simple. At the end of the day, only three factors affect the income stream a market can generate:

Let N = the number of consumers who purchase the product
Let U = the number of product units consumed per consumer in the period for which the calculation is made, and
Let P = the price at which each unit is purchased.

Then, income = $N \times U \times P$

Demographics determine the outer limit of N. No market can be bigger than the total population of potential consumers. When that number declines, the only way to increase sales is to sell more units per customer or increase the price per unit. The law of supply and demand suggests that one tends to offset the other.

Demographics also have other effects. They determine the size of the labor force and the relative size of the working versus the retired population. Average per capita income is GNP divided by total population, a demographic variable.

The cost of feeding, clothing, and educating children depends on the number of children per household. Combined with physical limitations on space, demographics determine whether housing and transportation are spacious or crowded. There is no aspect of the market that demographics do not affect.

Like the other nations involved in World War II, Japan experienced a baby boom once the war was over. But compared, for example, to the United States, where the upsurge in births lasted from 1946 to 1964 (Wilkie 1994:64), Japan's baby boom was much shorter. Japan's Baby Boomers were all born between 1947 and 1949. Starting in 1950, Japan's birthrate began to decline. After rising slightly in the late sixties and early seventies, it again continued to fall.

Sakaiya Taichi notes that his 1976 novel *The Baby Boomer Generation (Dankai no Sedai)* anticipated many of the problems confronting Japan today. What he did not expect, however, was the birthrate falling as fast as it has (Sakaiya 1997:18–19). Figures assembled by Ken Okamura, a strategist at Dresdner Kleinwort Benson, show the dramatic difference between population estimates made in 1986 and the actual population figures for 1995. An especially striking difference appears in the aged zero to four category, where instead of the 7.8 million children predicted in 1986, the actual 1995 figure is only six million (Figure 1.1), a shortfall of 23 per cent.

The combination of the short baby boom, a declining birthrate, and a life expectancy that is now the world's longest has resulted in a population pyramid that is no longer a pyramid (Figure 1.2). The top has the usual triangular shape. Below the Baby Boomers, however, the sides dip in. With the birth of the Boomer's children, we see a short bulge. Then the sides dip in again. Because the birthrate is still declining, there is no further expansion in sight.

These simple facts point directly to social issues of critical importance to Japan. Growing numbers of Japanese marry later or not at all. By early in the twenty-first century, one in four Japanese will be 65 or older. The Baby Boomers (aged 49 to 51 in 1998) are now approaching retirement, and the strain they will put on pension, medical, and welfare systems is cause for great concern. Studies that deal with these themes make up a large proportion of HILL research and especially of the studies covered in this book.

The Impact of Urbanization

Postwar development made Tokyo the undisputed center of Japan. Like London in relation to the U.K. or Paris in relation to France, Tokyo is where the

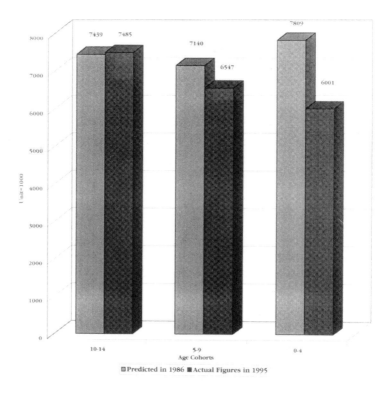

Figure 1.1 Impact of Declining Birthrate on Youngest Age Cohorts

headquarters of government, business, and the mass media are concentrated, where the nation's most prestigious universities are located, where styles begin and new products are introduced. HILL research reflects this pattern. Most of the studies translated for this book are based on surveys whose subjects live or work in the Tokyo metropolitan area. Research in Osaka or in other communities is virtually always presented in relation to what is going on in Tokyo.

For all these reasons we need to take a closer look at the course taken by urbanization as Japan's postwar economy developed and, in particular, at how Tokyo rose to its current preeminence. The following account is taken largely from Kuniko Fujita and Richard Child Hill, *Japanese Cities in the World Economy* (1993).

During the Tokugawa period (1603–1868), Edo, the city now called Tokyo, was the center of government. Osaka, a strategically located transportation center, became the commercial capital. Kyoto, the Japanese emperors' ancient capital, retained its status as a sacred or cultural center.

Focused on stability, Tokugawa policy had deliberately restricted migration between the domains into which Japan was divided. Following the Meiji

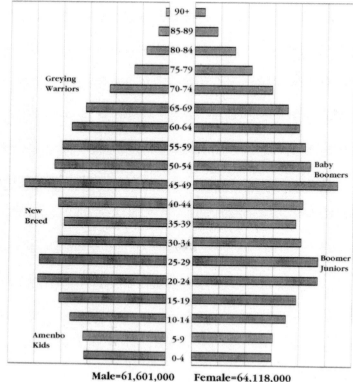

Male=61,601,000   Female=64,118,000

Figure 1.2 Japan's Population Pyramid, 1997

Restoration (1868), when barriers to internal migration were eliminated, industrialization attracted migrants to cities in four coastal regions where ports simplified the importation of raw materials and export of finished products. The largest was the Keihin (Tokyo and Yokohama) region. Second largest was Hanshin (Osaka and Kobe and the area between them). The others were Chukyo (centered on Nagoya) and Kita Kyushu (including the city of Fukuoka).

During World War II, the populations of all of Japan's major cities fell sharply. Between 1940 and 1945, the population of Tokyo, where Allied bombing was concentrated, fell by 13.84 per cent. Because of wartime evacuation, by the end of the war, only 28 per cent of Japanese lived in cities. Urbanization was at a level no higher than that of the United States in 1890.

By 1970, the year of the Osaka Expo, 72 per cent of Japan's population was concentrated in cities, the same level of urbanization as the United States. In only twenty-five years, Japan had 'caught up with the U.S.A.', but the costs had been high. 'Central government policies had emphasized investment in industrial infrastructure over social consumption and exacerbated pollution, housing shortages, and congestion' (Fujita and Hill 1993:6). Housing stocks devastated by wartime bombing left cities ill-prepared to cope with massive rural-urban migration. The result was the creation of housing that remains to this day both cramped and shoddily constructed compared with that in other parts of the developed world.

Osaka developed in a pattern similar to that of many American cities, in which the doughnut-shaped distribution of nighttime population reflects the decline of the inner city. Those with money left in search of a better environment in the suburbs, leaving the less advantaged behind. A falling population, declining tax revenue, and a rising proportion of dependent residents created financial problems for the city.

Tokyo is a different story. In Tokyo, the massive concentration of corporate, political, and media power in the inner city has made it too expensive for all but the wealthy to live there. The concentration of corporate headquarters raised land and housing prices and drove the middle class, together with low-income workers, out of the city center, a process accelerated by real estate speculation. The ebb and flow of central Tokyo's population is staggering; in Chiyoda ward in the center of the city, the difference between day and night population is over a thousand to one. But Tokyo is like a jelly donut. The cake is in the suburbs, but the sweetest part is the middle.

Dividing the index of urban land prices in Japan's six largest cities by the Bank of Japan wholesale price index and starting with 1956 as the base year produces the following figures:

Urban Land Price Index/ Wholesale Price Index

1956 (March)	1.0
1959 (September)	2.2
1962 (March)	6.1
1971 (September)	15.0
1973 (March)	20.2
1986 (March)	25.2
1990 (March)	68.2

(Tsuru 1994:160)

These figures reflect nationwide changes that were more extreme in Tokyo than elsewhere. Assume that the average aggregate income of a college graduate over a lifetime of employment is 166 million yen. Make the further assumption that the purchase of a home should cost no more than one-fifth of the buyer's annual disposable income. As of 1990, the college graduate in question could not buy even one *tsubo* (approximately 36 square feet) of land in central Tokyo (Tsuru 1994:169).

Thus it was that average Japanese who worked in Tokyo were forced to search further and further out in the suburbs for housing they could afford. The functional division of urban space into separate zones for work, shopping, and families that is characteristic of modern cities took firm hold. As daily mass-transit commutes of two hours or more became commonplace, shopping and entertainment centers grew up around train and subway stations.

The combination of commuting with long hours at the company transformed the traditional relationship of patriarchs to their families. Working fathers were separated from wives and families who spent their days in the suburbs. Wives took control of their households. With father absent all day, mother became the parent responsible for her children's education. In the new Japan where passing entrance examinations and attending the right schools had become the primary route to the enviable status of the salaryman with a job in a major corporation, the children's success or failure became the mother's success or failure.

What, Then, is The Essence of Modern Japan?

In *The 1940s System*, Noguchi Yukio (1995) asks his fellow Japanese a pointed question – suppose that what we take to be institutions deeply rooted in Japanese culture are, in fact, the product of a moment in history that we would rather forget? Japanese are taught, he says, that following World War II Japan was reborn as a totally transformed, peaceful, and democratic nation. Proponents of this view point to the postwar constitution, the arrests and dismissals of wartime public officials, the dissolution of the *zaibatsu* (large groups of diversified businesses owned exclusively by single or extended families) (Morikawa 1992: xvii), the land reform, and the legalization of labor unions. But while some systems were changed and new leaders appeared, Japan's core institutions and the thinking behind them remained, says Noguchi, the same.

Japan's financial system, in which the Bank of Japan controls a limited number of major banks and other financial institutions through 'window guidance', still rests on laws passed in 1939 to centralize government control over Japan's financial system, as part of the war effort.

Before the war, Japanese corporations operated much like those in other parts of the world, for the benefit of their shareholders. Starting in 1938, however, limits were imposed on dividends. As the nation mobilized for war, the corporation as a social unit contributing its strength to society as a whole became more important than shareholder rights. One result was corporations' increased dependence for funds for capital investment on borrowing from banks instead of profits or sale of stock. Since the banks themselves were under firmly centralized control, this dependence contributed much to holding the whole structure together.

Lifetime employment and the seniority wage system had appeared in Japan shortly after World War I. It was during World War II, however, that both became widespread in Japanese industry. Patriotic Industrial Associations formed during the war became the company unions prevalent after the war. It was also during the war that subcontracting became important, as military demand outstripped manufacturers' in-house production capabilities.

Noguchi is by no means the first to notice these things. Nakamura Takafusa had already described them in the work I have cited above (Nakamura 1995) on the postwar Japanese economy. Chalmers Johnson, citing Nakamura, describes Japan as one of the two great prototypes of a radical alternative to both the Marxist-Leninist totalitarian model in which the economy is absorbed by the state and the free-market model in which, in principle, the state keeps its hands off the economy. Like Germany under Bismarck, Japan successfully combined 'the absolutist and bourgeois streams of development' (Johnson 1995:30).

The slogan of the Meiji Restoration had been 'rich country, strong army' (*fukoku kyōhei*). Defeated in World War II, Japan had abandoned the latter goal to concentrate on the former. But while the Imperial Army and Navy were demobilized and discredited, the troops who had filled their ranks found new employment in government bureaucracies and large corporations. As Johnson acutely observes, however, the result was not peculiarly Japanese.

> The Japanese economic strategy is comparable to the American pursuit of a military strategy; and many norms of Japanese economic life – long hours, service to the group, wearing uniforms, equitable pay and long-term goals – are perfectly familiar to the American military.
>
> (Johnson 1995:37)

No student of corporate life will be surprised by Johnson's findings. As Anthony Sampson points out, military models have shaped the way that corporations are organized since the building of the first British railways. The two world wars accelerated this trend. By the end of World War II, he writes, 'American companies had been influenced not only by the huge military orders but [also] by the disciplines that went with them, including long-term planning and logistics' (Sampson 1995:93). Critics of American white collar workers writing in the 1950s sound eerily like those who savage the habits of Japanese salarymen today.

> The literary scholar Edmund Wilson had defined capitalist society as 'a vast system of passing the buck'; and the sociologist C. Wright Mills developed the charge: 'All managers are "middle-managers" who are not organised in such a manner as to allow them to assume collective responsibility.... The capitalist spirit has been bureaucratised and the enterprise fetishised.... The name of the firm is all that matters'.
>
> (Sampson 1995:96).

Seen in this light, Noguchi's question to his fellow Japanese takes on a peculiar and ironical force. What if those famous 'Japanese values' come down to the proposition 'You're in another army now'? And what if the army in question is now more *Beetle Bailey* than a mighty military machine?

What Happened to the Economic Miracle?

Richard Katz (1998:3) begins his analysis of Japan's current economic difficulties by writing, 'Generals are always prepared to fight the last war, it is said; that is why they lose the current one. The root of the problem', he writes, 'is that Japan remains mired in the structures, policies, and mental habits that prevailed in the 1950s and sixties' (Katz 1998:4). Japan's export sector is healthy, its skills honed by competition in the global market place. As Katz remarks, however, 'most Japanese live and work in quite another Japan – a Japan that neither exports nor imports' (1997:155). In this Japan where, for example, the food processing and textiles industries are found, Japanese productivity is only one-third of that in the United States. In wholesale and retail sales, which employ eleven million Japanese, productivity is 44 per cent compared to the American level. Even in telecommunications, a high technology segment considered vital to Japanese ambitions, it reaches only 77 per cent. But how did things get this way?

In *What Comes Next* (*Tsugi wa Kō Naru*), published in 1997, Sakaiya Taichi develops the thesis that what postwar Japan made of itself in the 1950s and 1960s is the world's most perfect modern industrial society. No country has ever more completely adapted itself to a world whose economy is dominated by mass-production factories and governed by large, white-collar bureaucracies. No other nation's educational system does a better job of turning out the masses of cooperative, loyal employees those big organizations need.

But that is precisely why, says Sakaiya, that Japan as we know it is doomed. Value now resides in innovative software instead of mass-produced hardware, and the dogged persistence and 'We're all in this together' for which the Japanese are famous are no longer an edge in global markets.

Sakaiya is not the only one who feels this way. One of the more poignant chapters in the *Nikkei* series 'Warning Bell from the Year 2020' is titled 'The Sinking of Dejima – Withered Brains in a Country Closed to Research' (*Dejima no chimbotsu: kenkyū sakoku de shibomu zunō'*) (Nihon Keizai Shimbunsha 1997:43–46). It begins by describing a Japanese research institute where foreign researchers never stay long. They are always in the minority and never one of the gang. It then describes a Silicon Valley institute where Chinese, Indians, and Americans of many ethnic backgrounds rub against each other, often fight with each other, and come up with new concepts. The saddest observation in the chapter is a statement by the Silicon Valley institute's manager. We've tried Japanese, he says. They didn't contribute. They didn't fit in. Printed in Japan's foremost economic daily, this statement captures perfectly the fear that Japan will be isolated and seen as a non-contributor as the world turns in other directions.

Again we might ask, how has this happened? One answer may be to take more seriously Chalmers Johnson's equation of Japanese economic strategies with military strategies and his statement that Japan's famous bureaucrats are, in effect, an economic general staff (Johnson 1995:68). There may be more at stake than Richard Katz's observation that generals are trained to fight the last war.

Armies that have won their wars return to garrison life. Warriors are replaced by those more skillful at bureaucratic infighting than winning battles on the battlefield. Military ethics are based on the principle 'mission, unit, self'. When the battle is won and the mission accomplished, the soldier's life ceases to be the great adventure that war made it. Protecting the unit too easily becomes fighting for bureaucratic turf. As morale slips, covering up and corruption can too easily become a way of life. Competing interests once united may start to fall apart.

Political Dimensions

According to Chalmers Johnson, Japan is one of the two great prototypes of what he calls the 'developmental state' (1995); the other was Bismarck's Germany. T. J. Pempel agrees that the early Meiji Japanese state was

> A classic conservative-authoritarian regime based on alliances between a centralised state, rural landlords, oligopolistic businesses, and an expansionist military that was viscerally hostile to political democracy and explicitly opposed to any significant increase in the economic or political power of organised labor and the political left.
>
> (Pempel 1998:84)

In these respects, Meiji Japan was similar not only to Germany but also to Austria and Italy.

In contrast to Johnson, however, Pempel rejects the view that the successors to the militarists who led Japan into World War II simply continued these tendencies which, even after Japan's defeat, persisted in the 1940s system down to the present day. Instead of uninterrupted continuity, Pempel sees massive changes of direction, regime shifts that grow out of the past but move in strikingly new directions.

Thus, for example, the new constitution written during the Occupation shifted the fundamental premise of Japanese politics. Sovereign power was vested in the people, to be exercised by the Diet, a freely elected parliament. The emperor, once the source of all authority, was reduced to a symbol of national unity. The military, rural landlords, and hereditary aristocrats – all three important elements in the prewar coalition – were stripped of both social position and power.

The centralized national government bureaucracies to which the 1940s system thesis points were one of that coalition's surviving major elements. The other was big business, whose leaders met on September 3, 1945, the day after Japan's formal surrender, to begin the discussions that led within less than a year to the August 16, 1946, creation of Keidanren (the Federation of Economic Organizations). With a membership made up of one hundred of the largest trade and industrial organizations and the 750 largest companies in Japan, Keidanren would become not only the voice of Japanese big business but also a major source of funding for the Liberal Democratic Party (LDP).

There was a brief period, shortly after the war, when it seemed that Japan might become the kind of social-democratic state exemplified by Sweden, Norway, and Denmark. In the early days of the Occupation, militant labor unions were formed and provided core constituencies for both the Japan Socialist Party

(JSP) and the Japan Communist Party (JCP). It was fear that the JSP would become the single largest party in the Diet that motivated the creation of the LDP through the merger of two smaller conservative parties.

'From its formation in 1955', writes Pempel, 'the LDP was a vote-gathering wonder' (1998:65). For nearly forty years it consistently captured between 55 and 60 per cent of the seats in both houses of the Diet and dominated local and prefectural governments by even larger margins. There is, however, a mystery here. The LDP achieved near-total dominance of Japanese politics despite the fact that its popularity, as measured by public opinion polls, was never much higher than 40 per cent and declined to a low of 25 per cent in the mid-1970s (Pempel 1998:5).

The answer to the mystery was a new coalition, in which bureaucrats and big business joined hands with farmers and small business. Crudely speaking, the bureaucrats provided the continuity and expertise, big business a large share of the funding, and farmers and small business people the votes that kept the LDP in power. Labor and the parties it supported, the JSP and JCP, were left out in the cold. It wasn't, however, all that cold. The enormous economic success achieved during the high-growth period meant both a rising standard of living for everyone and plenty of pork for political distribution as well.

Pempel sums up the results in the introduction to *Regime Shift*.

> For most of the postwar period, Japan had differed considerably from the other OECD countries. Politically, a single conservative party dominated Japan's electoral and governmental spheres in ways unmatched in any other industrialised democracy – two-to-one majorities over the next largest party; complete control of virtually all cabinet posts; and government influence over wide swathes of the economy.
>
> (Pempel 1998:2)

What, then, went wrong? We have already seen many of the answers. Urbanization drained voters from the countryside, making gerrymandered electoral districts look more and more unfair. The growing gap between the ultra-efficient export industries that provide Japan's face to the world and sluggish domestic sectors widened. As successful firms invested overseas and became less dependent on manufacturing and markets in Japan, their interests and those of the stay-at-homes who preferred regulated comfort diverged. A plummeting birth rate and rapidly aging population, combined with under-funded pension schemes, began to make the future look grim. The postwar coalition began to come apart at the seams. What will replace it is hard to say.

Another Perspective

To proponents of the 1940s system thesis, the centralized institutions created as Japan prepared for total war are the core of the developmental state that managed Japan's spectacular postwar development. To those more concerned with trying to explain Japan's economic stagnation since the end of the Bubble, these same institutions are now a drag on further growth. But to both they remain the heart and soul of Japan's political economy.

Harada Yutaka rejects this fundamental assumption. The following paragraphs are translated from the introduction of his *The End of the 1970s System* (*1970 Nen Taisei no Shūen*), a book whose title deliberately echoes Noguchi Yukio's *The 1940s System*.

> According to the 1940s system theory, a system created around the year 1940 centralised political control over Japan as the country went to war. This system remains in place today and accounts for Japan's economy being closed to the outside world. But given the changes imposed by the Occupation after Japan's defeat, the theory that this system continued unchanged to the present day doesn't make sense. If this argument were correct, the same system would account not only for Japan's postwar recovery and the period of high growth that extended through the sixties but also for the present situation in which Japan's economy seems to be stuck.
>
> One can, of course, argue that the system was just right for the catch-up period but is now behind the times. In fact, however, the so-called 1940s system was never a success. It wasn't effective during wartime. It had, moreover, nothing to do with the postwar, high-growth period. High growth after the war was due to the elimination of centralised control over the economy and the liberalisation of both trade and capital.
>
> (Harada 1998:1)

It was, argues Harada, the freeing of Japanese industry from wartime restrictions that opened the way for postwar Japan's remarkable growth.

> Then, however, in the 1970s, people were satisfied with Japan's economic recovery. They wanted stability instead of more development. A variety of systems were put in place to ensure that stability. Those systems created for the sake of stability have become fetters on Japan's economy.
>
> (Harada 1998:2)

Astute readers may question Harada's wholesale embrace of free-market principles to explain Japan's postwar economic miracle. After all, if they worked so well in Japan, why did they work only half as well in other OECD countries? Those who have read Katz's analysis of the growing gap between Japan's hyper-productive export sector and its under-productive domestic sector – together with Pempel's interpretation of the formation, success, and then fragmentation of Japan's postwar political regime – may find Harada's proposition that people were satisfied with Japan's postwar recovery and desired stability instead of further growth too sweeping a generalization. Clearly it lacks the articulation of economic mechanisms and political machinations that Katz and Pempel provide.

Still, there is something here. Both economic mechanisms and political machinations belong to a larger cultural context that includes a structure of feeling as well as the principles governing the distribution of goods and the distribution of power. As Japan moved from preparation for war to postwar recovery, from high growth to slow growth to bubble to bust, the emotions that colored the ways in which Japanese people perceived and felt about themselves also changed. The HILL research reported in the next chapter addresses precisely this issue.

2

EMOTIONAL RESPONSES

Chapter 1 explored the economic, demographic, and political dimensions of the 'economic miracle' that transformed Japan from a country devastated by war into the world's second largest economy. We traced a history whose basic steps are familiar to all Japanese who think about Japan's postwar development. It begins with the struggles of the first decade, when Japan was just beginning to recover. Next came the period of rapid growth that stretched from the mid-fifties until the first oil shock in 1973, when double-digit growth was the norm. Following the first oil shock, the pace of economic growth retreated to single digits. It remained, however, twice that of Japan's OECD rivals. The second oil shock, in 1979, was another brief setback, but Japan's recovery in the 1980s was nothing short of spectacular. During the economic Bubble of the late eighties, Japan Incorporated seemed invincible. The land in central Tokyo on which the Imperial Palace sits was, it was said, equal in value to the whole of California (a mild exaggeration perhaps, but it captures the mood of the period). The collapse of the bubble and the onset of near- or sub-zero growth brings us up to the present day.

The scholars whose work we reviewed in Chapter 1 are concerned with the material conditions that affected and produced these changes. In this chapter we explore them from a different perspective. Here we focus on two HILL studies. One examines the lyrics of popular songs, the other advertising copy. To the broad strokes and abstract logic of economic, demographic, and political analysis, this research adds an important emotional dimension. It offers insights into how the eras into which Japanese divide their pre- and post-World War II history felt to those who experienced them. They remind us, too, of how memory as well as experience is shaped by age, generation and gender.

The Culture Industries

Reader beware: In reading both these studies we must not forget that neither popular music nor advertising is an innocent expression of popular sentiment. Both are the products of what Frankfort School critics called 'the culture industries', which in the case of Japan can be very big business indeed.

According to music historian Hosokawa Shūhei (1997), Nippon Columbia and Japan Victor, both founded in 1927, were the first big names in the Japanese recorded music business. The industry is oligarchic and strongly linked with the film industry, publishing, and other forms of entertainment. From the start, Japan's recording industry has maintained strong control over the singers, composers, lyricists, arrangers, and orchestras who produce the music it sells.

During the Occupation, music, film, and radio were all subject to censorship. Antidemocratic or militaristic themes were officially taboo. The result, says Hosokawa, was songs whose themes were 'a vague romanticism or longing for family and home'. In the mid-1950s Japan embraced rock 'n' roll. A decade later, the Japan tour by the Ventures in 1965 stimulated the formation of hundreds of new electric-guitar bands.

Local tastes soon shifted from raucous rockabilly to softer, sweeter ballads (Schilling 1997:10), but no one musical type is now clearly dominant. Today's Japanese music scene includes local versions of every conceivable form of Western and world music: from cool jazz and Mozart to reggae, Latin, and heavy metal. Traditional musical forms performed on traditional instruments have increasingly become the preserve of small circles of connoisseurs.

Behind all the more popular musical forms are production companies linked with television and other mass media. Television is seen in Japan as an intimate medium. Television's small screen induces a sense of equality that contrasts sharply with the class distinction between star and audience produced by the movies. On TV, celebrities cease to be bigger-than-real and become instead boys and girls next door. The result, says Andrew Painter (1996), is a 'quasi-intimacy' that enables the issues of the day to be aired by people who are both familiar personalities and safely distant from their viewers.

The overlapping appearances of a limited number of celebrities in talk shows, TV dramas, fan magazines, and advertising create an extended neighborhood in which everyone knows the latest gossip and scandal. Popular songs are a good index of what the neighbors are thinking and feeling. The ads that bombard them are a vivid demonstration of what advertisers think is going on.

But that, of course, is precisely the issue that has to be kept in mind. Neither songwriters nor advertisers directly attack the core values of their audiences. Both look for dissatisfactions, for unsatisfied yearnings to sing about or new needs to be filled. In their constant search for something fresh, they look to the edges where society is changing. The changes they detect may sometimes signal major transformations. Then again, they may be nothing more than fads. What these studies do for us is to sketch an historical framework that HILL researchers can safely assume their Japanese audience shares. Japan has been changing, and for those of us who look over their shoulders, these two studies give us a sense of how change felt to those who were living through it. We must be very careful about the conclusions we draw.

The Sounds of History

In 1989, the death of the Showa Emperor brought to an end a tumultuous era (1926–1989) that had seen the rise of militarism, World War II, the Occupation, recovery, high growth, the Nixon and Oil Shocks, the Bubble Economy, and visions of Japan as No. 1. The collapse of the Bubble was still two years in the future.

In 'Showa High-Frequency Hits', HILL researchers examine the lyrics of popular songs to explore how Japanese hearts changed as the period unfolded. Their method was to measure the frequencies with which words in the opening lines of songs rose and fell by decade. In addition, a survey explored perceptions of Showa songs by men in their thirties and forties (the core of the Japanese workforce), women from 20 to 59 (Japan's most important consumers), and male and female college students (young people on the verge of beginning adult lives).

In this study, Japan's recent history is divided into four main periods. The prewar and wartime years are seen as a dark and wintry era in which ordinary Japanese were forced to repress their anger and endure the unendurable. In these years, songs were filled with words like 'flower', 'dream', 'night', 'love', and 'tears'. They evoke a melancholy mood, an awareness of the transience of life, love, and material things. They suggest the world of the demimonde, where men, at least, could escape for a while – but only a while.

The postwar and high-growth periods are seen as an era of manly men. 'I' and 'you', words that signalled the rise of individualism, had begun to rise in the charts, but 'flower', 'night', and 'love' remained one, two, and three. HILL's researchers conclude that, 'On the surface, values had changed, but prewar feelings were still strongly rooted in Japanese hearts'.

The 1970s and 1980s are described as an era of individualism and feminism. 'You' and 'I' replaced 'flower' and 'night' at the top of the charts. If the latter pair belonged to a world of clear male dominance, the former reflected a growing egalitarianism in relations between the sexes. They also expressed a weakening of the group orientation so often said to be a core Japanese value.

In retrospect, the 'Rebirth and Revival' attributed to the last stage in this scheme seems more a forlorn hope than the result of careful analysis. This study appeared in 1989. Searching for signs of change, HILL researchers perceived what might be a return to a stronger position for men. When the Bubble burst, however, Japan's salarymen saw their egos as well as their assets deflated. The renewed pride they had felt when Japan's becoming No. 1 had seemed a plausible expectation now looked like hubris instead.

How Japanese Advertising Sees the Japanese Consumer

A year later, in 1990, HILL undertook a study similar to 'Showa High-Frequency Hits'. Here, however, instead of the lyrics of popular songs, the topic was advertising copy. For 'Copy Mirror', HILL researchers also used word counts to trace changes over time. In addition, however, they analyzed the content of headlines to infer how copywriters perceived the consumers to whom they were writing.

Of particular interest in their findings are the ways in which the images of men, women, and children changed as markets evolved. In this study the larger historical thesis that an era of manly men gave way to individualism and feminism becomes more concrete. The focus is on the households in which advertisers' products are consumed and on the changing roles of men and women, parents and children within them. The time frame has also shifted. The period covered is 1945 to 1990; the prewar years are not included.

Once again, reader beware: What we are reading here is a researcher's interpretation of the images of men, women and children implicit in the headlines that copywriters have written. The researcher is a woman. The copywriters were mostly men. We should be careful, moreover, not to assume that all of the ads produced in a given period had the characteristics the researcher discovers in her sample. In Japan, as in other parts of the world, there is wide variation in creative approach, depending on the product, the advertiser's preferences, and the target to whom the product is sold.

That said, as the researcher sees her results, the manly men of the postwar years gradually became first 'warriors fighting in the shadows', then uncultured buffoons, the butts of jokes, and finally the clumsy and feeble objects of solicitous care for their health. Men's new role in the family is captured with particular poignancy in the 1986 headline which reads, 'Husbands should be healthy and out of the house'.

In contrast to the men depicted in ads, the women became increasingly independent. This study describes an evolution in the primary image of women from housewife to mother to liberated woman that implies not only increasing freedom for women to do what they like but also an increasing concern for personal style and erotic appeal in the image they present to others.

The children depicted in ads undergo a similar evolution. From unwanted babies mentioned in birth-control ads their image is gradually transformed to that of lively and impudent 'Latin young'. They become young adults whose presentation of self is the very antithesis of the strong, silent, self-contained patriarch who was, it is said, the typical Japanese household head only a few decades before.

All of these themes will be elaborated in other HILL research included in this book. But because of the timing of these studies, special care is needed in reading them. 'Showa High-Frequency Songs' was published in 1989, 'Copy Mirror' in 1990. Not quite a decade earlier, in 1981, Tanaka Yasuo's novel *Somehow, Crystal* (*Nantonaku Kuristaru*) had described a generation whose members defined themselves through shopping for famous, ideally Western, brands. As the Bubble expanded, the attitudes the novel describes had become increasingly commonplace. George Field's title *Gucci on the Ginza* (1989) captures the mood when these studies were conducted. Following the Bubble's collapse, the attitudes of the eighties swiftly became history.

As we use these studies for a backward look at how Japanese consumers felt about the changes they experienced, we mustn't forget the future that neither consumers nor HILL researchers anticipated, the future that is now.

Showa High-Frequency Hits
Lifestyle Times, August 1989

The Art: The illustrations, shown in Figure 2.1 are the faces of famous singers. In the box in the middle of the page are lyrics made up of the most frequently used words in Showa-era songs.

Love in the Night with You

You (1), you (1), love (3) in the night (2)
I (4), I (4), love's (5) flower (6)
You (2), you (2), someone's (8) dream (9)
Tears (10) in my heart (11), a woman (12) and a man (13)
Alone (15) in the city (14), the wind (16) and me (17)
The song (19) of the rain (18), filling a couple's (12) breasts (21)
Separated (23) from someone (22), now (24) that's me (25)
The sky (26) is red (27). Is that you? (28).

You (1), you (1), love (3) in the night (2)
Me (4), me (4), love's (5) flower (6)

The Research Design: This issue of the *Lifestyle Times* reports results from two studies. The first is a content analysis designed to measure the frequency with which words are used in the opening lines of 2,700 Showa Era songs. The second is a survey whose sample is described as follows: Male, 30–49, n = 200; housewives, 20–59, n = 220; male college students, n = 60; female college students, n = 116. (Conducted June, 1989.)

Boss, give us a song.
 'No, not me,' the division chief demurs.
 'Come on, don't say that'.
 'Oh, well, OK, I'll do it, but only if our Miss ... will join me. My song's a little old-fashioned'. The song is 'Tokyo Night Club', the one he always sings.
 Then, it's 'Section chief, it's your turn'.
 'All right, here's one from when I was young'. The song is 'Forever with you'. There are lyrics that nobody understands, even if he does rub his nose like Wakadaishō, the star who made this song famous. For the singer, however, the song is full of memories.

Figure 2.1 Cover, 'Showa High-Frequency Hits'

Songs Move the World. The World Shapes Its Songs.

Songs reflect the eras in which they are sung. Now that the Showa Era is over, we wondered how Japanese hearts have been changing. To find out, we examined the lyrics of 2,700 popular songs, counting the words used in their lyrics. Our method was the one we use each year to analyze the New Year editions of newspapers and magazines. The songs include a variety of genres, from Japanese *enka* ballads to pops and new music. We took the first line from each song (stopping where it seemed appropriate in those where the lines were not clearly marked) and wound up with a sample of 60,588 words. We also conducted a survey of perceptions of Showa songs, using a sample of 596 men and women.

36

'You', 'The Night', and 'Love' Are the Words That Touch Japanese Hearts

The most often used word is 'you' (*anata*) with 926 instances. Second is 'night' (*yoru*) at 665, followed by 'love' (*koi*) with 656. That is why our song's title is 'Love in the night with you'. Fourth is 'I' (*watashi*), fifth is 'love' (*ai*), sixth is 'flower' (*hana*).

The lyrics of our song are emotional, not logical. In the struggle between the sexes, 'Man' in twelfth place and 'woman' in thirteenth are separated by only ten appearances. Showa was the era of women. 'Alone' in fifteenth place ranks higher than 'couple' in twentieth; loneliness was a stronger thread than bright hopes for life together. 'Now' and 'tomorrow' are 34 and 49. Getting by was more important than dreams about the future.

'You love me, Baby'

The most frequently used English words are 'you', 'love', and 'me', which appear in the same order as the Japanese *anata, koi,* and *watashi*. But 'You love me, baby' has a lighter, brighter feeling than its Japanese equivalent. That may explain the recent proliferation of English words in popular songs.

Tokyo is the place to be

Tokyo far and away tops our list of place names. Districts within Tokyo also rank high: Ginza is second, Shinjuku fifth, Akasaka tenth. Other cities that make a strong showing include Nagasaki, Yokohama, and Hakodate. All three are port cities that evoke nostalgia.

The eye and the mouth

If we look at body parts, 'chest' is first; second is 'hand', third is 'face'. Then come the pupil and the eye, which rank above 'lips' in eighth place, and 'mouth' in twelfth place. Words for the face and its parts rank high overall. 'Nose' is an exception. In our sample of over 60,000 words, it appears only five times.

Three dominant colors

The color that appears most often is red, followed by blue and white. Passionate red, the blue of sea and sky, and pure, unstained white – these three words rank far above other words. Colors must have a clear image to communicate strong feelings.

Songs evoke 'tears', 'partings', 'drink'

When we asked survey subjects to tell us which words they associate with Showa songs, the most common replies were 'love' (*ai*) 'tears', 'love' (*koi*), 'parting' and 'drink'. What comes to mind when people think about these songs is the 'wetness' of Japanese ballads, suggested by tears, partings, and liquor.

Repression and Endurance

When the Showa Era began, Japan had not yet recovered from the Great Kanto Earthquake of 1923. Then came the Financial Crisis of 1927, followed by the Manchurian Incident in 1931. As Japan walked the dark path toward war, people had no way to express their anger and fled instead into erotic, grotesque nonsense. But even in the gloom of Showa's first decade (1926–1935), the most popular word in songs was 'love'.

Then came the February 26th Incident, the Sino-Japanese War, and, in 1941, the start of the Great Pacific War. As wartime institutions took hold, freedom of speech was lost. During the next decade (1926–1935), the most frequently used word was 'flower'. 'Love' fell to ninth place.

In the combined rankings for Showa's first two decades (1926–1945), 'flower' was in first place, second was 'dream', third was 'night', fourth was 'love', and fifth 'tears'. At no other time is 'dream' one of the top three. In a time without dreams, dreams were what people longed for.

Song lyrics speak of things that people lack. They communicate illusions simply and frankly. In the second decade of Showa, 'dream' ranks sixth. When the era of high growth began, it fell to ninth place. Then it fell again, to sixteenth. As Japan's economy continued to grow and life became materially richer, the desire for dreams declined. In the Showa fifties (1966–75), 'dream' remained stuck at sixteenth. Then, in the Showa sixties (1976–1985), it rose again to fifth place. Once again, people lacked dreams.

'Spring', in seventh place, is another of the words whose position varies dramatically from one decade to another. After Showa's first two decades, 'spring' never again made it into the top twenty. Like 'dream', 'spring' also seems to express the hope of escaping from the grim realities of a dark and wintry era.

The Era of Manly Men

On August 15, 1945, the war ended. As a hundred million people reflected on what had happened to them, prewar values underwent a radical transformation. But the words most often used in songs continued prewar trends. 'Flower' was still in first place. 'Night', in third place before the war, was now second. 'Love', fourth before the war, had risen to third place. On the surface, values had changed, but prewar feelings were still strongly rooted in Japanese hearts.

Signs of new values included 'I' and 'you', ranked seventeenth and nineteenth. During the 1960s, these markers of individualism would rise to the top of the list.

'Red', which made it to ninth place, reflected the burning passion of postwar reconstruction. It never again made it into the top twenty. Cooler 'blue' appeared more frequently during the prewar and war years and became more popular after the Oil Shocks.

Urbanization was another highly visible trend. The glamour of the city was reflected in eleventh-ranked 'town'. While not in the top twenty, 'Tokyo' rose to twenty-second. The use of such loan words as 'madras', 'neon', and 'Hawaii' also increased rapidly.

The 1956 *Economic White Paper* proclaimed the end of the postwar period. The Japanese became 'a hundred million idiots'. The Nichigeki theatre staged its first Western Carnival. Rockabilly swept the country. In 1960, demonstrations against the U.S.–Japan Security Treaty erupted. High growth began in earnest with the announcement of plans to double the nation's per capita income. Soon it would be 1964, the year of the Tokyo Olympics, when Japan once again took its place on the world stage.

In Showa's third decade (1946–1955), the top-ranked word in songs was 'night', followed by 'love' and 'flower'. The order was different but the top three words were the same as those in the previous decade. But third-ranked 'flower' was on its way out. It would fall to thirteenth, then to eighteenth, and leave the charts altogether during the late 1980s. The Japanese feeling captured in the phrase 'to fall with the flowers' (*hana to ochiru*) vanished as Japan's economy took off.

As rapid growth began, 'man', the corporate warrior, took center stage. *Ore* (a rough, masculine way to say 'I') had never before been in the top twenty. Now it was in fifth place. In ninth place, 'man' (*otoko*) was now in the top ten. The frequency with which 'man' was used gave the decade a strong, romantic image. It was also, however, the period in which the English phrases, 'I love you' and 'Let's go' entered the language.

Individualism and Feminism

In Showa's fourth decade (1966–1975), the high-growth period was fully underway, and people were intoxicated. The Beatles' first visit to Japan was in 1966. Japanese ballads became more diverse, shifting away from their mainstream roots in *enka* to include group sounds and Western-style 'folk'. In 1967, the Blue Comets, an 'electric guitar' band, won the Recording Grand Prix. Group sounds took off.

By 1968, Japan boasted the world's second largest GNP. Pollution was now a major issue. In 1969, riot police were called in to expel student radicals who had taken over the Yasuda Amphitheater at the University of Tokyo. Soon economic growth would slow. Groups of young folksingers appeared outside the west gate of Shinjuku Station, their songs filled with emotion. Music and society were more closely linked than in any other decade. EXPO '70 marked the peak. Then came the Nixon Shock in 1971 and the first Oil Shock in 1973.

Values were in flux. This change is reflected in our word counts where 'you', 'I', and 'love' (in Japanese) ranked first, second, and third. None of these words had made the top ten in previous years. Songs became more overtly subjective, expressing in a simple and innocent fashion the singer's personal feelings. There was a sharp proliferation of songs with such 'I-novel' lyrics as 'You did X' or 'I did Y', in which words like 'alone' (*hitori*) and 'as a couple' (*futari*) appeared. The age of the individual had begun.

Showa's fifth decade (1976–1985) saw further transformations in values. 'Woman' (*onna*) had never before been in the top twenty. Suddenly it was in seventh place. Women's liberation had arrived in Japan in 1970. As 'woman' rose, 'man' fell sharply. Ninth during Showa's third decade, it declined to twentieth place. Then, as the era drew to a close (1985–1989), it seemed that 'man' might be making a comeback.

Showa's fifth decade (1976–1985) was the period of Japan's biggest postwar recession, a ripple effect of the Oil Shock. As unemployment passed the one million mark, the country's mood was dark. The International Year of Women Congress in Mexico City marked the start of the Era of Women worldwide, and, by 1976, those born after the war had become the majority of Japan's population. The karaoke boom began in 1977. Public attitudes were shifting. Music was something to sing, not just listen to.

During Showa's fifth decade, 'you' (*anata*) still heads our list. 'I' (*watashi*) is second, 'people' (*hito*) is third, 'love' (*ai*)) is fourth and 'night' (*yoru*) fifth. Four of these words were in the top five during the previous decade; the fifth decade resembles the fourth. We note, however, the decline in childish forms like 'I' (*boku*) and 'you' (*kimi*) and the increase in vulgar forms like 'I' (*ore*) and 'you' (*omae*).

'Alcohol' (*sake*) entered the top twenty in nineteenth place. Combined with *ore* and *omae*, it suggests a more adult image. We must not, however, forget 'sea' at twenty or 'summer' at twenty-six. The seventies were a time of extremes; both heavy and light.

Rebirth and Revival

As Showa's sixth decade (1986–1989) began, the rankings beginning to change again. 'You' (*anata*) remained in first place. Second place was shared by 'love' (*ai*) and 'you' (*kimi*). The last time *kimi* was in the top five was during Showa's second decade. 'I' (*watashi*) remained in fourth place followed by 'dream', returning to the top five for the first time since Showa's first two decades. 'Man' in eighth place and 'wind' in eighteenth are now making a comeback, reflecting perhaps the current retro boom and a growing conservatism.

The use of English has increased dramatically, with 'You' at seven, 'Me' at ten and 'Love' at twelve. It has not been unusual in recent years for more than half the songs that make the charts to have English titles. Internationalization has penetrated the world of song.

In our survey, when we asked people to describe recent changes in song lyrics, many remarked on the growing use of non-Japanese language. That included the shift from single words to sentences and from English alone to other languages, for example, French. Critics decry the way in which 'People think it's better to use a foreign language'.

Other critics complain that 'Lyrics used to have deep, mysterious meanings. The new ones seem too commonplace'. 'In the past, lyrics were deep. Now they are light and lacking in feeling'. 'When you heard a song, you started to imagine a scene. Words these days are just lined up in rows'. We hear a lot of nostalgia, and a tendency to beautify the past.

Songs Evoke Memories

We hear a song in the background of a TV commercial. 'Oh, I remember that one!' The past comes alive in our memories; the connection between sound and memory is strong. But we aren't the dogs who drooled when Pavlov's bell sounded. When we hear certain songs, we become instead time travelers returning for a moment to the past.

In our Showa Song Survey, only two per cent of our subjects claimed to have no songs that evoked memories for them, and each generation remembered its own songs. Men in their forties remembered the songs sung by Ishihara Yūjirō. Men in their thirties remembered Kayama Yūzō. Women in their late twenties mention singer Mattoya Yumi. Age clearly affects the songs that people remember. For men in their thirties and forties, the songs they remember are those they heard when they were twenty-four. For women 20 to 59, the critical age is twenty-one. When asked about songs that hold memories for them, our subjects recalled their youth, the years when they were coming of age.

Women Remember Love; Men Don't

What kinds of memories do people associate with songs? Men and women differ sharply. Overwhelmingly, women associate songs with memories of love. Some typical comments include 'How much fun it was with the first boy I loved' (housewife, twenties); 'He was the one I went out with when I was in school. We were playing that cassette when we took our first drive together' (housewife, thirties); 'He was the one I loved most of all my college boyfriends' (housewife, forties); 'Just like in this song, I didn't get the one I loved' (housewife, fifties). Regardless of age, what women remember is first love, unrequited or lost love. Only nine per cent, however, recalled love-related incidents associated with their husbands.

In contrast, only sixteen per cent of men associate songs with love. Eighteen per cent remember songs associated with growing up. Examples include 'The one I heard played a lot when I was cramming for entrance exams' or 'The song everybody sang at our graduation party'. Among middle-aged men, nineteen per cent remember 'The first time I sang karaoke'; 'The songs they played in coffee shops and pachinko parlors when I was young'; 'The songs they played at the drinking spots I went to when I was single'.

Looking at these differences, we wonder if men are smug, indifferent or simply dull. Compared to women's memories, men's seem impoverished.

Karaoke Brings Back Memories

Karaoke and memories are closely linked. While the first couple of songs people sing are likely be recent hits, the more they get into it the more they are likely to sing songs from when they were coming of age.

Getting people to sing karaoke has traditionally taken three factors: applause, drink, and lighting. Now, however, this pattern is breaking down. There are karaoke rooms for rent, karaoke boxes, things we might call karaoke containers. Karaoke box fees range from 100 yen to 400 yen for thirty minutes, plus 100 yen per song. High school students, who wouldn't have the money to go to bars, can now get together for karaoke on their way home from school. Because of the boom, there are people waiting up to two hours just for a chance to sing.

The majority of karaoke box users are young people. For middle-aged men and women, however, they become time machines, transporting them back to the days of their youth.

Copy Mirror
45 years of consumer history as seen in 5,778 examples of advertising copy
Lifestyle Times, April 1990

The Art: On the cover (Figure 2.2), we see two faces. On the left is a woman who represents the consumer, on the right a man, a copywriter. His full beard and informal shirt – please note, there is no necktie – show clearly that he is creative and not to be confused with an ordinary salaryman.

The Twenty Most Frequently Used Words in Advertising Copy

1	*Watakushi* (I)	999
2	*Hito* (person)	980
3	*Otoko* (man)	697
4	*Onna* (woman)	560
5	*Nihon* (Japan)	556
6	*Anata* (You)	515
7	*Shin* (new)	445
8	*Haha* (Mother)	337
9	*Natsu* (summer)	336
10	*Jidai* (era)	316
11	*Sekai* (world)	313
12	*Chichi* (father)	312
13	*Nomu* (drink)	292
14	*Nen* (year)	259
15	*Terebi* (TV)	249
16	*Amerika* (America)	240
17	*Iro* (color)	239
18	*Kyō* (today)	217
19	*Utsukushii* (beautiful)	215
20	*Me* (eye)	213

The Research Design: This issue of the *Lifestyle Times* also reports the results of two studies. The first is a content analysis based on 6,000 examples of advertising copy taken from published collections. The second is a survey whose sample is described as follows: Housewives, 20–59, n = 204; university students, male/female, n = 129. (Conducted March, 1990.)

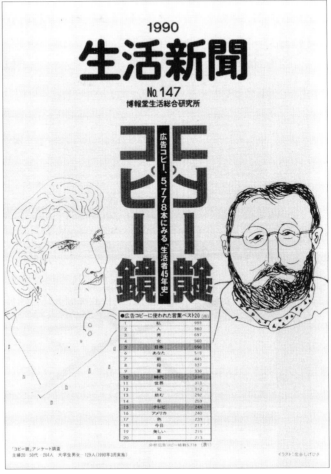

Figure 2.2 Cover, 'Copy Mirror'

Is Ad Copy the Mirror of the Age?

Yes, say sixty per cent of Japanese consumers. But how are changes in Japanese consumer behavior reflected in the mirror that copy provides? We wanted to know in particular how the image of consumers has changed in the 45 years since the end of World War II. To find out, we selected 6,000 examples of copy from the *Copy Annual,* published by Seibundō, and *Three Thousand Selected Headlines*, published by Shinkōsha. Using frequency counts of words used in headlines and analyzing the copy itself, we tried to discover how consumers were seen in each of the periods through which postwar Japan has passed.

Men Play the Leading Role

Since 1979, when ads first proclaimed the Era of Women, it has often been said that women are now on top. In our 45 years of copy, however, the word 'man' consistently appears more frequently than the word 'woman'. In our top twenty, 'man' is third; 'woman' is fourth overall. Only during the 1940s did 'woman' appear more frequently.

As society has changed, the consumer's image has also changed. In the five decades since 1945, the focus of ads shifts first from the housewife to the middle-aged male, and then from mother to youth to woman.

From 'Everyone' to 'I'

In the postwar period, the word most frequently used to represent consumers in ads was 'all of you' or 'everyone' (*minasama*). 'For all you cologne fans', for example, was the headline used to revive interest in Hechima Cologne. Ads spoke to a mass of readers and maintained a clear distance between the product and its users.

As we enter the 1950s, that gap shrinks abruptly. Now the term of address is 'you' (*anata*). Examples include 'Asahi beer is the beer for you' from 1953; 'You are the one I love' from 1955. 'The Dior line you honor us by wearing' from 1956. 'You' conveyed more intimacy; the consumer was now a strong presence, the one for whom products are made.

'You' remained at the top of the list throughout the fifties and sixties, while, in both decades, communicating product information was copy's most important task. In the seventies, it slipped to seventh place as 'I' or 'my' (*watakushi*) rose to the top, where it stayed throughout the seventies and eighties. Advertising appeals were shifting, first to 'feeling' (*kansei*) and then to 'personalization' (*kojinka*).

Examples include 'I [the woman] make it, I [the man] eat it' from 1975; 'Come back, my private time' from 1978; and 'The whiskey for my private life' from 1983. In ads like these, the message began to focus on individual lifestyles. Consumers were more than people with money to spend; they began to have lives of their own.

Men Start to Fade Away

In the 45 years since the end of World War II, the awe once accorded the paterfamilias has weakened year by year. As noted above, in advertising the word 'man' ranks third in frequency overall. In the 1940s, it was thirty-first. In the 1950s and 1960s, it rose to eleventh. It was during the seventies and eighties that the word 'man' rose to third and began to be used more often than the word 'woman'. It would be a mistake, however, to imagine that the men portrayed in ads are stronger than the women.

The male who was once an absolute presence has become an obscure figure, a warrior fighting in the shadows. This marks a sharp departure from the early postwar years when men were still portrayed as the prime movers in their families, as awe-inspiring pillars of the household. In the fifties, when people began to say 'It's not postwar anymore', the men depicted in ads were still strong. Already, however, their image was changing. Now they were 'uncultured dictators' (*mugei kampaku*). They lived only for work. For these men 'my home' included cute kids and a refrigerator stocked with 'Dad's beer'.

In the sixties the grey warriors appeared – salarymen riding the wave of high growth as Japan's economy took off. Now father was never at home. Typical headlines included 'Strong and long-lasting' from 1963. 'Oh! What passion!' from 1969; and 'Go! Go! Taisho-born!', also from 1969.

In the seventies, the dominant value shifted from the corporate warrior's burning passion to appreciation of beauty. Men for whom only work had value came to be seen as having nothing to say. This image appears in such lines as "Men should keep their mouths shut' from 1970; 'For the man who kills sweetness' from 1973; and 'Men aren't convivial' from 1976.

By the eighties, men mentioned in ads had no place to call their own, either at work or at home. They were like stray animals. Examples include 'How about telling your wife, "Follow me"?' from 1981. It was, however, important to keep men healthy. Another 1981 line said, 'I want Dad to have his calcium'. A 1986 headline sums up the trend with 'Husbands should be healthy and out of the house'.

Women Take Control

During this same 45 years, women shed their roles as virtuous wives and housekeepers. They took control of the household and claimed equality with men in public. They became independent and began to go their own way. In the forties, 'woman' ranks eighth in frequency; in the fifties it slips to seventeenth. In the sixties it disappears from the top twenty, replaced by ninth-place 'mother' (*haha*). In the seventies, the women's liberation movement brought 'woman' back to third place, a position it continued to hold in the eighties. Broadly speaking, the image of women had evolved in three stages, from housewife to mother to woman.

The forties were the decade in which the liberation of women was first proclaimed. One 1948 headline proclaimed, ' For the new woman'. Still, women were constrained by the 'good wife and wise mother' ideal expressed in such headlines as, 'Do you know the joy of baking bread?', from 1946.

During the fifties, when the 'my home' ideal was born, the modern American woman was the model. Copy designed to appeal to this type included 'Europe and America's most popular jet faucet' from 1954, and 'Hardworking machines that make leisure' from 1959.

Then, however, the spotlight shifted to mother. The sixties were the era of the monsters *(mamagon)* that Japan's mothers, obsessed with their children's education had become. From 1969 we have a pun on two phrases with the same pronunciation: 'It used to be "good wife, wise mother." Now it's "cooking, sewing, healthy mother."' A similar line from the same year was 'Not just an education mama, be a brain-training mama'.

The seventies saw the appearance of consciousness raising and the liberated wife. From 1975 we have, 'Why do you ask my age? Then in 1976, 'I don't want to be sweet'.

In the eighties, the liberated wife became Ms. Independence. One 1980 headline proclaimed that, 'Women's records may soon surpass men's'. Headlines from 1984 included, 'Isn't it OK to say "I love me"?' and 'A woman wants a wife'.

From Crawling to Independence

During the forties and fifties, children were rarely mentioned in advertising, except as unwanted fetuses in birth-control ads. During the sixties 'baby' began to appear more frequently. In the seventies 'child' ranked twenty-second. In the eighties, 'son' made it to twenty-eighth.

During the forties, when every one was working hard just to survive, 'You who give birth' (a pun on 'You who listen to our 3:00 show') were the targets of family planning campaigns. This trend continued into the early fifties, with children mentioned mostly in advertising for contraceptives. A headline from 1950 reads, 'First, a daughter; second, a son; third, contraceptive jelly'. In the mid-fifties the emphasis shifted to women with babies to raise. In 1953 we find, 'They're born small, let's raise them big'.

Then, in the sixties, as household electrical appliances became more widespread, toddlers were the focus of education ads. A typical example is 'Let's start English from age five', from 1966.

The seventies were a time swarming with children who no longer knew their place. Children were not just more independent; they were invaders rudely sticking out their tongues at adults. A typical headline from 1974 reads, 'If you can't understand what makes this jumper so good, Dad, I'm sorry for you'.

In the eighties, the children depicted in ads became increasingly individualistic. They grew up and became bright, lively 'Latin' youth. A headline from 1985 declared, 'I shouldn't say this so suddenly, but work is money'. From 1987 we have, 'Kids, let's choose for ourselves'. Children had become individuals with minds of their own.

Conversation with Shindō Kazuma
September 14, 1998

Shindō Kazuma was born in 1951, missing the Baby Boom by two years. He is married and has two sons, one a university student, the other still in high school. He joined Hakuhodo in 1974 and moved to HILL in 1986. Before moving to HILL, he was one of the creators of HAAP, Hakuhodo's proprietary model for optimizing media buying.

JLM: What did you major in at university?

SK: Business, at Keio. Marketing, but I didn't study that much.

JLM: What has been your favorite research theme?

SK: Salarymen. What would become of Japan's salarymen has always been the question that interests me most. We can think of them as consumers, but while I was in the R&D Division, I was also involved in the labor union. That was in the 1980s, when salarymen's attitudes were changing. It was a difficult time to be working with the union.

SK: Why was it difficult?

JLM: It was the eighties. Before then, Japan had been poor, and the struggle for wages was the big issue. Now, Japan was affluent; we no longer had that single goal. Some people wanted more money; others wanted more vacation time. Some wanted more welfare benefits. Wants became very diversified. Until then, if the union got more money, that was enough; the union leaders were praised. That had changed, and I was directly affected myself.

Japanese salarymen were called 'worker bees', but I couldn't see that. Their world was changing. So when I came to HILL, I thought it would be interesting to explore how it was changing.

JLM: Today we're going to talk about your study, 'Showa Hit-Frequency Songs'. Before we get into the content, could we talk a bit about the word-counting method you used?

SK: Every year we use the same method to analyse the New Year's editions of newspapers and magazines. We look at the words in their headlines, from which we learn what has happened and what directions the world is moving in. Recently, though, we haven't been using word counts in big studies focused on special themes.

Before we started, a few university professors had done similar projects, but they always counted small sets of words by hand. When people count by hand a lot of subjective bias gets into the process. It was shortly before we did 'Showa High-Frequency Songs' that computer software that could do word counts appeared, with a program called Happiness. We decided to try it out. There are lots of programs that do this now, but then it was revolutionary.

Our method is to count everything, to exclude subjective bias. Only after everything has been counted do we look at the results. Counting first and then thinking about the results is much better than thinking first and then counting.

Suppose you count all the words in someone's conversation. If a certain woman's name appears many times, you can infer that there is a strong interest there, even if the person who is speaking is unaware of the fact. That's what makes counting so interesting. It's a kind of depth psychology. When we look at what people have written, we can see things that the writer wasn't conscious of saying. We can see, era by era, how people's unconscious feelings have changed.

JLM: Why, then, haven't you done any big thematic studies since 1990?

SK: I've thought of doing a similar study [of song lyrics] for the Heisei era, but it wouldn't be interesting until enough time had passed. Now that it's been almost ten years .... But really, there isn't any reason. I just stopped for a while.

JLM: You haven't done another study, but how do you see what's been happening through your own eyes? How has Japanese music changed in the last nine years?

SK: Music? What we analyzed was lyrics. Now the number of totally meaningless words has increased. Melody and rhythm have become more important than the words. I said that I had just stopped for a while, but I wonder how meaningful counting words would be now. Lyrics no longer have the power they used to. Perhaps Japanese who listen to music have changed as well. Physical sensation (kankaku) has become more important. Words carry emotion but they are also intellectual ... today's songs have become ... perhaps the right thing to say is more directly felt. People listen to music for the feeling alone. If we had a way to count them, elements of melody and rhythm would now be more important.

JLM: Is that what Sekizawa calls resonance (kyōshin)?

SK: No. That involves shared feeling (kyōkan). Have you noticed that songs are becoming higher-pitched? It would be interesting to count the notes in songs. Every year they seem to be higher. Voices are becoming more falsetto, more forced. It could be the effect of the spread of karaoke. Counting is most interesting when something seems to be changing. If it doesn't show you what's going on in people's hearts, it's not all that stimulating.

JLM: What made 'Showa High-Frequency Songs' so interesting was counting words decade by decade to discover how Japanese hearts had changed. When you look at the music of the last nine years, how has Japanese society changed?

SK: Without counting I can't really say. If we counted ... at the very least, we would find evidence for what people are always saying, that Japan is becoming more globalized. That's true in songs, and not just in songs. The boundary between Japan and the rest of the world is disappearing. That's the big change. People now mix Japanese and English all the time.

JLM: Is this related to other social trends?

SK: Besides globalization? There's the greater salience of physical sensation in the way in which music and other things are being perceived. During the high-growth period, people were more rational. Now the pace of change is quicker, and the lifecycles of trends are shorter. People are also changing. It used to be that people would choose to buy a particular artist's music, and some artists had long careers. Now there are many who appear and disappear overnight. Consumers pick out things that impress them at the moment; the same thing is happening to brands. The particular product is more important than a name like Gucci or Vuitton. It's the same with music. People just buy whatever catches their fancy, and their CD collections are all over the place. People used to go out of their way to collect all of an artist's releases. Now their collections are random; my own kids are that way. They only buy songs they like. They don't collect a particular artist's or composer's work.

JLM: Shimamoto said something similar to me just a few days ago. He says that Japanese consumers have become very 'neutral' (See the 'Conversation with Shimamoto Tatsushi' at the end of Chapter 6).

SK: Yes, snacking or grazing *(tsumamu)* is more prevalent now. But while the behavior looks like snacking, we have to ask about the motive. More and more it's the first impression something makes. That's why people don't think first about who the artist is or what company released the CD. Now people buy music by artists from Taiwan or Korea. They don't ask where it comes from. It's all first impressions.

JLM: In the 1980s there was a lot of talk about *kansei*. What is the difference between *kansei* and physical sensation *(kankaku)*?

SK: *Kansei* is whether you like or dislike something. Thus, for example, someone might say 'I like Masuda Seiko. That is why I buy her recordings.' *Kankaku* is when the melody or the rhythm appeals directly to our feelings. It's more direct, more immediate. As we said in our book *The Age of the Five Senses* (*Gokan no Jidai*) (HILL 1994*)*, kansei still includes an element of rationality (*risei*). The issue now is whether a purchase will snap into focus for you (*pin to kuru ka konai ka*). We can't explain yet why something snaps into focus. The people we ask can't tell us why they buy things, and that lack of associations makes it hard to plan marketing strategies.

3

THAT 'TYPICAL JAPANESE', THE
BABY BOOMER SALARYMAN

In 'The Future That Has Already Happened', an essay written for the seventy-fifth anniversary edition of the *Harvard Business Review*, management guru Peter Drucker writes,

> In human affairs – political, social, economic or business – it is pointless to try to predict the future, let alone attempt to look ahead 75 years. But it is possible – and fruitful – to identify major events that have already happened, irrevocably, and that will have predictable effects in the next decade or two.

(Drucker 1997:20)

In March, 1982, the *Lifestyle Times* reported a study called 'Sneaker Middles' that provides dramatic proof of Drucker's claim. The subject was Japan's Baby Boomers, Japanese born in the years 1947 to 1949. In 1982, those born in 1947 were just turning 35. In 'Sneaker Middles', HILL researchers reviewed the Baby Boomers' impact on post-World War II Japanese society and forecast that they would be a source of enormous problems. Because of their sheer numbers, there would not be enough management posts for all of those, the majority, who sought success as salarymen in large corporations. Straining the system, they would break it, leading to the collapse of lifetime employment. Moreover, their retirement would impose a massive burden on the generations that followed them.

In 1997, as the Sneaker Middles born in 1947 turned fifty, those predictions had proved all too true. The aging population, the shrinking birth rate, and the fate of Japan's white-collar workers in an age of corporate restructuring were issues raised repeatedly in daily newspapers and weekly magazines, government reports and books by critics worried about Japan's future. I have mentioned Sakaiya Taichi, who argues that, following World War II, Japan created the world's most perfect modern industrial state (Sakaiya 1997, 1998). Economist Kimondō Kusaka remarks that over seventy per cent of Japan's labor force is employed as salaried workers who lack the self-reliance of their farmer and small-business predecessors (Kusaka 1997:29–30). Ohmae Kenichi (1997:17–46)

51

urges younger Japanese to become more politically active and reject the enormous burdens that their elders will otherwise impose upon them.

The Baby Boomer Salaryman

To read these critics and return to HILL's 'Sneaker Middles' study is to experience an uncanny feeling of *déjà vu*. After struggling through crowded elementary and secondary schools, Japan's Baby Boomers poured into colleges and earned a brief notoriety in the mass demonstrations of the student movements of the late 1960s. Then, they disappeared from view. As they found jobs and started careers and families, they were no longer newsmakers. They were, say HILL researchers, a generation unlikely to start new fashions or produce new heroes.

The Boomers preferred comfort to glitz and on weekends dressed in the jeans and the sneakers that suggested the name HILL gave to them. They preferred not being too visible. They liked being offered novelty more than creating new things for themselves. They would seek security and avoid risk. As consumers of information, they also preferred a variety of choices. They would cultivate taste instead of creativity.

The Baby Boomers became what both foreign observers and the Japanese man in the street would consider the 'typical Japanese'. In this familiar stereotype, we are talking about men who achieve the Boomer dream. They become successful, but not too successful, middle-class, white-collar workers. They are married, have one or two children. Their homes are in the suburbs. They commute long distances to the offices where, after working long hours, they go out drinking with their fellow workers. These are the men, it is said, who work so well in groups. They know the wisdom of the oft-cited maxim, 'The nail that sticks out gets hammered down'.

The ideal that the Baby Boomers achieved is, of course, older than the Boomers themselves. Writing in 1963, when the Boomers were still teenagers, Ezra Vogel traced the salaryman's roots back to the Edo period, when samurai warriors ceased to be soldiers and became, instead, bureaucrats.

Vogel observed that the samurai were bureaucrats with a warrior mindset. The ideal inculcated by training in martial arts was to be bold and courageous, capable of independent action. In contrast, the salaryman is more concerned with complex administrative and technical problems than with individual initiatives. 'He has less room for independent movement, and is likely to be more cautious and susceptible to influence' (Vogel 1963:5).

Vogel's analysis was based on fieldwork from 1958 to 1960, just as the high-growth period was getting underway. It was already clear, however, that the salaryman represented the future. The older middle class of independent shopkeepers, craftsmen, and farmers that Kimondō Kusaka remembers so fondly was losing ground to the new ideal. Able and enterprising young men could become much richer than salarymen, 'But', writes Vogel, 'most Japanese have no such confidence in their own talents and long-term economic prospects even if they were to have such an opportunity in the short run. For the vast majority of Japanese the life of the salaryman seems to represent as high a standard as they can reasonably hope for' (Vogel 1963:9).

We must not forget, moreover, that the Baby Boomers became salarymen under circumstances peculiar to their own generation. Rapid economic growth created jobs, making space for them at the bottom of growing organizations. Their fate would be to provide the army of subordinates that growing companies needed for the older generations whose members were starting to move up the corporate ladder. For themselves, however, lifetime employment would turn out, at the end of their careers, to be, literally, a pyramid scheme. The end of high growth and a shrinking number of younger men would make it impossible to continue the seniority-based promotions that made a salaryman's life seem so attractively secure.

The Baby Boomer's predecessor, the Greying Corporate Warrior, grew up during the late 1940s, a time of chaos and poverty. He found a job in the 1950s, as rapid growth was just beginning. His childhood memories were of times when basic necessities were scarce, there was widespread unemployment, and neighborhoods were still in ruins. What he remembers most is hunger.

> My grandmother had to sell the expensive kimonos just to pay for rice.
> (HILL 1991:85)

He would note the impact of the Occupation on Japanese education.

> At school, our textbooks were heavily censured. Anything that had to do with the divinity of the Emperor or about Japan's militarism was cut out. But pretty soon we got new textbooks, and we began studying about democracy.
> (HILL 1991:85)

He could tell you, too, what the beginning of economic recovery meant to him.

> My mother saved the money my father earned at the factory. Then finally she had enough to buy a refrigerator. She had to have the refrigerator because her neighbor had already bought one. And in those days, everyone wanted to keep up with the Satos.
> (HILL 1991:85)

The warrior worked long hours. He didn't spend much time with his family, and life was often tough. He did, however, have one thing that later generations would lack – a vision and a purpose. Japan would first catch up with and then surpass the West. At the time this report was compiled, he was in his late forties or early fifties.

The New Breed who came of age in the eighties grew up in affluence. Their parents were eager to buy them things that they had lacked when they were young. The birthrate had started to fall in the 1950s, so that families were smaller. While growing up, the New Breed salaryman had fewer siblings to compete with.

> He grew up expecting favors and material goods without having to work for them. He knew his parents were always ready to give him whatever they could afford. Their most important consideration was to make sure he was happy.

> (HILL 1991:88)

By the mid-eighties, the New Breed were in their late twenties and early thirties. From the Greying Warrior's perspective, they were doing outrageous things: demanding more time for themselves, taking longer vacations, cultivating friendships outside the companies in which they worked, even considering changing jobs.

'Sneaker Middles' is only one of studies focused on salarymen translated in this chapter. 'The Salaryman's Guide to Advancement' was published the same year as 'Sneaker Middles' and describes the alternatives open to Boomer salarymen for only a small fraction of whom a steady progress from junior to middle and then to senior management was possible. It also includes a typology of salaryman personalities, a useful antidote to the notion that Japanese salarymen are an undifferentiated mass.

'New Salaryman Constitution Proclaimed' was published five years later, in 1987. By then, the Baby Boomers were caught in the middle between the corporate warriors who ran the companies in which they worked and the New Breed whose tastes and habits were seen as a threat to the corporate cultures that the warriors had created. 'The Heisei Salaryman Constitution', published in 1995, shows the trends described in the earlier study accelerating. But by then it was the New Breed who were caught in the middle. The Bubble had collapsed, and the Boomers had become the 'Awakened Ones' who knew that their careers had taken them as far as they would go. A newer breed, the 'Bubbly Ones', had joined companies at the peak of the Bubble and seemed unable to shake its habits. The New Breed are caught between those two age groups; now married with young families and careers still to worry about, they are the 'Angry Ones'. They feel frustrated, overworked, anxious about the future, and enraged by what they see as the shiftlessness and corruption of both older and younger generations.

Sneaker Middles: The New Middle Aged
Lifestyle Times, March 1982

The Art: Figure 3.1 shows a photograph of a mass of solemn first-graders, lined up for their first day at school. The caption on the lower right reads,

> 'The length of the new class's lines was scary. We felt their power'. (From a person born in 1946, one year before the baby boom.)

The Research Design: The 'Sneaker Middle Survey' was based on a two-stage, stratified random sample of male and female individuals living in Tokyo and Osaka. The individuals sampled were divided into three age categories: 22–24, 32–34, and 42–44; total n = 2,000. (Conducted December, 1981.)

The Baby Boomers Are 35

When soldiers are sent to distant battlefields, the birthrate declines. When the battle is over, the men return home, and the following year the birthrate rises. This cycle has repeated itself throughout human history, and the years from 1947 to 1949 are no exception. An additional four to five hundred thousand babies were born, creating a massive wave of 7.13 million people.

They poured into elementary schools

In 1954, the *Asahi Shimbun* reported,

> The huge number of first-graders entering school this year, just as schools were starting to implement the new six-three (six years elementary, three years junior high) system, threw schools everywhere into confusion. Faced with shortages of classrooms and teachers, schools turned to split sessions. The number of temporary classrooms rose sharply. 'Blue Sky Classrooms', the outdoor classes now almost forgotten, reappeared.

'Rush hour classes' in Tottori packed in 77 students per class. In Toyama, halls and stairwells were used as classrooms.

Six years later, junior high

In 1960, that same huge wave hit junior high schools. Now the *Asahi* reported that 900 additional teachers had been shifted from elementary to junior high schools. Then, when the Boomers graduated from junior high in 1963, the

Figure 3.1 Cover, 'Sneaker Middles'

majority wanted to go on to high school. The newspaper headlined the story, 'There are almost no *rōnin* (students not admitted by any school). All are going to high school, says a Ministry of Education report'.

Then came college

The first cohort of baby boomers came knocking on the doors of colleges in 1965. As they poured in, colleges resembled snakes swallowing eggs. It is no accident that the student movement reached its peak in 1968. The generation was so big that its members found doors tightly closed. They pushed hard and broke them open.

- On January 19, 1968, the United States aircraft carrier *Enterprise* entered Sasebo Harbor and was greeted with angry demonstrations.
- On January 26, 1968, the University of Tokyo's School of Medicine began an endless strike.
- On August 27, 1968, Zengakuren, the all-Japan university student federation, was formed. Paris had had its 'Days of May'. Now Japan, too, would see its campuses erupt.

Going to work, getting married

As the Baby Boomers graduated and found jobs, Japan was approaching the end of the high-growth period that began in the 1950s. Expo '70 was held in Osaka. The hot topic of the day was Prime Minister Tanaka Kakuei's proposal to 'remodel the Japanese archipelago'. Then came the Oil Shock of 1973.

As the Boomers married and formed new households, they were flattered by talk of the 'new family'. They were still unsure if the phrase fit when it slipped out of use. The Boomers have been called the anti-war faction, the folk generation, the *dankai* (lump) generation. More recently, they have ceased to be noticed at all.

We Call Them 'Sneaker Middles'

This year first cohort of Baby Boomers turns 35. They are becoming middle-aged. Based on their lifestyles, we call them 'Sneaker Middles'.

There will not be enough management posts

Because there are so many Baby Boomers, they have started another wave rippling through society. This generation now accounts for seventeen per cent of all company employees, eighteen per cent in companies with more than 1,000 employees. If promotion by seniority continues, in a company of 1,000 employees, 30 will become division chief, 100 will become section heads, 40 will not be promoted. Since promotions on this scale are impossible, the promotion-by-seniority system will be under strong pressure to change. Many companies are now introducing early retirement schemes.

Growing numbers of Baby Boomers will not be promoted and will lose interest in work. If they find themselves locked like Europeans into a family-first approach to life, the vigor of Japanese industry will decline. That may not, however, be entirely a bad thing.

At work the outlook is gloomy, but for society as a whole, there may be a silver lining. Japanese society, long dominated by youth, may have the opportunity to achieve a more mature, European-style culture. In a middle-aged society, consumer behavior, marketing, and advertising may all become quite different from what they are now.

On the way to an aging society

Look for a moment at Japan's population pyramid for the year 2005. The severity of the problems facing the baby boomers on retirement is palpable. We foresee panic over the bankruptcy of severance pay and pension systems. Then, if we look ahead another ten years, we find that in the year 2015, one in five of Japan's population will be 65 or older. It will be a society with only three young workers to support each aged retiree.

People make a lot of noise about the 'mature years', but what's really being talked about is an aging society and the implications of the Baby Boomers' becoming senior citizens.

Yes – Gender Equality and Focus on the Family
But – Pragmatic and Reluctant to Stand Out

When we compare Sneaker Middles in their thirties with younger people in their twenties or the older middle-aged in their forties, we find the following characteristics.

- Equality of husbands and wives, living in nuclear families.
- Not wanting to stand out; they just get by.
- Always wanting to be with their families.
- Preference for practicality and comfort.
- Not trendsetters, but they do have the ability to choose what they like.

There is no single factor that determines what people feel. The times are one influence, generation another, aging a third. In the case of the Sneaker Middles, we shouldn't overlook the fact that they are now at the life stage with the least disposable income. First, then, let's sketch a profile.

Men

- Occupation: Corporate or government white collar   43%
- Schooling: Four-year college or higher degree   42%
- Lifestyle
  - Monthly household expenditure   ¥239,000
  - Savings   ¥2,719,000
  - Cash for personal use   ¥35,400
- Housing: Own home 44%   Rent apartment or house 52%
- Class identification   'Middle of the middle' 46%
- Satisfaction with lifestyle, on a scale of 10
  - Home   7.7 (Male average 7.4)
  - Job, work style   8.2 (Male average 7.9)
  - Income   7.0 (Male average 6.7)

Women

- Occupation:
Work outside the home	24%
Self-employed, cottage industry	18%
Full-time housewives	56%
- Schooling:
Jr. college or higher degree	24%
High school graduates:	57%
- Lifestyle
    - Monthly household expenditure   ¥255,000
    - Savings   ¥3,318,000
    - Cash for personal use   ¥12,500
- Housing: Own home 56%   Rent apartment or house 40%
- Class identification   'Middle of the middle' 51%
- Satisfaction with lifestyle, on a scale of 10
    - Home   7.7
    - Job, work style   7.4

Heart

1. Men desire information, intelligence, comfort, and something to do. More than other generations, they have faith in intelligence.
2. Women desire simplicity, naturalness, and equality. Most seek happiness in home and family.
3. Men care more about comfort than how others see them.
4. Both men and women like new things.
5. A majority describe themselves as people who crave company and feel lonely if left alone.

Clothing

1. Prefer comfort to trendy styles.
2. Wear good-quality basics that last a long time.

Food

1. Love to eat and will spend money on food.
2. Like going out to eat with their families.
3. Sneaker Middle housewives dislike highly processed frozen and instant foods. To save time, many do, however, use semi-processed foods and ready-made seasonings.

Housing

1. Again, comfort is primary. Concern about external appearance is low.
2. They do not insist on owning their own homes and move to fit their life stage. Housing standards are low. Practicality is a top priority.

Work

1. Men work for the sake of their families.
2. Their company loyalty equals that of the older middle aged, but work isn't everything.
3. Compared to other generations, more Sneaker Middle housewives feel that housework isn't just for women.

Schooling

1. Men show intelligent curiosity.
2. Women are less interested in study.

Older women support culture centers, lectures and classes in cultural subjects. Few Sneaker Middle women are now involved in study, but the latent demand is large. They will be the next generation going to culture centers after they let go of their children.

Conversation

1. Almost 60 per cent of husbands and wives converse with each other.
2. The four most frequently discussed topics are household finances, the children, housing, and work.

Money

1. Spend freely on things they like.
2. Most of the women regret wasteful or impulse purchases.
3. More women (25 per cent) than men (17 per cent) claim to use money well.

Sneaker Middle housewives have a tough time with household finances. They tend to be more careful about money than men are.

Knowledge

1. Eagerly absorb all sorts of information.
2. Selectively evaluate information from a wide variety of sources.
3. Men encounter more different media. Women's media contacts occur while they are doing something else.

Buying Habits

1. Men are concerned about brands and how other people see them.
2. Sneaker Middle housewives are more strongly involved in purchases and have more authority over decisions than older housewives.
3. Comfort is basic, but men want information. Dependent on brands and others' evaluations, they are easily taken in.

Friends

1. Socialize with family and neighbors.
2. Men socialize actively and have strong likes and dislikes.
3. Women are less socially adept. Interest in class parties or other group activities is low.

Gender

1. Compared to other generations, more Sneaker Middles of both sexes deny that a woman's happiness depends on getting married.
2. Most see themselves as manly or womanly.
3. Both sexes believe strongly that men and women are equal in ability and, thus, that both should have equal rights. This belief is especially strong among single, self-employed, and highly educated women.

A majority of men, however, think that sexual freedom is only for men. The publishers of pornographic magazines and owners of no-pants coffee shops are mostly younger middle-aged males. Using women in this way shows the selfishness of men.

Power

1. The husband speaks for the family and makes major decisions, but the wife holds the purse strings.
2. Compared to older couples, husbands and wives are more likely to be friends.

Recreation

1. Both men and women have shifted to middle-aged hobbies and recreations.
2. Men prefer to spend leisure time outside the home (spectator sports, mahjong, pachinko). Women prefer practical, at-home recreations (knitting, handicrafts, baking).

The Sneaker Middle male is more likely than older men to appreciate music. Men have a greater interest in leisure than women. The majority would like to do something with their families but lack both the money and the free time.

Sweat

1. Sneaker Middle men like sports.
2. Half of Sneaker Middle women do not participate in any sport.

Men seem more middle-aged in the sports that they prefer, women more youthful.

Music

1. Favorite types of music are the same as those of older people: Japanese ballads, Japanese pops, and songs from movies.
2. Like the older generation, almost 70 per cent play no instrument.

Here we see a strong contrast between the younger generation and both the Sneaker Middles and the older middle-aged.

Our 1947–49 Class Reunion

What we saw

'What do I remember from my elementary and junior high years? TV. We had just bought our first set'. (Woman, 32)

'Fridays at 8 o'clock there were live broadcasts of professional wrestling matches. Thirty of the neighbors would cram into our house to watch. Some stood outside and looked in through the windows'. (Man, 32)

'I remember the TV commercial for M company. Their vacuum cleaner was used to clean the ring. It was a really cheap commercial'. (Man, 32)

'The way Fred Brassy bit his opponents impressed me. There were old people so shocked that when they saw it, they died'. (Man, 35)

'There were open drainage ditches all over Tokyo. I remember falling into one on my way home from a movie'. (Woman, 32)

'There were still air raid shelters in empty lots'. (Women, 34)

'When I was in high school, there was a lot of excitement about filling in Kobe Bay. Did that become Port Island?' (Woman, 33)

'The Osaka Expo was held the year I entered the company. I regretted not having a summer vacation'. (Man, 35)

The sounds we liked

'When I was in elementary school, Misora Hibari and Shimakura Chiyoko were the rage. I mimicked them a lot'. (Woman, 34)

'There were people excited by the Beatles and others not excited at all. It was a pivotal moment'. (Man, 34)

'I really liked Japanese ballads better, but if you didn't say you liked the Beatles, you were seen as out of it'. (Man, 34)

What happened to us

'There were so many of us wanting to go to kindergarten, we had to draw lots. I will never forget the tears on the faces of the ones who didn't make it'. (Woman, 34)

'When we entered elementary school, there were more than 10 homeroom classes'. (Man, 33)

'Split sessions were taken for granted. Some schools had three shifts'. (Man, 34)

'It may have been the Tokyo Olympics. Gymnastics exercises were all we did for physical education'. (Man, 32)

'Because of the Tokyo water shortage, there was one summer when I didn't get into the pool'. (Woman, 34)

'From the time we entered elementary school, people were always saying that we would have a tough time in exams'. (Man, 34)

'Because there were too many of us, our coming of age ceremony was canceled'. (Man, 35)

'I got a notice from the town office that I wasn't invited'. (Woman, 34)

'There were so many of us who entered the company that year that "Oh, you're from the same year" was something we heard all the time'. (Man, 34)

What we ate

'I can still remember how much candy a one-yen note would buy at a cheap sweet shop'. (Woman, 33)

'Rolls were our afternoon snack'. (Man, 32)

'School lunches started around the time we entered school. They tasted awful'. (Man, 34)

What we did

'There weren't any toys'. (Man, 34)

'All the girls wanted baby dolls that drank a bottle and wet their diapers'. (Woman, 32)

'Hula Hoop. Some people did it too much and got sick'. (Woman, 33)

'When the new bullet train passed, we ran to look, even in the middle of class'. (Man, 34)

'I didn't understand the fuss about the Security Treaty, but "Oppose the Security Treaty" became something we all said'. (Man, 34)

'When I was in high school, a lot of us formed bands. In those days the very words "electric guitar" were exciting'. (Man, 32)

'There were many who imitated the Ventures'. (Man, 33)

'College was student movements and rock bands'. (Man, 34)

'The first Go-Go boom. I was a regular customer at Ashibe in Shinjuku'. (Man, 32)

'I went to jazz coffee shops almost every day'. (Women, 32)

'It was an interesting time to be young. There was always something happening'. (Man, 34)

'To get by we all had part-time jobs. It was a great time to be alive'. (Man, 34)

'We experienced all sorts of things. I wore everything from micro minis to long skirts'. (Woman, 34)

Our friends

'We were called latchkey kids'. (Man, 32)

'Tokyo municipal high schools were at their peak. Everyone got together and went to a city school'. (Man, 33)

'The first wave of Ivy League fashions, that was our generation'. (Man, 34)

'When we found jobs we were called single aristocrats'. (Man, 33)

'Our honeymoons were all at the same time. It was crowded wherever we went'. (Woman, 32)

'Ten years from now, we will all be window-watchers on the sidelines. But since it will be all of us, it's nothing to be afraid of'. (Man, 34)

'There were so many of us the same age I wasn't able to marry'. (Woman, 34)

And now

'Our generation was educated using multiple-choice tests. Even now, trying to write is a pain. Multiple-choice does limit the ability to express yourself'. (Women, 34)

'It's good to have choices'. (Man, 34)

'I hate handmade things. When I was a kid, we didn't have anything, so everything was handmade. This is something my wife and I fight about'. (Man, 34)

'I don't object to ready-made things. If anything, I desire them'. (Woman, 34)

'There are so many of us, we have friends everywhere. We can feel safe because our networks are wide'. (Man, 34)

'But we're always treated as a mass. I hate that'. (Man, 34)

'I don't like sticking out and being too visible, but I don't want to be exactly the same as the neighbors either'. (Woman, 34)

'To me there is a huge difference between getting together and being exactly the same as the neighbors'. (Man, 34)

'As a market, we're huge, but we also have our differences'. (Man, 33)

The Salaryman's Guide to Advancement
Lifestyle Times, June 1982

The Art: The cover (Figure 3.2) portrays salarymen as schoolboys. They are sitting at their desks, waiting for the teacher to appear. The copy on the blackboard reads, 'The Salaryman's Guide to Advancement, the public type? Or the private type?' Figure 3.3 shows the light and dark aspects of the salaryman's four faces. The vertical axis ranges from outside (*soto*) to inside (*uchi*), the horizontal axis from public roles to private self. Reading top to bottom, on the left we see the salaryman at work and at home, playing public roles. On the right, we see him socializing and, then, in the private time he has for himself. When socializing he escapes the constraints of prescribed roles at work and in the family, but this is still an external self, the persona the salaryman presents to the outside world. Figure 3.4. shows the good and bad sides of being promoted to section chief, the first major advance in a corporate career. The left shows the benefits: new tailored suits, applause from his family, deference from subordinates, better housing, playing the role of go-between at a wedding. The right shows the downside: sweating with anxiety and irritation over subordinates who are loose cannons, mandatory business entertaining, returning home late at night, having to take work home, being excluded from subordinates' gossip.

The Research Design: In addition to desk research using secondary sources, interviews with 72 middle-rank salarymen, plus 31 additional interviews with newly appointed section heads.

Public or Private?

How should a man live? Where should he take a stand? For a salaryman the choice is between public and private. To explore this issue, we enlisted the aid of 72 mid-career salarymen aged 30–49.

The salaryman has two faces: public and private. The public face has two sides: at work and at home. The private face appears at times when he frees himself from the duties society imposes.

Consider the man who is brisk and energetic at work. He quickly surpasses his age mates and is first to be promoted. He is successful in public. Others focus on private life, participating in community affairs or consumer movements, or cultivating a hobby. Let's start, however, with public success, which is what most salarymen desire.

Figure 3.2 Cover, 'Guide to Salaryman Success'

One in Two Wants to be a Manager

There is more to being a manager than carrying a business card with the title section or division chief, being able to sit in a chair with armrests, and having authority inside the company. It's having a position in society.

Nearly half of our subjects said that their aim is a higher management position. Only 30 per cent want to be specialists with expertise in particular fields. The remainder want no problems at work, preferring instead a well-rounded social or family life. The largest group, then, is those competing for higher positions.

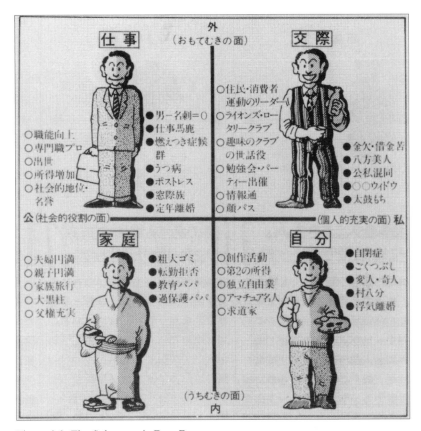

Figure 3.3 The Salaryman's Four Faces

How salarymen are sifted

Division chiefs are only 1.3 per cent of the total labor force. Section chiefs account for 4.4 per cent. For new university graduates, the chances of becoming either are slim. For Baby Boomers born between 1947 and 1949, the lack of openings makes the competition more than usually severe.

You are, perhaps, familiar with the 2-5-2-1 principle. Ten years after joining their companies, salarymen are sorted into four groups. About 20 per cent are the talented people on whom the company depends. The 'three *zu*' type who are never late (*okurezu*), never take vacations (*yasumazu*), and never work (*hatarakazu*) account for half. The rest are composed of the 20 per cent who are 'scrap' and the 10 per cent who are parasites and actively harm the company. In companies big and small, this kind of sorting goes on. It's not only hard to get ahead these days. Simply surviving may be difficult.

Figure 3.4 The Bright and Dark Sides of Becoming a New Section Chief

Tension on the job increasing

A wave of change of enormous proportions is bearing down on the workplace. Besides lack of positions, salarymen now have to worry about TQC (total quality control, including administrative functions), OA (office automation), selective promotion, changes in job classification, merit-based advancement, internationalization, women in the workplace, and the danger of being sidelined. As the wave of change grows bigger, tension is rising.

Public life also includes the public side of family life. The media are filled with stories of men tossed out of the house as oversized trash. Selection pressures are high at home as well as at work. Reports of mental illness, alcoholism, and divorce following retirement increase the tension that salarymen feel.

The Salaryman's Four Faces

When we think about 'public' and 'private' in connection with salarymen, we tend to equate them with 'work' and 'family'. But the real meaning of 'private' is the salaryman's private time, something increasingly hard to find, even when he is at home. Even there his public roles as household head, provider, husband, and parent take up most of his time (Figure 3.3).

Work is public squared

Success at work means either promotion or winning recognition as a specialist. Position and fame are the bright side. On the dark side we find the equation 'man minus business card equals zero'. Work is a man's heaviest responsibility.

Home is public, too

On the bright side are the public roles of the good father and husband and the pleasures provided by home and family. On the dark side are fathers who interfere or push too much and, when others cease to listen, are tossed out as oversized trash.

Private social life

What is social life? Here we mean involvement in community affairs and study groups unconnected with the company. Social life connected with work is work, not something the salaryman does for himself. Fewer than ten per cent of our sample participate in real social life. Something is missing here.

No face of his own

Today's salaryman lacks a personal face, unconstrained by public roles at work or at home. Those who achieve a professional level in pursuing their hobbies, who write books or music, have this kind of face. The most personal faces of all belong to those who do well in both public and private roles.

Seven Types of Salarymen

The Homing Pigeon flies back and forth between workplace and home. Just under 30 per cent of our subjects belong to this type. As one 42-year-old put it, 'Work is the way I contribute to society and the way I ensure a peaceful life at home'. This type is a good company man and a good husband and parent as well. He has no interest in becoming a specialist. He would like to be promoted, but it's not the most important thing.

He enjoys hiking and likes to take trips with his family. He wants to be a good father. One, 38, says, 'I pay attention to my children. I am always ready to talk with them'. It takes a lot of energy to fulfill obligations both at work and at home, but this is one classic approach to salaryman success.

The Sunflower is always looking toward those above him. Accounting for more than 40 per cent of our subjects, this type believes that a man must work and is eager for success as a manager or specialist. Most of his social life is work related. One, 42, says. 'I participate in every group activity I can'. He doesn't have much time for his family. 'I leave household matters to the wife. For a man, work is No. 1', says another, 44. This path is the way to the business elite, but disappointment may cause mental illness. Since only half these men share interests with their wives, the likelihood of their winding up as oversized trash is high.

The Celebrity isn't the 'I'm a star' type. He's the one who is always polishing his skills and using them as weapons at work. One, 43, says, 'A company should be a place where you can do something for society but also something for yourself. If work isn't satisfying, you can't keep employees from slacking off'. He rejects the idea that people should sacrifice themselves for the sake of the company and feels strongly that a man's work should make use of his abilities. His participation in company-related groups is minimal. He prefers, instead, to spend time on his own interests. One, 36, likes climbing mountains and reading books. Another, 47, says that he wants to publish a book. A third wants to add a private study to his house. For all three, what they want is their top priority. This type makes up only 10 per cent of our sample, but this path may become increasingly attractive for those with valuable skills. (Is this type more common in the West?)

My Friday is the man for whom every night is Friday night. His social life with his buddies is more important than work, family or hobbies. Accounting for only ten per cent of our sample, he regards his work as nothing more than a way to make money and spends more time on social life outside the company than on joining company groups. When asked about his family, one, 39, replies, 'I try to stay healthy'. The high risk here is extravagance leading to bankruptcy. We can't recommend this path to those who lack self-control.

My Home is the fellow to whom his family is more important than anything else. This type is unexpectedly rare, only one in forty of those we studied. One, 43, says, 'The company is a way to make a living, a place to make money, but that's all. Home is where the love between husband and wife is complete. Travel with wife and children? Yes, I want to spend as much time as I can with them'. The danger here is becoming too interfering. His children or wife may want their independence. We also wonder how confident he is that the way he has chosen is best when he sees others being promoted.

Bonsai's life is like a miniature garden in a box. It is small but contains mountains and rivers. It's a world unto itself with everything he needs: work, family, friends, all kept in careful balance. He may, however, sometimes feel a strong urge to break out. One, 33, says, 'Most men would like to use others instead of being used. But those with that strength are rare. I need a place where I can train and make myself stronger. If I had the guts and a better offer, I'd change jobs instantly'. 'I'd like to take a year off and go back to school, preferably overseas', says another, 40. People say that working women are often of this type. Among the men we talked to, we found only one in 25.

Mr. Leisurely does a certain amount of work, but since he won't be fired, he doesn't let work interfere with family or friends. He has fallen behind in the race for promotion. To those still longing for public success, he seems a failure. But, he says, 'Because of lifetime employment, I can still enjoy my lifestyle'. The leader of a bird-watching club, he also likes mountain climbing, soccer, and golf. He has plenty of time for his family. To walk this path takes enough confidence not to worry when people scold you at work. It might be a problem if too many wanted to live this way, but our sample contained only one.

Is Becoming a Section Head Sweet or Sour?

Becoming a section head is the first step up the management ladder, but how does it taste to be sitting at last in a section head's chair? To find out, we asked thirty-one newly appointed section heads.

The most frequently mentioned new perks were a manager's chair with armrests (24), a bigger desk (21), and a larger expense account (16). Next came a locker of one's own (7), a cabinet (6), a direct-line telephone (6), taxi coupons (6) and a company credit card (2). Only one got a personal secretary. Two got nothing but a new title and increased responsibility. None received a company car, a private office or a private meeting room. There were bonuses and increases in base pay, but with companies cutting costs and use of computers becoming more common, the material rewards of becoming a section head weren't lavish.

A typical section head

We asked how life changes when a man becomes a section head. What increases most is 'the amount of work I take home'. The biggest decline is in paid vacation actually taken. The lives of new section heads are a struggle to manage their time.

THINGS THAT INCREASE
(1) Work taken home
(2) Work-related responsibility
(3) Work-related authority
(4) Time spent in meetings
(5) Discussions with colleagues, subordinates
(6) Opportunities to meet people
(7) Work-related expenses
(8) Work-related stress
(9) Number of subordinates
(10) Income

THINGS THAT DECREASE
(1) Use of paid vacation
(2) Private time
(3) Time to do one's own work
(4) Number of business trips
(5) Time to think

In the past these men might have looked with envy or cold ambition at the chairs they now occupy. But to find oneself sitting there is an unexpectedly stressful change. Chances for family communication become more infrequent; time for hobbies disappears. The number of business trips declines. The section head who wants to rise further can rarely leave his chair.

Over time it goes stale

According to a Daiichi Kangyo Bank survey, 43 per cent of section heads are satisfied with their jobs; sixteen per cent are not. Satisfaction decreases with age: 50.6 per cent of those forty and younger are satisfied. At age 45, this figure shrinks to 44.0 per cent. At 55, it shrinks further to 33.4 per cent. The longer a man is a section head, the more he wants to speak out. The stronger his commitment to public success, the greater his dissatisfaction becomes.

Trampling the flowers, facing the storms

In Japanese firms, section heads work the hardest of all. Upper management determines overall direction. Division heads pass down top management's orders. They are the ones who get to say, 'Do this, do that', while scolding the section heads to spur them on. The section head bears a heavy burden. If he can carry it off, he can hope for quick promotion. Then, as a division head, he, too, will have more scope for self-expression. The section head who is aiming at public success has no choice but to do his job as well as possible.

Becoming a specialist

When the burden is too heavy and a section head realizes that he isn't upper management material, he may shift to a second track. By demonstrating unusual skills, he can shift his career onto a specialist course. Specialization will, we believe, become more common. But for those who have been section heads, that special flavor is hard to forget.

New Salaryman Constitution Proclaimed
Lifestyle Times, October 1987

The Art: The cover (Figure 3.5) depicts a political meeting. A document is being read. Banners in the crowd are decorated with neckties, shoes and pens. All are salaryman symbols. Except for the figures on the stage, we see no faces, and the face of the speaker is hidden behind the document he is reading. The three figures sitting behind the speaker all have beards or moustaches but are otherwise expressionless.

The Research Design: The subjects of the survey from which the data reported here are taken were four groups of one hundred each: New Breed males (age 25–29), men in their thirties (aged 35-39), men in their forties (aged 45–49), and office ladies (aged 20–24). All work for companies with 1,000 or more employees. Total n = 400.

Salarymen Are Changing

In 1962, salarymen were singing about planting gardens and making an easy living. Japan's high-growth period was in its early stages. Twenty-five years later, the salaryman's life has changed tremendously. The worker bees who sustained rapid growth and were given lifetime employment and seniority-based salaries in exchange are now approaching retirement. A New Breed has appeared. Caught between them, the Baby Boomers are now middle management. All three generations confront fundamental changes in the ways their companies operate, including a shortage of management posts.

Three distinct generations

The Old Breed were in school during postwar reconstruction. The Baby Boomers were students during the high-growth period. The New Breed have grown up in a world of peace and plenty.

The Old Breed directly experienced high growth. They look back on Japan's economic miracle as something they achieved and feel strong pride in what they accomplished. In contrast, the Baby Boomers and New Breed found jobs in years when growth was steady but slow.

Figure 3.5 Cover, 'The New Salaryman's Constitution'

Values are changing fast

While all companies have work rules, only twenty per cent of salarymen follow them religiously. To most, the rules seem superficial and not to be taken too seriously. What is it, we wonder, that salarymen take to be commonsense?

When we try to answer this question, we are likely to jumble together our three generations and create a false picture. Because of the different eras in which their lives are rooted, these three generations are very different. Note, too, that the Baby Boomers, who share some of the New Breed's attitudes, are now approaching forty. They and the New Breed now outnumber the Old Breed. Attitudes that were changing slowly will now change more quickly.

Skipping After-Five

'After-five' implies work-related drinking, mahjong, or dinner. When we look, however, at drinking (said to be the most typical form of salaryman social life), we find that if asked to go drinking, men will go only 60 per cent of the time, office ladies (OLs) only 40 per cent. Only 40 per cent of either group go out at least once a month with their bosses. Twenty per cent of the men and 40 per cent of OLs refuse to go out with the boss at all.

The New Breed go out with their bosses only 1.7 times a month (versus 3.3 times with their colleagues). They hate work-related socializing and don't want to go out with their bosses.

If we look at who picks up the check, we find that nearly half the New Breed won't chip in if taken out by their bosses. They go to get a free drink. When members of the older generation go out with their subordinates, they are stuck with bills for ¥10,000 or more. The usual pattern is to go to one or two places and drink for about three hours.

Invitations and refusals

What happens, then, when the boss invites someone for a drink? The style of both invitations and refusals varies depending on the sex of the recipient. To a man, the boss will start by saying, 'Just a moment', 'We don't often get the chance', or 'It's nothing special, but'. When you hear one of these three phrases, it is time to be on the alert. The boss will continue, 'Shall we go drinking?' or 'Shall we have just one?' What often happens is a steadily escalating, three-step pattern: 'Wouldn't you like to go drinking?', then 'Let's go drinking', then 'We are going drinking!'

In contrast, when inviting women to go out, the boss will use a softer opening. Examples include, 'Do you have any plans tonight?' or 'I've found this really great place'. Some bosses will ask directly if a woman has a date planned. They are hoping that she will say no and give them an opening.

There are, of course, ways to refuse an invitation. The most common are 'I've still got work to do' or 'I am not feeling well'. An increasing number of men claim that they have to work overtime. Here we list some smooth refusals, and then some that break the rules.

SMOOTH REFUSALS
- My wife has made chestnut rice, she's waiting for me.
- The doctor has told me I can't drink.
- My child is sick.
- Yesterday would have been OK, but ...
- It's too bad, I'd really like to go, but ...
- I'm sorry, I can't go ... Do invite me again some time.
- My grandparents have come up from the country.
- I have twisted my ankle and can't walk.

CLUMSY REFUSALS

- I've made a date with my lover.
- I've got no reason to go drinking with you.
- I don't have to tell you why.
- If I can have tomorrow off.
- Silence.
- What, you want to go drinking again?
- My boyfriend is waiting for me.
- When I go drinking with you, the liquor turns my stomach.

30 per cent dislike company trips

Division chief, section chief, group chief, ordinary salarymen: off they go together for a two-day company trip. This jumbling together of work and private time is an intensified version of workplace social life. More than 80 per cent of our subjects go on company trips, but not happily. For the salaryman on a company trip, what the boss defines as 'Today let's relax and get rid of the stress of everyday life' amounts to losing a day off and having to spend his own money on something he doesn't want to do.

50 per cent oppose company sports days

Even junior high and high schools have stopped having sports days, but what about companies? Half of our subjects say that sports days are a waste of time. Only 37 per cent of the Old Breed agree. They typically feel that everyone should enjoy getting together. About 40 per cent of companies still have sports days and force Baby Boomers and the New Breed to participate. Nearly 30 per cent, however, don't.

Please don't invite me to weddings

Year by year the scale of weddings is getting bigger. Many worry about who from the company has to be invited, but what about those who receive invitations? Our survey revealed that 48.3 per cent, or nearly half, don't want to be invited. This feeling grows stronger with age; 56 per cent of older managers share it. Since they get invited to many weddings and have to spend large sums of money on wedding gifts, they would happily pass up invitations issued just because someone thinks that they have to be invited.

Unless you were close, it's a waste

As you grow older, you attend more funerals and wakes. Older salarymen go to three or more funerals a year. Each time they give between ¥5,000 and ¥10,000 in condolence money. It's supposed to be a form of mourning; but if you have never known the deceased (one of your colleagues' parents, for example), what are you actually feeling? Nearly half our subjects think that going is a waste. Isn't this figure rather high for something we do as a duty?

Men Smoke, Women Redo Their Make-Up

Nine out of ten of our subjects agree on the need for breaks. Few still say, 'You must concentrate on your work' or 'Home is the place to relax'. Most agree that breaks are necessary 'to refresh your spirits' or 'to increase efficiency by alternating work and time off'.

The ways in which men and women take breaks are very different. The vast majority of men smoke a cigarette. Women go to the toilet to redo their make-up or chat while sitting at their desks. Here's another interesting contrast: men take breaks by drinking tea; women take breaks by making tea.

Ninja Breaks

The Smoke Screen. When you need a breather, light up. Since women don't like to smoke at their desks, it is men who started this trend. Don't smoke so much that what you produce is a real smoke screen.

Hiding in the Snow. The toilet is the only private space in the office. There you can take a nap, read a magazine, or do whatever you like. But Japanese-style toilets are no good; your legs go to sleep.

Go On Patrol. Walk around pestering others: 'You're hard at it, I see'. Pretend to have business in other departments. Be careful, however, that you aren't discovered having nothing to do.

Be Deep in Thought. The difficult thing is keeping your brow furrowed. The idea is look as if you have just stopped for a moment and are now thinking hard. Be careful not to snore.

Confer with Someone. Women used to gather around the village well; now they gather at someone's desk. Be careful to avoid loud voices and laughter.

Hide in the Clouds. Say, very softly, 'It's time to leave'. Then just disappear without telling anyone where you are going. Be careful though that people don't start talking about you never being around.

Goofing Off

There are a few ways of taking a break that we see as going too far. A new employee goes home while supposedly out on sales calls. A woman does her sewing on the job. A middle manager falls asleep at his desk for two hours in a row. A programmer with a 39-degree fever goes to sleep in the computer room on a mattress made of computer printout.

Beyond the Illusion of Common Sense

There is always a gap between attitudes and behavior. Seventy per cent of people will say 'It doesn't matter' but would never do whatever it is they are talking about themselves. The tables below show the top five items for which the gap between what people say and what they actually do is greatest.

They say it's OK, but what they actually do is different.

	OK	Did It	Gap
1. Invite someone of the opposite sex for drinking or dinner one on one	83.8	40.0	43.8
2. Don't bring back local products as souvenirs from a business trip	88.8	49.3	39.5
3. Go on an overnight business trip with a member of the opposite sex	40.3	4.3	36.0
4. Don't bring back local products as souvenirs from a vacation trip	88.3	56.3	32.0
5. At lunch, eat something better than what the boss has	80.3	50.5	29.8

They know it's wrong, but they do it.

	OK	Did It	Gap
1. Making personal phone calls from your desk	39.0	68.0	−29.0
2. Yawning during a meeting	36.0	56.0	−20.0
3. Private conversation during working hours	71.0	88.0	−17.0
4. Napping during working hours	8.0	21.5	−13.5
5. Slipping out for private business (e.g., going shopping)	29.5	41.8	−12.3

The Old Breed and the New

The largest gaps between attitudes and behavior are found among New Breed OLs, followed by the New Breed and then the Baby Boomers. The older generation is more consistent. The New Breed seem confused about how far they can actually go.

Of the 63 items in our list, 32 were labeled unacceptable by a high proportion of the older generation. Baby Boomers condemned only twenty, the New Breed only eleven. When, however, we look at individual items, we find that the older generation is not uniformly rigid. There are several items for which the New Breed are more likely than the older generation to condemn the behavior in question.

Neither the New Breed nor the Baby Boomers see anything wrong with private conversation or touching a female colleague on the shoulder. Here Baby Boomer attitudes are continuing in the New Breed.

The New Breed are often confused by what the older generation consider commonsense. The older generation are perplexed by being seen as old-fashioned and rigid.

Generation Gaps

More New Breed Say OK

(Percentage difference, New vs. Old)

1. Private conversation in the workplace — 31.6%
2. Coming to work with a hangover — 29.5%
3. Touching female employees on the shoulder — 26.8%

More Old Breed Say OK

(Percentage difference, Old vs. New)

1. Not inviting co-workers to a wedding — 14.5%
2. Not going out drinking with co-workers — 13.5%
3. Not bringing back souvenirs from vacation — 13.4%

More Boomers say OK

(Percentage difference, Boomer vs. New)

1. Private conversation in the workplace — 16.0%
2. Touching female colleagues on the shoulder — 12.0%
3. Reading sports newspapers at your desk — 8.0%

More Old Breed Say OK

(Percentage difference, Old vs. New)

1. Not inviting co-workers to a wedding — 11.0%
2. Not going out drinking with co-workers — 11.0%
3. Coming to work in casual clothes on holidays — 11.0%

More New Breed Say OK

(Percentage difference, New vs. Old)

1. Demanding entertainment from business partners — 27.1%
2. Coming to work with a hangover — 25.5%
3. Going to funerals and wakes — 19.4%

More Boomers say OK

(Percentage difference, Boomer vs. New)

1. Reading business magazines at your desk — 6.0%
2. Going to a movie while you're out on business — 5.7%
3. Crossing your legs during a business conversation — 5.5%

The Unacceptable

Below we list behaviors that virtually everyone labels unacceptable, but four to five per cent of salarymen do these things. On July 28, for example, we observed a couple sitting in Hibiya Park for an hour starting at 3:00 p.m. The man was wearing a blue suit and seemed to be about 25. The woman looked like a college student and was wearing a pink dress. It looked like dating during business hours. On September 14, we observed the crowd leaving the Scala-za Theater at 2:30 p.m. after the noon showing of *Fire Dragon*. About twenty per cent of the 166 people we checked appeared to be salarymen. Salarymen generally account for half or more of those playing in the afternoon at the pachinko parlors under the tracks at Yurakucho Station.

Unacceptable Top Five

	No-no	*Do it*
1. Going to a sauna during working hours	95.8%	4.3%
2. Dating while out on business	95.3%	3.5%
3. Going to a movie while out on business	95.0%	5.0%
4. Playing pachinko while out on business	93.8%	8.5%
5. Listening to headphone stereo during working hours	91.5%	5.5%

Fuzzy Zones

Fuzzy zones occur where the gap between the commonsense rule and actual behavior is small. When it comes to things like 'Going to a bookstore during working hours' or 'Taking a day off to play golf', most people find it hard to distinguish right from wrong. The New Breed score higher than Baby Boomers on some items. On others the Baby Boomers score higher than the older generation. Overall the results are mixed. There are no definite trends.

Adulterous office affairs are something that most people still find unacceptable, but generations differ slightly. Two-thirds of all our subjects find office affairs unacceptable. Only 60 per cent of the New Breed and 58 per cent of OLs agree with this opinion.

The Heisei Salaryman Constitution
Lifestyle Times, February 1995

The Art: The cover (Figure 3.6) is a simple graphic design with no illustration. The Japanese characters for the title are arranged vertically on what appears to be a small handbook.

The Research Design: The survey for this subject duplicated the one from which the data for 'New Salaryman Constitution Proclaimed' were taken. Subjects were divided into four groups of one hundred each: New Breed males (age 25–29), men in their thirties (aged 35–39), men in their forties (aged 45–49), and office ladies (aged 20–24). All work for companies with 1,000 or more employees. Total n = 400.

After the Bubble

It has been seven years since the start of the Bubble in 1987. To find out how salarymen have changed, we replicated our earlier study. The trends we found then have grown stronger.

Increasingly, the individual is respected more than the group. Boundaries between male and female, senior and junior are disappearing. A spirit of egalitarianism is rising in the workplace. The common sense that had governed the Japanese workplace since the end of World War II is collapsing. More and more people say, 'Well, why not?' Norms are becoming more relaxed.

The Bubbly, the Angry, the Awakened

Those who entered companies around 1990, when the Bubble Economy was at its peak, are now in their late twenties. These relaxed, fun-loving, 'Bubbly Ones' are trapped in the Bubble's illusions. In contrast, the New Breed, those who entered companies around 1980, when Japan's economy was in recession, are now in their late thirties. They are now the 'Angry Ones' who bear the company's weight on their backs and are filled with rage against their bosses. The Baby Boomers, who found jobs around 1970, when the high-growth period was drawing to a close, are now in their late forties. The shadows of the student struggles of the sixties have disappeared from their faces. Now the 'Awakened Ones', they have come to accept the world as it is. In the data reported below, figures in parentheses are for men aged 25–29, 35–39, and 45–49 respectively.

82

Figure 3.6 Cover, 'The Heisei Salaryman's Constitution'

The Bubbly Ones: 25–29

Tend to be a bit selfish. They take it easy and can't forget the Bubble's sweetness.

- If work is done properly, dress and attitude don't matter. (31%, 12%, 11%)
- Taking breaks is natural. (98%, 89%, 87%)
- Being a salaryman is an easy way to make a living. (28%, 23%, 21%)
- Prefer time off to a higher salary. (35%, 27%, 30%)
- It was hard finding a job. (13%, 28%, 27%)
- If something painful happens, I'll cry. (14%, 1%, 3%)
- I'd like to change jobs. (45%, 31%, 36%)
- But, I'd like to succeed while staying at the company. (73%, 57%, 57%)

The Angry Ones: 35–39

They don't flatter their bosses.

- I don't send Mid-Summer or New Year's presents to my boss. (76%, 86%, 69%)
- I don't send New Year postcards. (29%, 41%, 37%)
- You should do what your boss tells you. (54%, 49%, 61%)

They do have a lot of self-confidence.

- I take time off while I still have some energy. (65%, 73%, 63%)

They are angry because nobody else – part timers, full time employees, managers – seems to work as hard as they do.

- You carry the company on your back. (46%, 68%, 61%)
- Women have it easy. (33%, 60%, 46%)

The Awakened Ones: 45–49

Their attitude is cool.

- Loyal to the company. (60%, 80%, 86%)
- Follow their bosses orders. (54%, 49%, 61%)
- Flattery is necessary. (31%, 31%, 41%)
- Want to stay in the same company until retirement. (29%, 58%, 69%)

Progressive.

- Merit-based evaluations should be more thoroughly implemented. (65%, 65%, 71%)

But also traditional.

- You should come to work even if you have a hangover. (61%, 63%, 69%)

Money is important.

- Prefer a higher salary to more time off. (41%, 39%, 52%)

Conversation with Sekizawa Hidehiko
February, 1998

JLM: How has salaryman life changed since HILL published 'The Guide to Salaryman Success'?

SH: The biggest difference is that in today's Japan, meritocracy has become the rule. No longer is everyone equal. There can be differences in salary and conditions even between people hired at the same time, so competition is stiffer. Even though Japanese salarymen are said to work hard all the time, the number who put more importance on their families has increased. There is also more stress on the individual.

JLM: Has the family-like, we-are-all-in-this-together feeling of company life broken down as much as 'The Heisei Salaryman's Constitution' claims?

SH: In this study, the focus is on generational as opposed to age differences. Age matters, but there is also something else going on. With company systems changing and more emphasis on merit, things are different now. Personal achievement has become more important. It may be even more important that individuals now want their work to be interesting. Japanese salarymen are no longer the classic workaholic, group-oriented types who see work as an obligation.

Another big difference is not being bothered when they see others behaving differently from themselves. Also, the number of people who say they aren't disturbed by being seen as different has increased enormously. Still, only about 20 to 30 per cent are actually behaving differently. While attitudes have changed, around 80 per cent are still conformists.

JLM: More people say that they want to enjoy their work, but ...

SH: Whether or not people actually enjoy their work varies from one workplace to another. If people today find their work boring, or the workplace irritating, they quit their jobs. Even when economic conditions are tough, they quit and look for other jobs. The rate of job-hopping is still low compared to the rest of the world, but it's gotten much higher than it used to be.

JLM: Is it true that boundaries between male and female are breaking down?

SH: Compared to Europe and America, there is still a lot of discrimination.

JLM: What about the falling rate of OL participation in company activities?

SH: Japanese women's commitment to companies does seem low.

JLM: Is this a post-Bubble phenomenon? It's harder now for women to find jobs.

SH: There is no denying that it has gotten more difficult for women to find jobs. That's a mistake on the part of corporate management. It may also be that women are looking for a more human way to live. To make money, they work at part-time or temporary jobs. Then, when they've saved a bit, they study abroad or try to secure some additional qualification. Men will put up with boring work, even if they aren't much interested in it. Women won't stick it out no matter what. So it's both a matter of companies pushing women out and women's deciding to leave. Society is more forgiving of women who decide to leave and try something else.

JLM: What does 'more enjoyable work' mean to men?

SH: More than the content of the work, isn't it a matter of being able to do what you want to do because you want to do it? More than what you do, isn't it how you do the work? What's bad is a boss who doesn't know anything about the client or the current situation insisting on your doing things his way. But that's changing. More and more companies are saying, 'You are the one in the front line. You know what's going on. You do it your way'. That's a big change. So if you succeed, it's your success; if you fail, it's your failure. In that respect, work has become more fun. 'Fun' means more involvement and having the right to make decisions.

JLM: Where it used to be the team that won or lost, now it's the individual player.

SH: That's it exactly. In this respect the Japanese system has changed a lot. It will probably go on changing. It may become more like Europe ... but it won't be like America. Group-orientation will decline as individuals are given more importance. Heavy and manufacturing industries will have a smaller role. Even in the automobile industry, for example, the position of those who have redesigned factories and made manufacturing more efficient will decline. The weight will shift to product development, to people who decide what kinds of cars should be made. The creative sections will expand. People in these sections can't do things just because that's the way their bosses are used to doing them. They have to be sensitive to consumer trends and consumer desires. They have to have more individualistic, more flexible attitudes.

JLM: I can easily understand that in the case of advertising agencies, but making ads is still a craft-like business where one or two people do the work. But car companies, for example, where so many people have to be involved?

SH: In talking with many companies, I have noticed a difference between those where proposals are filtered through the chain of command from section chief to division chief, only to be rejected by the president, and those where a project team can present its work directly to the president. The management of the latter is quick and agile. The management of the former is slow and clumsy. When the quick and agile win, the slow and clumsy are forced to change their ways.

JLM: Quick and agile sounds like fun, but what about the guys in their 40s and 50s?

SH: For the ones who have always just done what they were told and taken no responsibility, it's going to be very hard.

JLM: What about these categories: the Bubbly Ones, the Angry Ones, the Awakened Ones?

SH: The Bubbly Ones entered the company during the bubble years. They have always had it easy, having fun in Azabu or Roppongi.

JLM: The Angry Ones are easy to understand. They had a good time, but now they are in their thirties. Times are tough.

SH: That's true, but people in this generation still have a strong interest in new products. A typical member of this generation has probably bought a digital camera, a digital camcorder, a personal computer, an electronic organizer ... or a station wagon. He still likes new things. It's at work that he's angry.

JLM: What about the Awakened Ones? Is this related to Zen?

SH: Doesn't 'awakened' just mean that they know things can't be helped? I wonder if those in this group really are awakened? On the positive side, they have experienced a lot of different things and know what life is about. But pure acceptance reflects a loss of life force. That's the result of aging. This passive type is the one who has the hardest time in American-style companies where he can be told he's no longer needed. There are lots of these people in Japanese companies. This group is the one whose members are most likely to be thrown out. That will be very tough.

Interview with Shindō Kazuma
February, 1998

JLM: What was going on in 1987 when you did 'The New Salaryman's Constitution'?

SK: Japan's traditional lifetime employment and seniority systems were starting to break down. That was the effect of the Baby Boomers. Because of them, the old system of organizational pyramids had to change. If lifetime employment and seniority systems hadn't changed, Japanese values wouldn't be changing the way they are now.

JLM: What has been the biggest change in the last decade?

SK: The disappearance of the older generation. What we'll see from now on is basically the continuation of the new postwar patterns. Things won't change that much from now on.

JLM: Won't we see radical changes in the social environment? With the aging population and fewer children?

SK: Lifetime employment and seniority systems were connected with the idea that the company is a family. That connection is breaking down. The aging society and fewer children seem like smaller problems. There have already been Japanese companies with too many older employees and too few younger ones. Ways have been found to deal with these problems. But firing long-time employees or not giving people the raises they expect – these reflect big changes in values.

JLM: The older generation have mostly retired, but a small group have become the top executives of Japanese corporations. Isn't there a tremendous gap between these top executives and the younger generations?

SK: In Japan, we are very group-oriented. The top executives may have the old values and really want to change things. But they can't avoid being influenced by the younger people. That's why things won't change that much. There aren't many Japanese executives who can act like American executives and make drastic changes. Japanese-style management depends on building consensus. In Japanese institutions, the top doesn't get to pull the bottom wherever it wants to go; instead, it waits to see which way things are moving and then goes along. The way you become a top executive is by being good at noticing what's happening and going along with what younger people want to do.

JLM: What about this 2-5-2-1 idea?

SK: It looks a little strange to me. I've often heard that only ten per cent are on the fast track. But surveys of worker attitudes show that nearly half of Japanese salarymen feel that they are important to their companies.

JLM: What about their three-*zu* type who are supposed to account for 50 per cent?

SK: Japanese salarymen are more likely, I think, to act like managers, reading the newspapers and wondering what's happening to Japan's economy. They all say 'our' company. That's something only an owner would say. That is one of the benefits of the lifetime employment and seniority-based promotion systems, having everyone advance together so that we all feel that way.

I'd say that 80 per cent of Japanese work hard. There may be twenty per cent who are worthless, but for those who work, lifetime employment is just right. With restructuring, that 80 per cent is going to shrink until only a minority work hard. That is when the Japanese way of doing things will really change.

JLM: Another idea that appeared in 'Guide to Salaryman Success' was the proposition that since only a small fraction of Baby Boomers could become section chiefs or division chiefs, most would have to look for other kinds of careers, other ways to find meaning in their lives.

SK: That study was done just after people became worried about the shortage of management posts. That problem has been solved. People have found other ways to be happy. If you can't be a division chief, you can still be a specialist. People who worried about not becoming division chiefs were still thinking like old-fashioned salarymen; to them not being promoted was failure. When values changed, not being promoted ceased to be a problem.

JLM: You are saying that salarymen have found new paths inside the company. Others say that, not being able to find satisfaction inside the company, they have become more family-oriented.

SK: To me it seems old-fashioned to pose the choice in this way. Problems at work are solved at work. Satisfaction at work and satisfaction in the family are different. If you are not happy at work, you can't be happy at home. You need to think about how to be happy both at home and at work. Becoming a division chief isn't as important to your status as it used to be. It means a lot of paper work, and many people don't want the responsibility. It doesn't make much difference to your salary.

JLM: What will happen, though, if there's more restructuring, with a shift to merit-based pay?

SK: If that happens, things will change.

JLM: In 'The Heisei Salaryman's Constitution' we find the words the 'Bubbly Ones', the 'Angry Ones, and the 'Awakened Ones'.

SK: The Bubbly Ones are the problem these days. They entered the company during the Bubble, when standards weren't very high. It isn't that there were too few of this group. Companies hired too many. Top companies were hiring two hundred instead of the hundred they usually took, so they got a lot of third-rate people. Other companies got even less-qualified people. Older people look at this generation and say that they're worthless, they can't do anything.

JLM: In 1987 the majority of the New Breed were unmarried. Now they are the Angry Ones.

SK: Even back then, they rejected established standards and were very picky about the brands that they bought, the things that they liked. They were always uppity. Many don't want to become managers. They hate the idea of becoming administrators.

JLM: But it is true, isn't it, that the New Breed now have families and are caught in the middle at their companies?

SK: Times are tough. But because they always wanted to do their own thing, they may be finding it especially tough. This is the worst possible time for people who aspire to their kind of lifestyle.

JLM: What about the Awakened Ones?

SK: Here life stage may be the biggest factor. People in this generation are now approaching retirement. Things won't change much for them from now on.

JLM: The Boomers experienced the student movements of the sixties; later generations haven't had this experience. Is this significant?

SK: Later generations don't understand what it is to fight. That's something we noticed in the New Breed. Boomers believed that they could make a difference, and they did, in fact, have an impact on society. They radically changed the family, for example. Later generations tend to see things as unchangeable. They are easily bored but don't feel that they themselves can make a difference. That is why they seem so cold.

4

WOMEN SPREAD THEIR WINGS

'*Onna no jidai*' or 'the era of women', is a catch phrase heard often these days in Japan. The implication is that, having attained a large measure of equality in a highly affluent society, Japanese women today are able to choose freely from a variety of options in their pursuit of an active and fulfilling life. At the same time, women are portrayed as being more vibrant, more independent, more in tune with new ideas and new values, and enjoying a happier, longer, more balanced lifestyle in comparison with their male counterparts, who are often portrayed as holding on to old-fashioned views on everything from marriage to the environment and tied to the dull, stultifying routine of the salaried white-color worker, or *sarariman*.

(Fujimura-Fanselow 1995: xvii)

The feminist who writes these words has good reason to doubt the image they portray. Women are, she writes, still far from achieving 'real substantive equality in nearly every sphere of life – the family, schools, the workplace, the media, and politics' (Fujimura-Fanselow 1995: xix).

There is, however, one sphere in which the prominence of women is clear – consumption. In Japan, as in other advanced capitalist economies, woman is, above all, the consumer par excellence.

Men earn, women spend. In Japan, as elsewhere, the stereotype is clear. In Japan, moreover, it is reinforced by the widely disseminated images of the free-spending, single office lady and the married housewife who controls her household's purse strings. The former is fashion-conscious, shops in trendy department stores, dines in gourmet restaurants, and frequently travels abroad. The latter is a careful spender and tight-fisted 'minister of finance' who returns to her salaryman husband a meager allowance from the income he earns. Behind these widely accepted images, there is, however, a history.

The Legal Status of Women

In the Meiji Civil Code, promulgated in 1898, women were granted few legal rights. The Confucian ideology which underlay the Code made woman a perpetual minor.

> When [a woman] married she entered her husband's family (and the family register) and control of her property was transferred to her husband. Custody of the children was held by the father exclusively. A husband's illegitimate sons (if any) had prior rights to the family estate over legitimate daughters.
>
> (Kaneko 1995: 4–5)

Article 5 in the Police Security Regulations of 1900 explicitly forbade women from joining political organizations. They were forbidden to initiate, hold, or attend meetings at which political speeches were given (Kaneko 1995: 4).

These laws would remain in force until after World War II. Then, at the insistence of SCAP, the Supreme Commander for the Allied Powers, General Douglas MacArthur, the enfranchisement and legal emancipation of women began. In 1945, women's suffrage was approved. In the Japanese Constitution, proclaimed in 1946, Article 14 bans discrimination on the basis of race, creed, sex, social status, or family origin. Article 24 explicitly states that marriage must be based on the consent of both individuals. In the revised Civil Code issued in 1947, the *ie* system, which embodied the restrictions described above, was abolished.

The next major change in women's status was the 1985 passage of the Equal Opportunities Employment Law. Its implications are, however, far from clear. The law stipulates that firms shall endeavor to treat women equally with men in hiring, placement, and promotion. There are, however, no penalties for violations. 'The law's effectiveness was left to firms' goodwill and administrative guidance by the government bureaucracy' (Kawashima 1995:284). Following the collapse of the Bubble, many firms cut back on hiring women as full time employees and eliminated many part-time jobs held by women.

Working Women and Wise Mothers

During the Meiji period (1868–1912), rural women were an important source of factory labor as Japan industrialized. It was not, however, until the Taisho era (1915–1926) and the first bloom of Japanese consumerism that the kinds of service industry jobs that so many Japanese women now fill emerged in urban areas (Skov and Moeran 1995: 14–15). The rise of militarism before and during World War II led to suppression of nascent feminist political movements and brought renewed emphasis on the proposition that a woman's proper place is in the home.

At the same time, however, efforts to mobilize women in support of the war improved the status of women – as mothers – as men went off to war. By embracing the state ideology of separate spheres for men and women, women's groups were able to construct 'more authoritative roles within the family for housewives and mothers and, by extension, new public roles for women within the state' (Garon 1997:144). Feminists who had previously promoted the independence of the modern woman went along with the new regime 'for the simple reason that it was the first time that [the state] had promoted a *positive* image of women' (Skov and Moeran 1995:15). It was during this period that the roles of women as bearers and educators of children while men were away from home took on a heightened significance in Japan's national project of becoming a world power.

For men who grew up before or during the war, Japan's defeat in World War II would be the death of ideals for which many would literally die. Survivors would become the corporate warriors who would fight new wars on economic battlefields. Women, meanwhile, were left with the choices of remaining at home as 'good wives and wise mothers' or pursuing careers outside the home. The consequences would fuel debates for years to come (Plath 1980:173–174).

Women in the Labour Force

Starting around 1965, the year after the Tokyo Olympics, rapid economic growth created a labor shortage. The shortage grew more severe when growing numbers of junior high school graduates went on to high school instead of looking for jobs. 'Women, especially housewives, were sought as a new labor supply' (Kawashima 1965: 271). By 1996, over twenty-six million, or 48.1 per cent, of Japanese women were gainfully employed for at least one hour a month.

Most Japanese women are not, however, hired as permanent, full-time employees (Kawashima 1995:278). Young women hired as office help leave their jobs to marry and have children. Returning to the labor force as middle-aged housewives, they find jobs that offer no hope of careers. Working here, working there, they move from job to job, fragmenting working lives that lack the narrative consistency of male careers and leave their lives centered in the home (Kondo 1990).

Educating Women

In 1872, a system of four years of compulsory education for members of both sexes was introduced to Japan. By the end of the century, elementary education was virtually universal, but education for men and women diverged sharply after the elementary level. The Imperial Rescript on Education promulgated in 1890 laid down the principle that women should be educated in a way that restricted their role to home and family (Hara 1995:97).

During the postwar years, higher education was a scarce commodity and one consumed primarily by men. According to Fujimura-Fanselow (1995:127), in 1955 only 2.6 per cent of females and 1.9 per cent of males went to junior college, while 2.4 per cent of females and 13.1 per cent of males went to university. The ratio of women to men receiving post-secondary education was one to three. It was one to six at the university level.

By 1970, as Baby Boomers graduated and entered the job market, 27.3 per cent of men were attending university, compared to 6.5 per cent of women. By 1994, however, a larger proportion of women than men were receiving some form of post-secondary education, 45.9 per cent versus 40 per cent.

In sum, while becoming more visible and vital as consumers, Japanese women have also become more educated and more likely to be employed outside the home. Not surprisingly, the position and possibilities of 'liberated' women have become hot issues in Japan as they have in other parts of the world.

Searching for Significance in New Lifestyles

It was 1970 when the words 'women's liberation' first appeared in Japan. That year would also see the death by ritual suicide of author Mishima Yukio and the holding of Expo '70 in Osaka. One was a literal death designed to have symbolic significance. Mishima's final words, 'Is there none among you who will join me ... ? Not even one ... ? So be it ... I have seen the end!' reproach the members of the Japan Self Defense Forces for having abandoned the romantic, masculine warrior ideal that Mishima sought to embody and revive. The other marked postwar Japan's debut as a major economic power, a society in which men would slip into the shadows as media began to highlight women.

The aggressive and aestheticized masculinity symbolized by Mishima's life and death would be pushed to the margins of Japanese society, where today it survives most palpably in the plaintive and raucous songs and speeches emitted from the sound trucks of right-wing political groups. As we have seen in Chapter 3, instead of a warrior, the ideal would be a salaryman, a self-effacing searcher for security – a man who prefers a comfortable life to a glorious death. In Japan's mass media, activity, independence, and aesthetic self-construction were increasingly portrayed as proper for women.

When Women Spread Their Wings

'What does my wife do with herself when she is alone in the middle of the day?' It is, say the HILL researchers who produced the 1982 study 'Housewives' Empty Nest Time', a question that husbands ask themselves. Suppose it turned out to be real, this 'Era of Women' played up so strongly in the press. With children away at school and husbands off at work, women would have more time of their own. The flood of household appliances and ready-to-eat, instant, or semi-processed foods and other convenience products produced by a rapidly growing economy would give them more control over that time. Coffee shops and culture centers, theaters and galleries, sports clubs and ever more lavish opportunities for shopping would tempt housewives to step out and enjoy themselves. Those who worked would have their own money, adding to their independence.

What, then, would become of women's traditional roles as wives and mothers? How would women themselves see the new possibilities that life seemed to offer? Would they all want careers? How would they manage their children? 'Housewives' Empty Nest Time' addresses these questions and identifies four types of Japanese housewives, women whose primary values are friends, family, house, and job, respectively, plus a fifth type who tries to have it all, including male friends besides her husband.

Two years later, in 1984, HILL published 'The Age of Women, Highlights and Shadows'. As in other parts of the world, it was the liberated woman who attracted the attention of the media; but what about the dark side? This study, based on research conducted in 1983, examined the fears and anxieties of women who saw themselves as ordinary, lacking the knowledge and ability to achieve the dazzling image the media presented to them. In 1993, HILL repeated the study. 'Cleopatra Complex' reports the results, paying special attention to successful but aging career women worried about preserving their looks along with the social position they had worked so hard to achieve.

Can Educating the Kids Be Fun?

It is not, of course, unusual that, as women become more liberated from traditional home-bound roles, their obligations as mothers become the focus of public debate. Postwar Japan, where the salaryman father goes off to work, leaving the children in the hands of their mothers, is certainly no exception. In the last of the issues of the *Lifestyle Times* translated for this chapter, HILL researchers examine the women they describe as 'Play Education Mamas'. The Japanese term is a twist on the term 'education mama', which refers to women, mostly middle-class housewives, whose lives are focused obsessively on their children's education.

In recent discussions of Japanese childhood, the education mama is a central figure. The salaryman father, whose long commute and long hours on the job make him a mostly absent parent, tends to be equally absent in the literature. Muramoto Kuniko's *The Lie Called the Happy Family* (*Shiawase Kazoku to iu Uso*) (1997) is a rare exception that focuses attention on fathers and their daughters. Far and away more frequent is the focus on mother and son, which is developed with particular poignancy in Anne Allison's *Permitted & Prohibited Desires: Mothers, Comics, and Censorship in Japan* (1996).

Allison is an anthropologist who, while doing fieldwork in Japan in 1987, was also a mother with a kindergarten-aged son. Like other kindergarten mothers, she had been given a calendar in which to keep track of her son's activities during his summer vacation. She hadn't taken the task seriously and, in fact, turned up at the kindergarten on the first day of the new term without it. She had, she writes, mistaken the calendar for a gift instead of the duty that it actually was. She found herself scolded by her son's teacher, who would not now be able to know what he had done with his summer. More serious still was the implication that this American mother had not sufficiently scheduled her son's activities and thus had failed to instill the routines needed for success in a Japanese school.

It must not be concluded, however, that the mother is expected to be a tyrant. On the contrary, her mission, Allison explains, is to make obligation desirable, to surround learning with acts of love and to make them 'so pleasant that they disguise and thereby instill the task at hand' (1996: 109).

The women studied by HILL go further. They not only want education to be more fun for their children. In wanting more fun for themselves as well, they violate traditional expectations that a good mother will sacrifice herself for her child. As a result, to HILL's researchers they seem like aliens – creatures from outer space – who have taken the place of real Japanese mothers.

Housewives' Empty Nest Time
Lifestyle Times, May 1982

The Art: Figure 4.1, the cover for this issue, shows a woman who is spreading her wings and flying away from the birdhouse in the tree to the right. The large head and little body seem childish, almost infantile, although they may, when seen through Japanese eyes, be only a common cartoon convention. The hair, the apron, the socks all signal that she is a mother. The title, *'Akisu'*, is a pun: while I have translated it as 'empty nest', it also means 'burglar' and suggests that women are stealing time for themselves. This issue opens out into a four-page spread (Figures 4.2–4.6) that illustrates the daily lives of four typical women and another type altogether, one who breaks the rules.

Figure 4.1 Cover, 'Housewives' Empty-Nest Time'

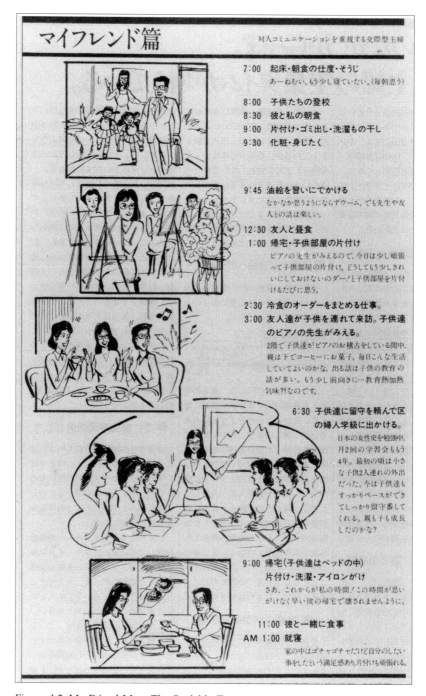

Figure 4.2 My Friend Mrs., The Sociable Type

Figure 4.3 My House Mrs., House-proud and Envied

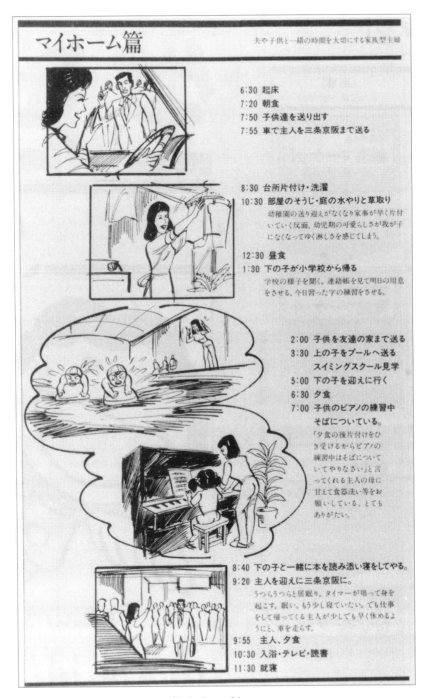

Figure 4.4 My Home Mrs., Family Is Everything

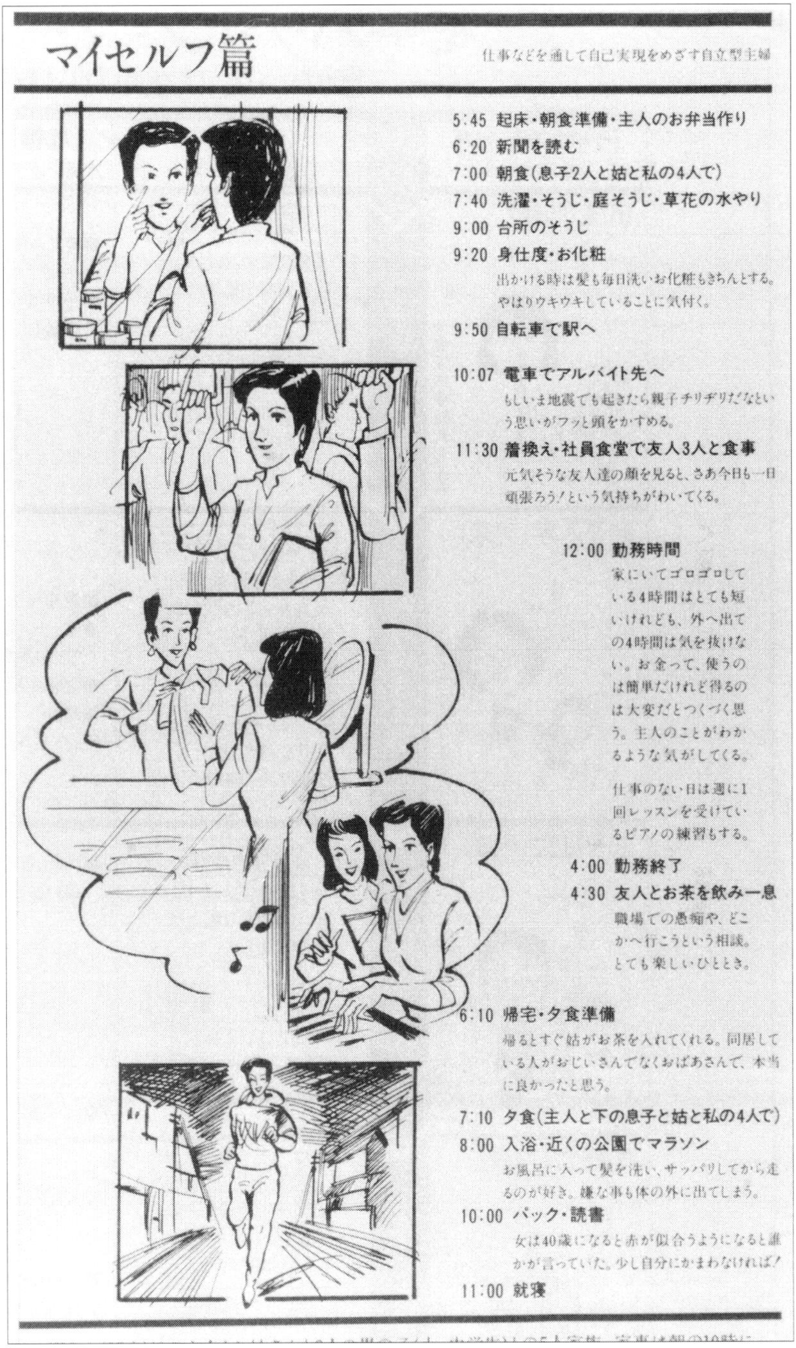

マイセルフ篇　　　　　　仕事などを通して自己実現をめざす自立型主婦

5:45　起床・朝食準備・主人のお弁当作り
6:20　新聞を読む
7:00　朝食(息子2人と姑と私の4人で)
7:40　洗濯・そうじ・庭そうじ・草花の水やり
9:00　台所のそうじ
9:20　身仕度・お化粧
　　　出かける時は髪も毎日洗いお化粧もきちんとする。
　　　やはりウキウキしていることに気付く。
9:50　自転車で駅へ

10:07　電車でアルバイト先へ
　　　もしいま地震でも起きたら親子チリヂリだなとい
　　　う思いがフッと頭をかすめる。
11:30　着換え・社員食堂で友人3人と食事
　　　元気そうな友人達の顔を見ると、さあ今日も一日
　　　頑張ろう！という気持ちがわいてくる。

12:00　勤務時間
　　　家にいてゴロゴロして
　　　いる4時間はとても短
　　　いけれども、外へ出て
　　　の4時間は気を抜けな
　　　い。お金って、使うの
　　　は簡単だけれど得るの
　　　は大変だとつくづく思
　　　う。主人のことがわか
　　　るような気がしてくる。

　　　仕事のない日は週に1
　　　回レッスンを受けてい
　　　るピアノの練習もする。

4:00　勤務終了
4:30　友人とお茶を飲み一息
　　　職場での愚痴や、どこ
　　　かへ行こうという相談。
　　　とても楽しいひととき。

6:10　帰宅・夕食準備
　　　帰るとすぐ姑がお茶を入れてくれる。同居して
　　　いる人がおじいさんでなくおばあさんで、本当
　　　に良かったと思う。
7:10　夕食(主人と下の息子と姑と私の4人で)
8:00　入浴・近くの公園でマラソン
　　　お風呂に入って髪を洗い、サッパリしてから走
　　　るのが好き。嫌な事も体の外に出てしまう。
10:00　バック・読書
　　　女は40歳になると赤が似合うようになると誰
　　　かが言っていた。少し自分にかまわなければ！
11:00　就寝

Figure 4.5 My Self Mrs., She's Got a Job

Figure 4.6 The Exception, She Breaks the Rules

The Research Design: Desk research, ethnographic observation, interviews with 147 women.

What Are Housewives Up To?

'What does my wife do with herself when she is alone in the middle of the day?' There must be many husbands who ask themselves this question. In this issue of the *Lifestyle Times*, we explore what happens during this 'empty nest time'. Besides the members of the HILL Housewife Network, our subjects also include the wives of Hakuhodo employees whose children entered first grade this year. One hundred and sixty-five women answered our questionnaires.

The nest is empty in the middle of the day

We asked how women spend both ordinary days at home and those on which they go out to work or pursue personal interests. On ordinary days they spend 22 hours at home. On the days when they go out, they spend only thirteen hours at home, a nine-hour difference.

When housewives go out, they leave an empty nest behind. A veteran market researcher remarks that, 'It has become harder to do surveys that target housewives. If you try to visit during the day, you find that houses are empty'. (The researcher cited is herself one of those housewives who leave their homes to go to work on a regular basis.)

Housewives are making time for themselves

Most mothers agree that when children enter kindergarten or elementary school, it is time to loosen the apron strings. Letting go of children is one source of free time. On average, children are 7.4 years old when their mothers send them off by themselves and start to have free time of their own.

Starting this April, when the Japanese school year starts, more than thirty per cent of our subjects had more free time; twenty per cent were busier. Explanations for not having more free time were 'a second, young child' and 'no school lunch program, so the children come home earlier than they did from kindergarten'.

Separation is a chance to be free

There were two reactions to letting go of children. While some mothers breathed a sigh of relief, others felt lonely. Those who felt lonely hadn't planned how to use their free time; freedom left them feeling bewildered. In contrast, those who had looked ahead and planned how to use their free time were happy.

One lonely mother said, 'With the kids and their friends running in and out, it was always very lively. When they all entered kindergarten and then elementary

103

school, it was too quiet. The atmosphere felt heavy'. In contrast, a happier mother said, 'I couldn't wait. I had already started looking for chances to use my time more effectively'.

Housework, a Pandora's box

Smart approaches to housework also save time. Only fourteen of our subjects told us they don't have any free time at all. Fifty said their free time is broken up into short chunks less than 30 minutes long. One hundred and two, however, were able to make time for themselves.

Some did it by careful scheduling. 'I make preparations for dinner while doing the laundry and cleaning. I do several things at once'. Others get all their housework done in one concentrated push: 'Whatever it takes, I get everything done by 10:30'. One scheduler says, 'I do the laundry after putting the kids to bed. All that's left for the morning is hanging it out to dry'. One gutsy woman told us, 'I either do all the housework at once, or decide not to bother. I shut my eyes to the whole thing'.

For all these women, the goal is make more time for themselves. In the words of one, aged 36: 'I must have time for myself! The most important thing is to be really determined'.

What Do They Do With Their Free Time?

Most housewives do not use their free time to relax. Starting this April, more than 70 per cent of our subjects intend to work, pursue a hobby, take up a sport, or join a study group. Others will socialize with friends.

Even those stuck in the nest think about what they want to do. One says, 'Life is so long. I'd like to find something that will last me a long time'. These women are strong.

Sociable 'My Friend Mrs.' in the mainstream

She describes herself as fresh and full of life, brisk and relaxed. She pursues a wide variety of interests: hobbies, sports, or study groups. Many women of this type strive to balance the needs of body and spirit: 'The times I enjoy most are when I forget my cares and sing and talk in a loud voice'. 'When wearing a leotard, I can talk about silly things and let go of my stress'.

Most envied: 'My House Mrs.'

The most popular alternative for all of the other types is the My House Mrs. Many housewives have to find jobs because of financial difficulties. To those who feel constantly pushed around in the workplace, there may come a moment when, suddenly, they would rather stay at home. My House Mrs. is brisk and full of life. In her free time, she is able to relax and pursue her hobbies. To other women, she embodies fulfillment and stability.

Life is hardest for family-first housewives

It is My Home Mrs., who always puts her family first, who finds her life most difficult. She describes herself as tense and irritable. She worries, for example, 'When the children go to elementary school, they will start to prefer their friends to me'. Those who would like to enjoy a long, relaxed conversation with their husbands find a relationship that can be summed up by 'finish supper, take a bath, go to sleep' highly stressful.

Independence requires physical strength

Independent My Self Mrs. leads a physically demanding life. Because having a job doesn't release her from household chores, she winds up short of sleep. Compared to those who work and then stop work to get married or those in marriages where both husband and wife work, those who marry first and then find jobs wind up with the heaviest burden of housework. Their brisk, lively exteriors cloak a daily diet of irritation.

My Friend Mrs.

The most important thing to her is socializing with her friends.

7:00   Gets up, makes breakfast, cleans.
Oh, I'm sleepy. Wish I could sleep some more. (I think this every morning.)
8:00   Gets kids off to school.
8:30   Breakfast with husband.
9:00   Straightens up, puts out the trash, hangs out the laundry to dry.
9:30   Puts on make-up, dresses to go out.
9:45   Oil painting class
Doesn't come out the way I'd like, but chatting with the teacher and friends is fun.
12:30 Lunch with friends.
1:00   Goes home, straightens the children's room.
Because the piano teacher will come today, I'd better tidy up the children's room. It will look bad if it isn't clean.
2:30   Organizes frozen food order.
3:00   Friends visit, bringing their children. The piano teacher appears.
Upstairs the children are practicing the piano, while I have coffee and cake with my friends. I wonder if it's right to do this every day. What we talk about is mainly our children's education ... If we were a bit more ambitious, we might catch education fever.

6:30   Leaves children to mind the house, goes off to a women's studies group sponsored by the ward.

It's a four-year course on Japanese women's history that meets twice a month. At first there were two women who brought small children with them. Now the children can stay home by themselves. Doesn't it look like both mother and child are growing up?

9:00   Returns home (the children are in bed), tidies, does the laundry and the ironing.

Now is my free time! If he gets home too early, he'll mess it up.

11:00   Dinner with husband.

1:00   Goes to bed.

My home may be messy, but I have the satisfaction of doing what I like. And I do my best to keep it tidy.

Our example is Mrs. K, whose four-person household includes her husband and two elementary-school-age daughters. She spends eight hours a day (three in the morning, three in the afternoon, two in the evening) with her friends. She's divided her housework and does some in the morning, some at night. She lets things go if they are too much bother. Rigid about the time her children go to bed, she likes to have time for herself before her husband gets home at night. She does, indeed, have a knack for making time for herself.

My House Mrs.

She is proud of how well she manages.

5:40   Gets up, makes breakfast, prepares a lunch box for the live-in nephew.

6:40   Husband, daughter, and nephew eat breakfast.

6:55   Nephew leaves for school.

On a fine, clear morning, I wake up feeling energetic. They say people with low blood pressure have trouble getting up in the morning. I don't believe it.

7:15   Husband leaves for work, daughter leaves for school. Puts out the trash, does the laundry, makes the beds.

8:00   Has breakfast with her mother-in-law.

8:20   Cleans kitchen.

9:00   Scrubs and wipes down the bathroom, sink, and entrance hall. Pulls weeds and tidies up the garden.

I feel tense when I can't wake up in the morning and find myself daydreaming. When the engine starts, the body should move automatically.

1:00   Lunch.

2:00   Shops, goes to bank, department store.

3:00   Returns home, takes in laundry, does the ironing.

Prices are so high. Putting food on the table is so expensive. I spend a lot of time shopping, trying to find good quality protein, vegetables, and fruit to feed those hungry kids. Sometimes I'd like to buy something just because I want it.

4:00   Daughter returns home. Has homemade snack.
5:00   Prepares supper; prepares food for next day's lunchbox.
7:00   Supper with mother-in-law, daughter, nephew.
       It makes me happy when they say it's delicious and eat it all up. It's a commonplace pleasure. But that's OK, I think.
9:00   Daughter goes to bed.
       I sew and practice calligraphy while waiting for my husband to get home.
12:00 Goes to bed. Husband isn't home.
       I'm exhausted. I go to bed. My husband is out from early in the morning until late at night. Works hard, he does!

Mrs. T is 40. Her five-person household includes herself, her husband, her husband's mother, a daughter in elementary school, and a nephew in high school. She would like to find a job, but she doesn't believe that she could do both housework and a job well. She starts early on household chores and works efficiently. She likes to get a firm grip on her housework before the middle of the day when salesmen call and the phone starts to ring.

My Home Mrs.

The most important time in her day is the time that she spends with her husband and children.

6:30   Gets up.
7:20   Breakfast.
7:50   Sends off the kids.
7:55   Drives husband to the station.
8:30   Cleans up the kitchen, does laundry.
10:30 Cleans other rooms, waters and weeds the garden.
       Now that I don't have to deliver the kids to kindergarten and pick them up again, I can finish the housework earlier. But tiny kids are so sweet, and it's a little sad and lonely to see them becoming less cute.
12:30 Lunch.
1:30   Younger child returns home from elementary school.
       I write the necessary entries in his school notebook and check what homework he has to do. Today it's practicing calligraphy.
2:00   Delivers child to friend's house.
3:30   Takes older child to swimming pool, watches swimming class.
5:00   Goes to pick up younger child.
6:30   Supper.
7:00   Stays beside child during piano practice.

I leave the dishwashing and other chores to my mother-in-law, who has volunteered to do them while I supervise the piano practice. That's a real help!

8:40   Puts younger child to bed and reads to her until she goes to sleep.

9:20   Drives to station to meet husband.

I dozed off, but the alarm clock woke me up. I'm sleepy as I drive to the station, but this way my husband gets home earlier.

9:55   Husband has supper.

10:30   Bath, TV, reading a book.

11:30   Goes to bed.

Mrs. U is 33. Her five-person household includes her husband, her mother-in-law, and a boy and a girl in elementary school. Things became easier for her when, starting this April, she no longer had to deliver and pick up a child from kindergarten. But her eyes are always glued to her children. She goes with them to their friends' homes and to the swimming pool. Her free time also is interrupted by having to pick up her husband. She is a typical My Home Mrs., totally devoted to her family.

My Self Mrs.

Her job is something she does for herself.

5:45   Gets out of bed, prepares breakfast, makes lunch for husband.

6:20   Reads newspaper.

7:00   Has breakfast with two sons and mother-in-law.

7:40   Laundry, cleaning, gardening, watering flowers

9:00   Cleans kitchen.

9:20   Gets dressed and puts on make-up.

I shampoo my hair every day and make up properly. I'm feeling lively and bouncy.

10:07   Boards train to part-time job.

I suddenly wonder what would happen in an earthquake, with the family scattered all over the place.

11:30   Changes clothes, has lunch with three friends in company cafeteria.

Seeing my friends' shining faces makes me want to keep on working.

12:00   Work begins.

The four hours I spend at home go by very quickly. In contrast, I can't let go and relax during the four hours that I'm on the job. I realize that spending money is easy, making money is hard, and begin to appreciate my husband's situation. The one day a week I don't work, I have a piano lesson.

4:00   Work ends.

4:30   She takes a break and has tea with friends.

We enjoy grumbling about our jobs and discussing where we would like to travel.

6:10   Returns home, prepares supper.

As soon as I get home, my mother-in-law makes tea for me. My mother-in-law is a widow who lives with the family. That's a good thing, I think.

7:10   Supper with husband, younger son, and mother-in-law.

8:00   Bath, then running in the park.

I like to wash my hair while taking a bath, then go out running while I feel fresh. It's my way of getting rid of all the things that bother me.

10:00   Puts on facial pack, reads book.

Someone has said that a woman of 40 should look good in red. It shouldn't matter to me, but ...

11:00   Goes to bed.

Mrs. U is 37. Her family of five includes her husband, her mother-in-law, and two sons. She finishes all her housework by 10:00 a.m. By completing all her shopping and chores before noon, she makes time for herself in the afternoon. Since her sons are in school, she has started working at a part-time job and taking piano lessons. She has skillfully divided the housework and gets along well with her mother-in-law. She is the very model of the independent My Self Mrs.

The Rule-Breaker

She goes her own way.

4:30   Gets out of bed.

5:00   Takes the car and goes off to work at a bakery.

I've only had four or five hours of sleep, so I feel like a lump. In the morning, time moves so slowly. The job seems very long.

9:00   Returns home, eats, and does the laundry.

10:00   Takes car to go shopping.

I'm always busy, but today is especially busy because I'm meeting someone.

1:00   Meets a friend involved in sales and buys a brassiere with the hooks in front.

At work the straps keep slipping off my shoulders. I wanted one with straps that cross in back.

2:00   Goes to the station to meet a (male) friend.

Because I'm running late, my saleslady friend goes with me. What will she think?

2:30   Goes off for a private drive.

3:00   After eating at a restaurant, they continue their drive.

The man (36) doesn't have a driver's license, so when I wanted to buy a car he lent me ¥250,000. He says that he is attracted to me. Another male friend (24) has his own car and comes to pick me up when we go off to together. During these times, the children are left on their own at home, to do whatever they like. What kind of parent am I?

6:00   She sees her friend off at the station.
8:00   Husband returns home from work, supper.
9:00   Quarrels with husband. Their fight continues late into the night.
2:30   Goes to bed.

Mrs. X is 33. Her household includes her husband, a son in elementary school, and a daughter who hasn't started school. She is so independent that she has her own job and male friends as well as a husband. We take off our hats to a woman who has 24 and 36 year-old boyfriends and the strength to work at a bakery from 5:00 to 9:00 in the morning or from 5:00 to 10:00 in the evening.

Note: Mrs. X said to us, 'Because my husband always reads the *Lifestyle Times* before I do, please don't send this issue to us'. We agreed!

The Age of Women, Highlights and Shadows
Lifestyle Times, March 1984

The Art: The cover (Figure 4.7) shows a sketch of an anxious-looking young woman in a pageboy haircut. The women I have asked say that she looks about 29. Inside we find Figure 4.8 whose title reads literally 'The Tree of Women's Anxieties'. The title contains a pun: the word for tree sounds like another word, 'collection'. The text in the leaves describes issues that women are anxious about. The oblique boxes on either side are environmental factors: for example, changes in life cycle or the advent of the information society. The roots are descriptions of psychological states.

The Research Design: The data for this study were gathered in focus group interviews. First, three groups of full-time housewives living in Tokyo, Osaka, and Kōchi, a small city on the island of Shikoku, were interviewed. There were six women in each group, aged 35–44. Additional focus groups were invited to comment on remarks made in the first three groups. The additional groups were composed of salarymen in their forties, about the right age to be husbands of the women in the first three groups; women in their sixties, about the right age to be their mothers-in-law; and women in their twenties, about the right age to be their daughters. In the comments reported below, statements from the original three groups are in ordinary roman type. Comments from members of the other groups are italicized. Additional data was taken from a large-sample survey conducted in August, 1983. The two-stage random sampling for that survey produced the following sample: 300 full-time housewives aged 35–34; 298 full-time housewives aged 35–44; 297 full-time housewives aged 45–54; 284 housewives with part-time jobs aged 25–54; 294 housewives with full-time jobs aged 25–54; and 294 self-employed housewives aged 25–54.

The Tree of Women's Anxieties

We talk about the era of women. The number of working women is growing, an equal employment law may soon be passed, and women are increasingly visible in the workplace and in cultural activities. Culture centers and museums are their paradises. Those with sufficient leisure and strength of character have, it seems, nothing to fear. How far, however, can ordinary housewives spread their wings? Does liberation mean happiness?

Women's life-cycles and roles are changing. The classic 'good wife, wise mother' model is disappearing. Women who have spread their wings seem

Figure 4.7 Cover, 'The Age of Women, Highlights and Shadows'

glamorous, but when other women look at themselves, what they see is meals to be cooked and laundry to be done. They ask themselves, 'Is this all I can do? I, too, would like to spread my wings.' At the same time they wonder 'Can I do it? People may say that we have to live our own lives, but what if I can't find a job or lack knowledge and ability?' Husbands are totally absorbed in their work and don't listen to what their wives have to say. The time when the children will leave home gets closer.

Environmental Factors

The loss of a model: As women's lives become more diverse, those who can only be 'good wives and wise mothers' feel abandoned.

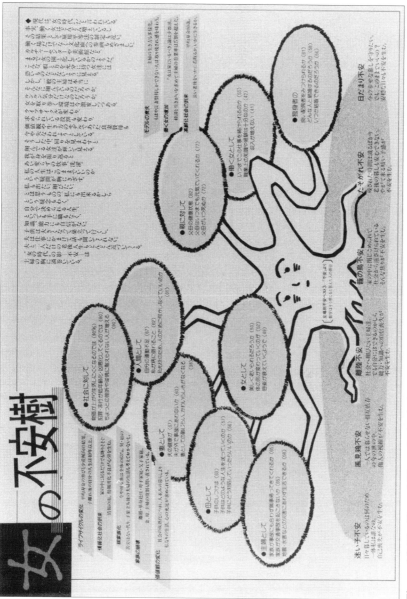

Figure 4.8 The Tree of Women's Anxieties

Working women: Few now feel that 'A woman's place is in the home'. For economic reasons or to find a meaning in life, more than half of all housewives now have jobs.

The aging society: The average life expectancy is 80 years. How to imagine a long retirement?

Changing life cycles: Women are now 40 or older when children leave home.

The information society: Even those who stay at home are deluged with information. There is too much to absorb.

The nuclear family: Nuclear families now account for 63 per cent of all families. The in-laws are no longer a problem. The issue is now husband and wife.

The collapse of the family: Divorce, husbands sent off on unaccompanied job postings, mother-child and father-child single-parent households.

Changing values: Wanting to be like others is being replaced by wanting a lifestyle.

Branching into Specific Topics

Society
Rising prices.
Crime and juvenile delinquency.
Growing numbers of people are unable to endure disappointment.

Everyday life
Not enough exercise.
Often feel sick.
Not doing anything for myself or for society.

As a wife
Husband's health.
Husband having an accident.
Ceasing to be attractive.

As a mother
Discipline.
The kind of life to provide for the children.
How to control the children.

As a homemaker
Will everyone get home safely?
Traffic accidents?
Earthquakes and floods?

As a woman
Will I stay beautiful?
My figure is changing
Will I lose my figure?

Parents
Health
How long will parents stay healthy?
When will parents die?

As a working woman
   How long will I be able to work?
   Do I have enough knowledge and experience?
   My income isn't rising.
If single
   Will I be able to find a good mate?
   What kind of man will I marry?
   Will I be able to marry?

The Roots of Anxiety

Fear of losing one's way
   Why am I living this way?
   Who am I?
   Death and dying.
Fear of being a weathervane
   Afraid of living alone.
   Afraid of what others are thinking.
Fear of being at a loss
   Lacks confidence.
   Disappoints herself.
Fear of being a caged bird
   Confined to the house.
   Irritated by not being able to go out.
Fear that night is falling
   Time is slipping away.
   Worried about retirement.
   Gloomy about the future.
Fear of sleeping in the sun
   Clinging to a happy life.
   But are things really all that good?
   Afraid that things are too peaceful.

Good Wife and Wise Mother, or, the Irritations of Independence
(Statements from the Focus Groups)

Education is a housewife's biggest concern. First and foremost she's a mother.

The number of working women has increased. More and more women are active in public. But even in this era of women, many of us feel anxious.

- I may have some latent awareness of anxiety, but I'm not conscious of it. My family's way behind economically; I'm full of dissatisfaction over that. But I suppose I'm better off this way than feeling satisfied yet anxious.

- If I started listing my complaints, I don't know where I could stop.
  - *Young people today are so extravagant. They grumble about how expensive things are, but they can't hold back if it's something they want.* (Mother-in-law, 61)
- We are looking at high schools and colleges. It gets tougher every year. If my son goes on like this will he be able to get into high school? Maybe a private high school ... yes, I'm anxious.
- Education costs a lot these days. The children want to go to cram school. That is why everyone's saving these days. We can't afford to get sick.
  - *A child is an iron bond holding a couple together, they say. When you think about the amount of money and time and worry children take, wouldn't it be more comfortable not to have any?* (Husband, 41)
- I'd like to live somewhere without cram schools, where children can play naturally. I'm not sending mine to cram schools. When they get bad grades, I keep on smiling, but inside I do worry.
- You would probably call me an egoist, but I want my child to start out with better chances than other children. That's what it means to be a mother.
  - *My youngest child is refusing to go to school. I can't ever take my eyes off the kid.* (Housewife, 41)
- We need to save up for their education, even if it's only a little at a time. I'll probably have to go out to work, even if it's only a makeshift job.

I want to work, but age limits and working hours are big barriers.

- The money, of course. But also, once the cooking and laundry are done, there is nothing left to do. That's when I like to get out. When the children get bigger, I am the only one who won't have anything to do. Yes, I would like to be more active.
- I feel the same way. That's why I read the help-wanted ads in the newspaper. But there are age limits.
- I want to be home when the children come home.
  - *If it were only from 10 a.m. to 2 p.m. and I didn't have to go every day, but the work was satisfying? If I could find a job like that, I wouldn't care what people said.* (Husband, 41)
- Friends have just suddenly made up their minds and gone out to work, but it does seem to upset their husbands and children. What's wrong with living thriftily within a fixed income and putting out the bedding to air?
  - *I don't want to destroy my image as a good wife and wise mother.* (Housewife, 38)
- If you have a child you can't go on working. But to hunt for a new job with a blank in your resume takes incredible courage.
  - *My friends say that work is just a chance to meet someone to marry. As long as you have similar family backgrounds and educational levels, you can be economically secure.* (OL, 24)

- I have a friend who found a job. She fell in love with another man. Now she and her husband are getting divorced. A tragedy, I think.
- There's too much information these days. I can't just stay put. My turn to work will come, even if I don't want it.
  - *People who talk about the anxieties of the full-time housewife blindly accept what the mass media and other people are saying.* (OL, 24)
- It is mostly women in their forties who go to culture centers and handicraft sales at department stores. Yes, if you've got the free time, you have to do something for yourself. You don't want to be out of it.
  - *Once the kids are independent, then I'll have to take care of my husband when he retires. If that's what my life is going to amount to, I can't stand it. I've got to find something else to do.* (Housewife, Kōchi, 36)
- Nervous disorders that affect many housewives grow out of their feeling that 'I've got to do something, but what can I do?'
- Today's young mothers go back to work as soon as their children enter elementary school. Won't this be a problem for their children's education? One's own life is important; but before taking a part-time job, that's something you should look at with a mother's eyes. I know this makes me sound like a granny.
  - *Even cabbage is now sold pre-chopped. I understand that a growing number of housewives work part time and don't have time to prepare dinner, but still this is strange. The ones who are chopping the cabbage are housewives working part time, aren't they?* (Housewife, Kōchi, 26)

Are a husband and wife husband and wife, even if they don't talk with each other?

- There are so many things about the children's education that I want to talk over with my husband, but the lord and master is never home until after midnight.
  - *When it comes to education, the family budget, things like that, I may be a coward. I run away.* (Husband, 41)
- He's like a boarder. The family is mother and children. Since I can do whatever I like, I'm not dissatisfied.
- We are a three-phrase couple. 'Welcome home', 'Supper?' and 'Time for bed?' Just those three phrases.
- My husband talks about his work but won't listen to what I have to say. When he said that husbands and wives don't need to talk with each other, I was shocked, but he's hopeless.
- My husband is fifty, the type who says, 'I leave the house to you'. Men in their forties are willing to help out. Younger ones will even take a day off from work to take the baby for a check-up. I keep telling my husband about these things, little by little. He doesn't like it, but he accepts it.
  - *When I hear one of my coworkers who's one of a young couple who both have jobs say, 'Today it's my turn to do the housework, I'm leaving early', it makes me really angry.* (Husband, 43)

117

- It doesn't matter what, I have to do everything. Even when I take all the responsibility, I still worry about something going wrong.
- We often have conversations sandwiched in between dealing with the children. But a while ago the children were gone for a week. The first two or three days were fine. Then we ran out of things to say. I suddenly realized how tough life is going to be after the children leave the nest.
- You are getting old, and there's nothing you have in common. Your thinking is totally different. You may have to go your separate ways.
- When I complain about my mother-in-law, he pretends he doesn't hear.
    - *I intend to think about both their positions, but in the end I just put up with it.* (Husband, 43)
- He's so lazy he won't ever say, 'Let's do this'. It's really sneaky.
    - *When my wife talks, she is so bright and lively. I become as silent and long-suffering as Oshin in the famous TV series. My role is just to listen.* (Husband, 42)

How to handle mothers-in-law

- When we reach our forties, we are in control. Mothers-in-law become very careful in the way they treat their daughters-in-law.
- Recently, it seems to me that whenever I talk with my friends, the subject is always retirement. Everyone's taking care of aging parents.
    - *As long as my body holds up, I want to live on my own. I'd hate being taken care of grudgingly.* (Mother-in-law, 60)
- This generation still feel that our parents have done so much for us, we have to look out for them.
- I don't think that our own children will put up with us forever. That would be an imposition, wouldn't it?
- Isn't our problem that we still want to do our duty as brides and daughters, but we also cherish our own free time?
- From now on, old people who can't endure loneliness will be in trouble.
- Still, I don't want to be a shrinking violet when I deal with my daughter-in-law. I'm a daughter-in-law myself, so I know how difficult it can be living together.
    - *There's too much information these days. Because I don't want to be an old-fashioned mother-in-law, I either have to restrain myself or pretend to be good, like a docile child. Both are impossible. My generation acts this way and causes suffering for themselves.* (Mother-in-law, 61)
- Even if you do the same things you would do for your mother, your mother-in-law's response is totally different. Why shouldn't her own daughter take care of her?
- Even one's own parents can be too demanding. Living with elderly people is always a problem.

- It's all right as long as they are healthy. I worry about them becoming bedridden. Now, there's the housing problem and housewives going out to work. Old people are being stuck in hospitals. It's like throwing away your parents.
  - *Because we've lived apart so long, I'd feel anxious living together. They've got their own lives now. Would there be a place for me?* (Mother-in-law, 67)
- If medical care for the aged becomes something we have to pay for, taking care of them at home will become more common again.
- Me, I want to save up enough money to be able to hire someone to look after me. The national pension isn't enough to live on, so I've joined a personal annuity scheme, too. Not being able to depend on the children is something I worry about when I think about the economics of being retired.

Where should I fly? What can I do?

- I want to be independent when I'm old. But in the city there aren't many chances to meet other people as couples. I worry about what will happen when it's just me and my husband, forced to be together.
  - *In household affairs, especially when it involves the neighbors, I don't have the right to say a thing.* (Husband, 43)
- Young couples are clever in the way they socialize. Because they dress informally and don't prepare anything special to eat, they can get together whenever they like. We tend to entertain more formally.
- My husband's post-retirement plan seems to be to play golf in his own dufferish way. I haven't found a hobby I could stick with. I worry about being left alone.
- I do chorus, swimming, and gardening, but, at the end of the day I don't know what I really like or want to do.
- We move a lot. Whenever my husband gets a new assignment, it affects the way I live. Study and work are both just bits and pieces.
- I do flower arranging, but it doesn't look like I'll learn enough to be able to make money teaching. Still, when my friends and I are old, it will give us something to enjoy together.
  - *A happy mother is essential for having a happy family. That's why I fill my time with things to do.* (Housewife, 39)
- When it's only you and your husband living together, you need something you both enjoy. Otherwise, you are likely to throw him out.
  - *It isn't that I'm dissatisfied with my husband. I like him a lot, but I'd like to take half the retirement money and be free to go my own way. I've always given up everything for my children and husband.* (Housewife, 36)
- Me, I can't believe that a hobby is a reason for living. I want to find some work that only I can do, that won't get done if I'm not there.
  - *Since I'm old, I have plenty of time for volunteer activities, but people won't let me participate. Even those a little bit younger are much happier.* (Mother-in-law, 64)

- You have to get out now. It's while the children are young that you still have the energy. When you start to get thick around the waist, you'll be satisfied with even a little happiness and give up trying. We're at a crossroads where doing nothing will only lead to irritation. What we feel is depression.
  - *When I look at my mother, I understand how much strength it takes to go on living.* (OL, 22)

Cleopatra Complex: Loss of Position and Beauty Is Frightening
Lifestyle Times, November 1993

The Art: Figure 4.9, the cover of this issue, shows a woman with a Cleopatra haircut. The stars around her head suggest that she is the shining height of fashion. She stands, however, on a shadow, whose face is that of a man. His head is bowed toward her. While she looks straight at us, he looks anxiously at her.

The Research Design: This issue describes the results of a study that replicated the survey reported in 'The Age of Women, Highlights and Shadows' using a smaller sample: 100 full-time housewives aged 35-34; 100 full-time housewives aged 35–44; 100 full-time housewives aged 45–54; 200 housewives with part-time jobs aged 25–54; 200 housewives with full-time jobs aged 25–54; and 100 self-employed housewives aged 25–54. The survey was conducted between September 20 and October 8, 1993, a decade after the earlier study.

From 'They Won't Let Me' to 'This Is What I Choose'

It wasn't so long ago that women were called the 'They won't let me' tribe. They complained that their husbands didn't care about them; their children wouldn't listen to them. They said, 'I want to go out to work', 'I want to express myself', 'I want to test my abilities'. The era of women had just begun.

Because of their sufferings, these women were ready for a call to action. The era of steadfast Oshin, who was able to persevere, no matter what, had lasted too long. Women had great reserves of strength. If the husband didn't pay attention to his wife, she would do as she liked. Some women chose 'Friday affairs'. Others demanded divorces. Even the majority, the cowards who stayed at home, became the 'I won't give it to you tribe'. Some chose 'de facto divorce'. While not legally divorced and still living with their husbands, they lived their own separate lives.

Frightened by these rebellious women and anxious to keep peace in the home, men steadily gave them more freedom. Thus, as time went by, women achieved most of the aims behind which they'd rallied. More important than any specific accomplishment was ordinary women's securing the freedom to decide for themselves how they wanted to live. 'They won't give it to me' has become 'this is what I choose'.

Figure 4.9 Cover, 'Cleopatra Complex'

Going out while the children were still too young to be separated from their mothers was no longer an underhanded move. To work or not to work, to go to a culture center, to leave housework undone, or to choose not to live with the in-laws are now all matters that women freely decide for themselves. Still, somehow, not all is well. Why should this be?

Words (Prize-winning words from the All-Japan New and Popular Words Awards)

- *Kurenaizoku* 'They won't let me tribe' (1984 silver prize, trendy words division).
- *Oshindorōmu* 'Oshin syndrome' (1984 gold prize, new words division).

- *Kateinai rikon* 'de facto divorce' (1986 creative prize, new words division).
- *Sekushiaru harasumento* 'Sexual harassment' (1989 gold prize, new words division).
- *Nureochiba* 'Damp fallen leaves' (1989 creative prize, new words division), refers to husbands who stick around demanding attention.
- *Obatarian* 'Mrs. Monster' (1989, gold prize, trendy words division).

Events

- 1975 International Women's Congress marks start of the International Decade of Women.
- 1983 Divorce rate and absolute number of divorces reaches new postwar peak.
- 1984 Tax-reduction bill for part timers becomes law.
- 1984 The number of working women exceeds the number of full-time housewives.
- 1985 Equal Opportunity Employment Law is passed.
- 1986 The Japan Association of Corporate Executives accepts its first female member.
- 1986 Doi Takako, a woman, becomes Secretary-General of the Socialist Party.
- 1987 Women are successful candidates in the eleventh combined nationwide local elections.
- 1987 Students at culture centers are 2.5 times as numerous as nine years earlier.
- 1987 Agnes Chan controversy erupts when actress brings baby to work.
- 1989 The number of women accepted by colleges (including junior colleges) exceeds the number of men accepted.
- 1991 Parental leave law is passed.
- 1992 Number of divorces exceeds previous record, reaches 179,191.

Media

- Magazines promoting new lifestyles for women proliferated during these years.
- 1977 *Croissant* (fashion, family, and career) and *More* (for the younger woman with money to spend) start publication.
- 1980 *Torabayu* (a job information magazine for women) starts publication.
- 1985 The TV program *Friday Wives III: Falling in Love* becomes a cause célèbre.
- 1985 *Orange Page* (homemaking tips and style for the working married woman) starts publication.
- 1986 *Lettuce Club* (cooking-centered lifestyle information) starts publication.
- 1988 *Nikkei Woman* (for the career woman) and *Hanako* (the quintessential style magazine for the Office Lady) start publication. *Fujin Kurabu* (Wives' Club; for good wives and wise mothers) stops publication.

- 1990 *Suteki na Okusan* (Stylish Wife; ways to make housework interesting) starts publication.

Advertising Copy

- 1975 *Watashi tsukuru hito, boku taberu hito,* 'I (the woman) make it, I (the man) eat it'.
- 1978 *Otto wo wasureru san jikan,* 'Three hours when I forget about my husband'.
- 1979 *Onna no jidai,* 'The era of women'.
- 1985 *Onna datte, nyōbo ga hoshii,* 'A woman wants a wife'.
- 1986 *Teishu genki de rusu ga ii,* 'A husband should be healthy and out of the house'.
- 1988 *Kono kuni de wa, onna dake ga shinsen da,* 'In this country, only women are fresh and vivid'.

Happiness Is Up, Anxiety Is Up

Our survey results surprised us. Women are more anxious now than they were ten years ago. They are also much happier. The age of proclaiming dissatisfaction and demanding relief is over, but women are worried about the future.

Fear of loneliness

Our subjects feel anxious about their value as individuals to parents, husbands, and children. They worry about the ways of life they have chosen. Women used to seem more light-hearted; now they seem more serious.

Women who want individual fulfillment are looking for something far harder to find than relief from dissatisfaction. Instead of 'They won't let me', women now say, 'I want to do something for society, something for other people'. Working women are the most concerned. The old equation, 'work equals involvement in society' no longer holds. It doesn't follow that because a woman has a job she is doing something to make the world a better place.

The Cleopatra Complex

Another noteworthy change in women has been a growing fear of losing their feminine allure. 'I am losing my looks' tops the list of anxieties that are stronger now than a decade ago. 'I am losing my figure' is third. These issues worry even wives and mothers. They hate being called aunties. They don't want to lose their sex appeal.

Some of the 40 items we used score lower than ten years ago. Fewer women now say that, 'It's bad luck to be born a woman' or 'I'm afraid of perverts'. Women are no longer weaklings.

Women have become, in effect, like empresses who, having seized power, now worry about their beauty. Their prototype is Cleopatra, the queen whose rule was absolute, who continued to refine her talents and her beauty. She is the archetype of the 'This is what I choose' tribe. The two things whose loss she fears most are her beauty and her position.

Anxieties no more

Other anxieties have evaporated in the last ten years. Reflecting the end of the Cold War, the item that shows the greatest decline is fear of Japan's becoming involved in a war. Anxieties about advances in high technology and an overabundance of information have also decreased as women have become more knowledgeable. Fear of immoral behavior and increasing individualism are also weaker. 'Each to her own' has become commonsense.

Antony Is Afraid

Cleopatra was the lover of three Roman generals, Cornelius, Caesar, and finally Antony. Antony, too, had things to worry about. Caught up in a struggle for political power, he had made a marriage of convenience based on political calculations but found himself unable to forget the woman he loved. Divorcing his first wife, he married Cleopatra and started a war.

Today if a man commits adultery, it isn't just his wife, it's the company that gets to know about it. The result is uproar in the workplace. If Cleopatra is the president of a rival company, and she and Antony try to merge their companies, it becomes an even bigger problem. Historians see Antony as a lightweight who was easily pushed around. Every man, however, has a host of enemies to overcome, including fear of sexual addiction, melodramatic adultery, and worrying about how others rate his abilities. Being a man is tough.

Ten years ago, women becoming full-fledged members of society simply meant their taking full-time, career-track jobs. Now they want to contribute to society, not just be part of it. Brothers! Arise! If we too are sluggish, their vision will defeat us!

Play-Education Mothers
Lifestyle Times, May 1985

The Art: Figure 4.10, from the cover, shows a mother and a baby as superhero-style figures. The baby looks tough. He clenches his fists and stares straight ahead. The mother's eyes are on the baby.

The Research Design: The survey reported in this issue was conducted on August 17–18, 1985. The subjects were 300 mothers of elementary and junior high school children and were aged twenty to 49. The method was a street intercept survey conducted in the Ginza, Shinjuku, and Shibuya areas of Tokyo.

Child-rearing Is Left to Others

In salaryman households, the second largest expense, after paying off the mortgage, is educating the children. If we break down spending on children and look at rates of increase, educational expenses are rising more quickly than others. It appears, however, that the psychological burden imposed by educational expenses is qualitatively different from that imposed by the housing loan.

According to the manager of the baby and toddler department at a major department store, these departments are cash cows. Amounts per purchase are up. Also increasing are the number of households that don't shrink from monthly expenditures on English, physical education, and other types of classes for toddlers. Expenditures on after-school education are six times higher than they were ten years ago.

A smaller number of children does not imply a shrinking child market. As parents' expectations rise, anxieties about 'Is this good enough for my child?' are also growing stronger. New businesses are finding ways to cater to that anxiety. Child-rearing is being outsourced.

Training to be the best

Whether measured in cash, care, or material things, the expenditure of resources per child is rising. When we asked 300 mothers between the ages of twenty and 49 about their childrearing plans, 37 per cent replied that they will spend more time and money. With a smaller number of children per family, parents are pushing their children to be not just better but the best. To send children to one or two after-school classes a week has now become the norm.

Figure 4.10 Cover, 'Play-Education Mamas'

Alien Mothers

From an old-fashioned mother's point of view, today's young mothers look like aliens. There are mothers who hand over their children to baby hotels while they go off to enjoy themselves. There are mothers who hire babysitters, even though they are full-time housewives. There are mothers who want to take their children to resorts where the grown-ups can leave the child-care to someone else. There are mothers who rely on schools to raise their children. There are mothers who pack their children off to cram schools or practice rooms and mothers who make free time for themselves by sending their children to summer camp. Not so long ago, that would have been unthinkable. These young mothers don't feel the slightest guilt about it.

Telephone counseling services report that there are many mothers who, while able to put up with being pregnant, complain about any additional suffering. The new generation of mothers has never learned to endure.

Mother wants to enjoy herself

Even childrearing and education, once thought to be completely serious subjects, now include an element of play. Upscale classes for mothers and kids and computer-aided education are both showing strong growth. Mountain village homestays and experience-farming camps are also doing well.

Play-education mamas want to enjoy the time they spend educating their children. Or, put another way, they want to enjoy the time with their children they reserve for themselves. Even those who are totally immersed in child-rearing don't want to be always doing things the same way as earlier generations of mothers.

But alien as they seem, it is precisely these sorts of mothers that 'play-education' businesses are looking for, and these new businesses are thriving.

Parents need more education

A director of mother-child creativity classes says, 'When mothers make something together with their children, it's the mothers who get something out of it. Today's children spend too much time under their mothers' control. Their mothers spend too much time looking after them. There used to be spaces where children could play by themselves. Because they don't exist anymore, the children have to come to places like this. If we don't teach the mothers, we can't teach the children. The first thing we say is, "Please don't help the child". It's important that children learn how to do things for themselves'.

'Today's parents get worried if their children seem the least bit out of the ordinary. We give those parents someone they can talk over their problems with. We also do summer retreats where mothers discuss their children. One mother is worried because her son seems obsessed by cars. Another is frantic over a picky eater. In fact, the one isn't really that obsessed, and the other does eat what he likes. These mothers don't know their own children', says a private school teacher.

Many teachers say the same sorts of things. They talk about changes in parents and changes in the children's environment. Because places for children to play have disappeared, children are under adult supervision too much of the time. Because there are too few children, kids are always being interfered with. Parents spend too much time trying to manage their children's lives. Teachers often report, 'It is unusual to hear a mother say that she wants her child to have more freedom. If we fail to educate parents, children become fragile. They become like little soap bubbles'.

Conversation with Kobayashi Yoshiko
September 25, 1998

Kobayashi Yoshiko is Managing Director of CAPCO, Hakuhodo's temp staff subsidiary. She is 45 and married to a journalist. They have one child, a son who is now in his third year of high school. She graduated from the University of Tokyo and joined Hakuhodo in 1976. In October 1980, she was appointed to the committee formed to set up HILL. Her previous Hakuhodo experience had been staff training with the Human Resources division. Four years ago, when Hakuhodo set up CAPCO, she left HILL to join the CAPCO start-up team.

JLM: As you see it, what was the basic concept when HILL was set up?

KY: As I am sure President Shōji has said, it was to understand the *seikatsusha* (the consumer with a life that includes more than consumption alone). On a personal level, I saw myself as an advocate. I was the only female researcher, and I saw myself as representing women, whose situation hadn't been considered before.

JLM: What were your research topics?

KY: First women and then children. I married just before joining HILL and had a child while working for HILL. My research grew out of my life. Through having a baby, I became interested in the relationship between mothers and babies. I was sure that there were other people who could empathize with my situation as a working mother with a baby, but I hadn't been able to find them. That's how I came up with the idea of the play-education mother (*yūiku mama*) who would be able to enjoy raising her child without sacrificing herself.

Then, as my boy grew up, I became interested in the attitudes of elementary and junior high school children. Eventually, I became interested in people's feelings about death. My father had just died when I saw an article in the *Nikkei* about living wills. My father had opposed using extreme measures to prolong his life, so this issue was important to me. That is why I wanted to research the relationship between the way that people live and the way that they want to die.

JLM: That was 'Last Identity'.

KY: Yes, and it was also my last *Lifestyle Times*. When I did the research, it had already been decided that I would move to CAPCO, so 'Last Identity' had a double meaning for me.

JLM: Did you notice any changes in HILL while you were working there?

KY: At the beginning, it was great. We did whatever popped into our minds. It was enough to discover one new key word. We didn't have to have a lot of data to back up what we talked about, so coming up with a new idea or a new word was enough to have impact.

Hakuhodo's marketing and R&D divisions were coming up with plenty of solid and rigorous results; but if you do too much of that kind of research, you lose the ability to come up with big ideas. When you test proposals A, B, C, and D, in a sample of a hundred people, only three may agree with the one you like. Back then, however, when the number of people at HILL was still very small, we could have faith that the three would become ten, the ten twenty, the twenty fifty. What was important was the idea itself. We didn't have the budget to do big surveys, and none of us was an expert in everything. I had come from human resources. By chance, at university I had majored in psychology, so I did know that we ought to do surveys to test hypotheses. But there were so few of us, and our mission was more to foresee the future than to pile up data about the present. So at first we didn't do surveys. We just looked at whatever seemed interesting.

After a while, however, other think tanks doing similar kinds of research appeared. Not so much places like the Nomura or Mitsubishi Research Institutes that did serious research, but special sections set up inside companies to do the same kind of thing we were doing. We had many visits from people wanting to get beyond data to do the kind of things we were doing in the *Lifestyle Times.*

We realized that, if we stayed at the same level, anybody could do what we had been doing. That's when we decided that we needed some numbers to talk about and started doing surveys. But they weren't surveys designed to prove an hypothesis. They were exploratory, designed to generate new ideas.

There was a stage at which we would ask – say, ten or twenty people – what they thought of an idea and discover that five would agree with what we were saying. Still, we weren't doing big surveys. We would just throw together a questionnaire and ask a few people. Then came the stage at which we decided to use samples ranging between 100 and 300 subjects. Then, finally, we developed the *Lifestyle Annual* surveys that use a very large number of subjects. That was because we believed that to be a proper think tank, we had to have that kind of data.

There was also the creative side. At first, we put a lot of stress on creativity. We started with words and images to which we attached data. Later, as we became more data-oriented, it became more boring. You can have an idea you really like, but when you do a survey the results are not what you were hoping for. Previously, you might be convinced you had spotted a trend, something that would, in time, become very big. Then, when you did a survey, you found that it had caught on with only a small percentage of people. So on the creative side, too, we also became increasingly cautious.

JLM: Was that in the second half of the eighties?

KY: Especially right around the Bubble years, in 1989, 1990, 1991. There was a lot of interest, then, in using numbers to trace the effects of the Bubble. During those years we did a lot of big-sample surveys. We collected more and more numbers. We had done big surveys before, for our annual research reports, for example, but by then even the reports in the *Lifestyle Times* had to have numbers to back them up. Recently, however, things seem to have changed a bit.

JLM: What's been happening?

KY: Honestly speaking, I haven't been reading every issue. But when people change, the questions they ask and writing styles also change. Once again they seem to be more getting out and moving around to see what's going on.

JLM: You have done a lot of research on women. What changes do you see in women's lives since 1981, when HILL was founded?

KY: The biggest changes have been the increases in freedom and independence. With the increase in freedom, the need for women to put up with things (*gaman*) has disappeared. I did a survey on the taboos that used to affect women. Now they are gone. In the past, it was, for example, taboo for someone like me to go on working. It was also taboo to go on working or playing past the time when the children were supposed to be fed. In this respect, women are now much freer, to work if they want, to be full-time housewives if they want, to go to school if they want. When women are compared to men, these have been the big changes.

It is also a fact that the number of financially and spiritually independent women has increased. This appears both in the ways that marriages work and in the workplace.

JLM: What about now?

KY: Now the way things are moving has changed a bit. Women don't have to struggle for freedom and independence now. Women who are now becoming adults take these rights for granted.

When I was a child there were still very clear expectations about what women could do. When I entered the company, women were expected to do only clerical work. You heard things like, 'Just sit over there', or 'You will get married and quit won't you?' I had to say, 'No, I want to go on working' and 'I really want to do this'. Unless we spoke up, made a point of things, and built up a record of achievement, nothing would have changed for us. It was only later that companies created the dual-track system, and women could choose to be 'regular' full-time employees or 'ordinary' (office lady, clerical) employees. Now women who have the ability and determination have a chance, but having a career has lost its appeal.

I feel strongly that the tide has turned. Now women are saying, 'Why should I have to work so hard?' Kids start so early these days going to cram schools and taking special courses. Everybody does it. You don't see kids having to ask to go to cram school because they want to get into a particular high school or university. The new generation has been given so much. When they graduate and get jobs, they don't have much perseverance. Somehow, they seem weaker now. They give up and quit so quickly. They are used to having what they want. The number of kids leaving school without graduating has also increased. They feel that everyone should be allowed to do what they like.

In my generation deciding to quit wasn't just a personal decision. Since quitting too soon would reflect on other women, we would vow to stick with it for at least six years. It didn't feel right to give up and get married without staying the course. Now they quit because they want to study abroad or because the company doesn't fit the image they had of it. I'm running a temp staff company. We have a lot of these people who register with us. They have been working for first-class companies but have quit within the first year. The feeling that you ought to stay and work for two or three years without complaining is gone.

I haven't done a proper study of this and don't have figures to back me up, but, for example, did you see that recent *Nikkei Woman* in which the whole issue was dedicated to temporary work? The magazine used to target OLs who weren't happy being office ladies and wanted to be career women. That's a tremendous change. I can't help feeling that the number of women interested in pursuing careers has declined.

5

IDEAL COUPLES
AND OTHER CHOICES

In the *ie*, the form of family and household organization legally sanctioned by the Meiji Civil Code, the role of women was simple: to obey. The theory that prescribed this role for women was articulated in the seventeenth century in the *Onna Daigaku* (Great Learning for Women) by the male neo-Confucianist Kaibara Ekken, who wrote: 'The only qualities that befit a woman are gentle obedience, chastity, mercy and quietness' (quoted in Hendry 1981:20). It is not hard, then, to understand how, from a feminist perspective, the emphasis on the 'good wife and wise mother' (*ryōsai kenbo*) image promulgated in the Imperial Rescript on Education in 1890 and celebrated throughout the war years could be seen as a step forward. Instead of a suffering servant automatically obedient to her husband and his parents (especially her mother-in-law), a woman affected by romantic ideals infiltrating from Europe or the United States might see herself as 'a better half on the European model, a companion and friend to her husband, equal to him and able to discuss his work' (Hendry 1981:26).

By the late 1950s, this new ideal was well-entrenched in the families of Japanese salarymen. Japan was no longer at war; its soldiers had come home. But those who became salarymen reproduced a basic wartime condition: the man of the house would spend his days away from home. In a nuclear family living apart from his parents, the salaryman's wife would be in charge of the household. She would, ideally, be deferential to her husband. Major decisions, however, required consensus, hammered out in discussion between them.

As women, as well as men, began to find jobs outside the home, adjustments had to be made. David Plath's *Long Engagements* (1980) includes two life histories that exemplify the choices required. Goryōhan lives to the full the life of a traditional daughter-in-law. She has spent years at the beck and call of her mother-in-law, who now, if truth be told, figures more largely in her life than her mostly absent husband. She finds considerable satisfaction in how well she performs her traditional role. Tomoko has led a different life. She married for love a boy she met in college. Both have gone on to successful careers, he as a research chemist, she as a TV producer. Managing both careers, keeping their household together, and caring for their daughter Tsuneko has required compromises from both spouses. He has taken on more of the housework; she has foregone opportunities to advance her career by moving to the network's headquarters in Tokyo. They share an interest in music and dream of once again having the time to play together the four-hand concertos they learned together in college.

Defining the Ideal Couple

In 1985, when the June issue of the *Lifestyle Times* examined the question of what makes an ideal couple in 'Husband-Wife Holons', the issues raised by choices like those described above were still, as they remain today, very much alive in Japan. As a possible solution to the tensions involved, HILL researchers considered the holon, a concept developed by Arthur Koestler (Koestler and Smythies 1969) to describe biological processes, then taken up by management theorists as a model for corporate organization.

During the mid-eighties, 'holonic' became a buzzword as management gurus attempted to sketch new forms of corporate organization that would somehow manage to combine commitment to the corporate whole with more independent and creative behavior by individual employees. The holon, a biological system in which individual elements (cells, tissues, structures) act autonomously but combine to form well-integrated wholes, provided an attractive metaphor.

Japanese corporations had often been described as modeled on the *ie*, with its stress on self-sacrifice for the good of the whole. A holonic paradigm would, it was hoped, give employees more freedom to act on their own while retaining their identification with the group. Applied to marriages, it suggested the possibility of couples composed of individuals who lead their own lives but retain the commitment to the whole that the *ie* epitomized.

The *ie*, however, was a corporate group with enduring assets passed down from one generation to another. While farmers have land, entrepreneurs have businesses, and independent professionals have practices to pass on to their children, the best that salarymen can hope for is to pay for their childrens' education. Without working assets to form the core of a corporate unit that will last beyond their own lifetimes, the couple involved in a salaryman marriage is thrown back on other, more personal resources to form a meaningful relationship. What those resources might be is the subject of 'Husband-Wife Holons'.

But Why Get Married at All?

In January 1998, the *Japan Times* reported that, according to Health and Welfare Ministry Statistics, divorces in Japan had more than doubled, from just over 95,000 in 1970 to 206,955 in 1996. It went on to note that divorced people are 'the new darlings of the Japanese media'. Their lives provide the plots of prime-time TV dramas and topics featured on morning talk shows. Magazines depict divorced women as 'striding confidently into the future'. Women are more likely than men to ask for a divorce (Sakurai 1998).

Ideally the lives of husband and wife may overlap enough to forge a bond between two social networks and create a larger network for the couple conceived as a whole. But if husbands and wives lead largely separate lives, why get married in the first place? The *ie* system provided an answer, to perpetuate the household. In a world of more fluid modern families dependent on non-transferable salaries, where ties between family members are fragile, the single life, however lonely, may seem a better alternative. In 'The Unmarried' and 'High-Singles Society', HILL researchers explored that possibility.

Husband-Wife Holons
Lifestyle Times, July 1985

The Art: Figure 5.1, from the cover, reproduces the form of the classic wedding photo, with the couple in the spotlight, sitting front and center with their families and friends surrounding them. Oddly enough, they are faceless, suggesting that we don't know who they are.

The Research Design: The sample for this survey was three hundred married couples living within a 40-kilometer radius of the center of Tokyo. Three age categories, 25–29, 35–39, and 50–54, each contained one hundred couples.

Holons? What Are They?

The words 'holon' and 'holonic' were coined by Hungarian-born science writer Arthur Koestler, by adding the suffix 'on' to the Greek 'holos' in a way that suggests the name of a new atomic particle. 'Holonic' is the adjectival form. Originally the words were used in biology to describe the way in which cells, tissues and nerves are connected to form self-regulating wholes.

The holon concept, with its functional harmony between the individual and the whole, has appeared in discussions of corporate management. The words 'holonic management' pop up in discussions of corporate strategy, corporate revitalization, new product and business planning, and other areas of corporate life. Holonic strategies assume that autonomous individuals will act on their own initiative and thus transform business units, making them more dynamic. Could the same be true of marriages?

The husband-wife holon is a 'COUPLE'

Looking at recent social trends, we find that the subtle balance between Holos (solidarity) and On (self-assertion) vectors is broken. With the rise of me-ism, the spread of the nuclear family, and the growing frequency of divorce, the centrifugal pull toward separation has become too strong. We need to ask again what it means to be husband and wife, what it means to be a couple. The husband and wife must be independent. The individual must be respected. But their relationship doesn't have to be chilly; the husband and wife can talk to each other. While affirming their relationship, they participate in society in a light-hearted and playful way.

Figure 5.1 Cover, 'Husband-Wife Holons'

They

- Talk with each other   =   **C**ommunication
- Are tolerant of each other   =   **O**pen-minded
- Are independent   =   **U**nit
- Can be excited   =   **P**assion
- Give firm guidance   =   **L**eadership
- And have playful hearts   =   **E**ntertainment

The young are in love, the Guppies sedate.

We began with a typology of couples. One dimension divides couples who are always together from those who lead separate lives. Another divides those for whom socializing outside the family is more important from those for whom family is always their top priority.

In the younger generation, the largest group by far consists of those who are always together and for whom family relationships are more important than those outside the family. In only one in ten couples do husband and wife lead separate lives. At the opposite extreme are the Guppies (grown-up urban professionals). Here, too, the largest single cluster is composed of couples who stick together. Nearly as many, however, lead sedately separate lives. The group whose members place a premium on socializing and the group in which family members pursue separate interests are both relatively large. The Sneaker Middles fall between the younger generation and the Guppies.

In the younger generation, who will be boss is not clearly defined. Thus, when couples disagree, there is no easy way to make decisions. Among the Guppies, husband and wife each take the lead in their own domains. Here the issue is lack of passion. The Sneaker Middles face problems both in public and in private. Since, however, they are the most flexible in the way that they handle their relationships, their marriages should be happy ones.

Communication

With the growing frequency of divorce and of men being posted away from their families on business assignments, we hear a lot these days about the need for husbands and wives to spend more time talking with each other. Our research shows that many couples in all generations do, in fact, talk with each other. But the frequency of dialogue is highest among the young.

In other research we have noted that the younger generation are sociable but vulnerable when faced with silence. Among the members of this group, this trend continues after marriage Among the Guppies, monologue is more common (46 per cent) than dialogue (40 per cent); Fourteen per cent don't talk with each other at all.

The three generations also clearly differ in the way they make purchase decisions. It does seem a bit ominous that wives now have so much say in selecting life insurance.

Open minds

The younger generations get together with other couples. The Guppies also enjoy this form of socializing. In contrast, more than 60 per cent of the Sneaker Middles lack these contacts. The usual reason is young children. This group, however, is the most broad-minded when it comes to either spouse having friends of the opposite sex.

Unit

'U' stands for the unit, respect for individual difference. Many young couples share similar hobbies and sports; taking trips with colleagues or classmates without the spouse is rare. At the opposite extreme are the Guppies. Each member of the couple has personal hobbies and sports, and going off with friends who share similar interests while leaving behind the spouse is common. In the young and Sneaker Middle groups, most trips taken alone are those taken by the husband.

Passion

As time passes, flames that once burned brightly weaken. Love becomes a ceremony. (According to anthropologists, even passion has its rules.) It seems only natural, then, to find that members of the younger generation frequently exchange gifts to celebrate anniversaries. Among the members of this group, the ceremony is still infused with passion. But the frequency of presents doesn't decline steadily with age. It is lower among the Sneaker Middles and higher again among the Guppies.

Leadership

Younger couples make everyday decisions democratically. Among the Guppies and the Sneaker Middles, either husband or wife takes the lead, depending on the situation. In one in five Guppie couples, the wife is clearly the boss. 'Fetch it for me' husbands are said to be common among those born in the Showa era (1926–1989). There are many couples, however, where the hen rules the roost.

Entertainment

We live in a playful age, and playful spirits are necessary for a marriage to function as a holon. The younger generation and the Guppies enjoy their relationships. The Sneaker Middles, unfortunately, rarely have enough time. Yes, small children do require a lot of care, but couldn't they be left with their grandparents? Yes, early middle age is a difficult time economically. Still, it is hard to imagine that a couple can't afford a few dates each year. Yes, Sneaker Middles do tend to do everything in families. They also tend to be practical. But both family and practicality can be taken too far. Shouldn't husbands and wives pay more attention to their marriages, the most basic of social relationships?

The Unmarried
Lifestyle Times, April 1982

The Art: The cover (Figure 5.2) shows a man and a woman sitting at separate tables. The opening spread headline is 'Unmarried! Does That Mean I Can't Get Married?'

The Research Design: The data reported here are taken from the same 'New Middle-Aged Survey' as 'Sneaker Middles'. That survey, conducted in December, 1981, used a two-stage, stratified random sample of male and female individuals living in Tokyo and Osaka. The individuals sampled were divided into three age categories: 22–24, 32–34, and 42–44; total n = 2,000.

'Unmarried! Does That Mean I Can't Get Married?'

'Single women', 'Women who refuse to marry', 'Women who spread their wings': we are hearing a lot these days about the problem of unmarried women. But it isn't just women. Singles of both sexes are increasing in number every year, and their impact on society has become a hot topic in the media.

The structurally unmarried

On average, Japanese husbands are three years older than their wives. Thus, if there is a difference between the number of women of a given age and the number of men who are three years older, we expect to find at least this number of unmarried people. We call this segment the structurally unmarried. Among people of marriageable age between twenty and 33, there are 1.39 million males and 1.1 million females in this category. (I get it, no partners!)

The proportion of structurally unmarried is especially high among the Baby Boomers born between 1947 and 1949. In this generation, the proportion of females who would be unmarried if their husbands had to be three years older is 25 per cent, or 870,000 people. One result was a rapid increase in same-age marriages, but even that has not evened out the male-female imbalance. There are still 490,000 unmarried women among the newly middle-aged. Single women are driving women's liberation. Their attitudes will change not only female lifestyles but consumer markets overall. Looking to the future, however, it is single men who will be the problem. One in five newly middle-aged men have not been able to marry.

Figure 5.2 Cover, 'The Unmarried'

The singles market

In America, the growing number of singles has created a singles market. As described in *Lonely in America*, singles bars, singles apartments and matchmaking services all cater to lonely singles. Singles bars are places where men and women get acquainted while pretending that 'it's the first time I've ever been in this kind of place'. (Apparently, you have to look like it's your first time, even if you are a regular.) In Japan there are now computerized go-betweens, a modernized version of the matchmakers who depended on local and kinship ties. There are many new opportunities for developing singles-oriented businesses.

New types of wedding parties

With the rapid decline in the number of marriages since 1972, the wedding halls that sprang up to handle Baby Boomer marriages are now in serious danger. As the number of weddings falls, wedding halls are trying to promote more expensive weddings. We have seen an explosion of competition to produce more dramatic performances with dry ice and lasers. Efforts to sell new packages that combine the engagement, the wedding ceremony, the reception, the post-reception party, and even a first-anniversary party are booming. We foresee the formation of 'Bridal Conglomerates', built around wedding halls but including travel agents, real estate and insurance companies, and doctors.

Divided selves

Working women are finding ways to split themselves between work and household chores, but even so it is difficult. So for women who work all day, there are businesses that will take care of shopping for accessories or other personal items. The housework outsourcing business is flourishing. In the future we expect to see services that today seem unimaginable.

Throw-away electrical appliances

Single women's apartments are often luxuriously furnished, but their electrical appliances don't fit the decor. The furniture is intended for use after marriage. The appliances will be thrown away when the women get married.

Tea for one

When people live alone, they don't purchase products in large amounts. Often, moreover, they shop late at night. What they seek is convenience. But low-class products won't satisfy these single aristocrats. In America, all sorts of 'tea for one' businesses have begun to appear, designed to make the single life luxurious.

Away-from-home-products

As the number of singles grows, demand for fashions, accessories, and other away-from-home products is increasing. Newspapers and weekly magazines read by commuters are also affected. An office lady offers a hint: 'We want the sports scores, but we don't like the pornography in sports newspapers. I would like something pocket sized or a newspaper that won't soil your hands'.

Bodyguards

Fear of being alone is more than fear of loneliness. Concern about personal safety is a high-priority issue for women. Computerized security services now market themselves to households. Low-cost security systems for singles would, we think, attract a lot of interest. Apartments for singles won't sell these days without measures to ensure security.

Unisex magazines

Among the unexpected results of our survey were the number of women who read men's magazines and the number of men who read women's magazines. Androgynous magazines, however, are not at all popular with either men or women. Women's magazines written for men and men's magazines written for women could attract substantial audiences.

No-kids kindergartens

The sharp decline in the birth rate is having effects on fields that range from baby products to education. A shortage of new toddlers is devastating for kindergartens. The run-of-the-mill kindergarten is going from bad to worse.

Wonderful or Depressing

Plus: rich singles

Singles have a lot of money, especially single females. Among single women between the ages of 32 and 34, one in five has savings of more than ¥5 million. The average for women in this age group is ¥4.575 million. By contrast, one in four married men with children in the same age group has savings of ¥500,000 or less. While new middle-aged households with a full-time housewife and an oldest child who has not entered school spend a total of ¥14,000 per month on clothing, unmarried women spend ¥20,000. (A married man has to cry.)

Minus: Christmas cakes

What are you saying! You flatter singles by calling us rich, but we have our problems, too. Have you heard the phrase 'Christmas Cake'? It's even appeared in cartoons. In one, an office lady says, 'Is this my fate, to be a Christmas cake?' When her boss asks, 'What are you talking about?' she explains, 'Christmas cakes are meant to be eaten on December 24, Christmas Eve. On the 25th, it's too late'. The boss replies, 'That's silly. It's good until the 31st, the last day of the year'. As he speaks, there are three other women, his assistants, present. The numbers 32, 33, and 34 are written on their heads. That's awful. After a certain age the door slams shut. There are no more offers of marriage.

Plus: The Hefner image

Many men would like to live like Hugh Hefner, the founder of *Playboy* magazine. They are tired of single men being seen as dull sticks. Their ideal is the 'swinging single' who seems more common in America. The playboy sees sex as a game. Half the fun is the competition. The winner makes points by going to bed with the largest number of beautiful women.

Minus: Eating alone

A single life isn't all fun. When you live by yourself, you eat out all the time. Your nutritional balance gets skewed. You deal with loneliness by drinking too much and could become an alcoholic.

Plus: Parents

One reason why the unmarried can live so well is that many live with their parents. Looking at the table below, we can't help thinking how many of our subjects are the 'mother-complex' or 'father-complex' types we see in Tokyo Broadcasting System's Sunday television drama specials. They resemble the daughter who won't marry because her parents love her too much. Still, being dependent on your parents when you reach your thirties – what's that about?

	Men, 32–34	Women, 32–34
Dependent on parents	27.1%	40.1%
Living with parents	48.3%	66.8%

Minus: Sick and lonely

A 28-year-old single salaryman says that it's better to live with your parents. 'If you live alone like I do, there are times when you are sick and lonely. This winter the flu was going around. For two days I was alone, sick in bed. When I opened my eyes in the darkened room and looked out through the knotholes in the ceiling, I felt so isolated'.

Plus: Heroines

There's an active type of woman who won't give in to the playboys. The liberated woman whose spread in America was ignited by *Cosmopolitan* has also come to Japan. In Japan, *Cosmopolitan* and *More* now have higher circulations than *Egao* and *Shinsen*. These new types of magazines are stimulating an increase in the number of women spreading their wings.

The proportion of women who experience sex by age 21 was sixteen per cent in 1974. In 1981 it had risen to 37 per cent, a 2.3-fold increase. The rate of increase for women was higher than that for men (Prime Minister's Office Survey, 1981).

Minus: Blind-alley love

It's great to be free. But when a career woman finds someone of equal social standing and intelligence, he always turn out to be married. Many of my friends are trapped in this kind of bitter love affair. Marion Zora's *All the Great Ones Are Married* (1981), a book recently published in America, describes the plight of the single career woman who falls in love with a man who already has a wife. In a very American way it offers a recipe composed of eight rules:

- Don't date other men.
- Don't stop working to please him or move to be close to him.
- Don't stop working and depend on him economically. Retain your self-respect.
- Don't meet friends and family from whom you are keeping the secret.
- Don't waste time fighting with his wife.
- Don't carry his phone number with you.
- Make sure he knows that you are not going to stop leading an independent life. Plan your life in the long run without him in it.
- Take care of yourself.

Plus: Temples of the unmarried

Singles have the money and time to travel. Temples popular with this group include Kyoto's Jikkō-ji and Gion-ji and Kamakura's Tōkei-ji, also called the *An Non* temples (because they are frequently mentioned in the young women's magazines *An-an* and *non-no*). When single women travel overseas, they have already done the usual places and now travel instead to Cebu, Fiji, and New Zealand.

Minus: After getting divorced

'I've never been to those "temples of the unmarried" or traveled overseas. Divorced women don't have that kind of time or money. We are frantic just trying to keep up with work and children'. In the last twenty years the number of divorces in Japan has doubled. Most involve those who married since 1955 and have now been married for five or ten years. It is harder now for a divorced man to marry a previously unmarried woman. Conversely, it is now somewhat easier for a woman who has been divorced to marry a previously unmarried man.

Plus: 'Un DK'

More and more singles are purchasing apartments. What are called 1DK (in French, '*un* DK') apartments in good urban locations are overrun with single women. In one apartment complex in Tokyo's Suginami Ward with good views of the city, single women have purchased 80 per cent of the apartments.

Minus: Being widowed

Buying an apartment and living alone has its points, but when you retire the outlook is grim. The bitter tea of single life may sound attractive, but the loneliness of old age is grim. Twenty per cent of singles households belong to individuals who are sixty or older, and this figure is growing. It is widows and widowers who seem least suited to living alone.

Plus: Marriage is superfluous

This conversation is getting gloomier and gloomier. We would like to end on a bright note. 'It's as superfluous as adding legs to a snake, but please marry me' says Kirishima Yōko, who has suddenly changed her mind about the joys of the single life. It seems that marriage, like beer, is also 'lite' these days.

High-Singles Society
Lifestyle Times, June 1993

The Art: The cover, shown in Figure 5.3, presents a small abstract figure with wings. Beside it there is a short verse.

Who has seen
the singles
character?

You
Me
We don't understand.

Still,
They're shaking up the way we live,
Singles are changing society.

The Research Design: This survey's sample was composed of 1,200 men and women, aged 25–39, living within a 40-kilometer radius of the center of Tokyo. The sample was composed of four groups of three hundred individuals each: unmarried men, unmarried women, married men and married women.

Who Are These Singles?

	1970	1990
Single men (%)		
• 25–29	46.5%	64.4%
• 30–34	11.7%	32.6%
• 35–39	4.7%	19.0%
Single Women (%)		
• 25–29	18.1%	40.2%
• 30–34	7.2%	13.9%
• 35–39	5.8%	7.5%

More and more people are staying unmarried. We ask ourselves why? The spread of higher education and the entry of women into the workforce have both affected the way society is structured. But we are also seeing a major change in the way that people feel about themselves. They are happy to be alone. That is why instead of making singles our theme, we decided to focus instead on singles attitudes that are eating away at the hearts of the married as

Figure 5.3 Cover, 'High-Singles Society'

well as the single. (Don't you know someone who plays around even though he's a family man?)

Our image is a virus. Like AIDS, the singles virus is changing families, companies, and consumption. Invisible, it works its way in deep, hidden places. That is why this survey report isn't called 'The Singles Tribe'. We aren't looking at demographics but at how attitudes affect behavior.

In Short

Our questionnaire examined views of marriage, family, work, clothing, living and eating habits, leisure and transportation, and, of course, shopping. Looking at our results, we find items that distinguish the unmarried from the married and

148

items that differentiate strong singles attitudes from weak. The latter contrast seems more important to us. With it, we sketch an image of what a society dominated by 'high-singles' attitudes might look like from inside.

- The self is a fenced-in paradise. There is pleasure in turning inward.
- Everyone has his own world; don't interfere with others.
- In relationships, keep a certain amount of distance, not too close, not too far.
- Keep a distance, too, from family and company, the groups to which you're attached. No stains, no smells; be self-deodorizing.
- Don't be caught up in old systems and customs. Break out of the standard models. Go your own way.
- Just drift along like tumbleweed. Don't get tied down.

These are the characteristics of the high-singles segment, a new paradigm for behavior in a society where singles characteristics are becoming more widespread.

But Doesn't That Mean Chaos?

You may be worried about a lack of law and order. But what we see is a new, more flexible social structure. We are used to rigid relationships, but in a high-singles society, relationships will be soft and easily broken off.

Change is sure to bring conflict. High-singles have always had problems with society. But that, we believe, is going to mean opportunities for products and services that repair the damage conflict causes – social shock absorbers.

High-singles don't want to be alone. It's just that their lifestyles don't fit the old system. We need to envision their future in a more positive way, thinking about how they can live richer, more creative lives.

Can You Actually Measure That?

Every individual has singles attitudes to some degree. There are high-singles and low-singles among both the married and unmarried. It was, indeed, very hard to measure what we are talking about. It is no easy task to find yardsticks for the human heart. In the end, we settled for three criteria: freedom, independence, and turning inward.

High-singles

1. Prefer freedom, i.e., not being tied down
2. Prefer to keep a distance from others
3. Prefer to avoid dependence on others

High-singles, those who answered 'agree' or 'somewhat' when we asked about these descriptions, make up 36.5 per cent of our sample. Low-singles, who said 'not much' or 'don't agree', account for 63.5 per cent. High-singles cut across age and gender categories. Their attitudes are reflected in their lifestyles.

	High-Single	Low-Single
• Stay in the company but act as if self-employed	68.9%	59.8%
• Don't interfere with spouse's friends of the opposite sex	66.4%	60.5%
• Want to live apart from parents	63.0%	55.6%
• Want to be left alone	59.8%	41.7%
• Like to gamble	47.0%	38.1%
• Want a marriage partner who 'won't tie me down'	30.8%	18.6%
• Would prefer living together with a big group of friends to getting married	22.8%	14.0%
• Prefer easy-to-break-off relationships	18.0%	10.4%

Will These Trends Affect Marketing?

Yes. The table below shows four types of singles, a typology created by crossing the married-unmarried dimension with the high-singles – low-singles dimension. This scheme provides a different perspective from conventional views in which the unmarried are seen as forming a homogenous 'singles market' while the married are seen as forming a homogeneous 'family market'. By dividing the unmarried into those who are high and low, we develop new target profiles. High-singles products for the married might be an interesting idea.

	Low-Single	High-Single
Unmarried	*Mishin,* the muddled single, 23.7%.	*Junshin*, the pure single, 26.3%
Married	*Mushin*, the un-single, 39.8%	*Gishin*, the pseudo single, 10.2%

- Pure single: Lives for his or her dreams (explosive). Lost in his or her own world.
- Pseudo single: Cold-blooded thoroughbred. Forward-looking, self-confident; but tends to think too much of himself.
- Muddled single: A duckling who wants to be a swan. Looking for a moratorium from the stress of independence.
- Un-single: Attached to both family and company. A firm believer in traditional values.

Conversation with Masuko Miki
September 21, 1998

Masuko Miki is thirty-one. She has been married almost two years and has no children. After graduating from Waseda University with a degree in marketing, she joined Hakuhodo in 1990. She moved to HILL in 1996.

JLM: What type of research would you most like to do?

MM: I'd like to study the effects of maternity. Women's attitudes change radically from before to after they have children. I'd like to see how they change, perhaps do a survey of mothers. Today's young women see 'me' as No. 1. When they buy things, they buy what they themselves want. In relation to their parents, they put themselves first. 'Me' is always the most important thing. But that will change when they become mothers. I am interested in how these selfish girls will change when they have children.

JLM: Will they really change?

MM: We talk about generations, 'Sneaker Middles' or 'Amenbo Kids'. But to human animals, the biological fact of having a child is more important, I think.

JLM: What do you think has been the biggest change in women's lives since HILL was founded in 1981? How have Japanese women changed?

MM: In the past, women were on their guard, ready to push, in both a good and a bad sense. Full-time housewives saw themselves as professionals with particular things they had to do. Women who went out to work felt that they had to work hard to prove themselves. Now, instead of forcing themselves, women have become more relaxed. If they work, they work in ways that please themselves. After becoming mothers, they don't give up having fun. They interact with their children while continuing to have fun themselves. The drive to struggle on (*gambaru*) has disappeared.

JLM: Is that what people mean when they talk about 'my pace'?

MM: It's more egoistic than that. (laughs)

JLM: Egoistic?

MM: Doing what I want to do. It's more deliberately contrary than 'my pace'.

JLM: So that is why, the last time we talked, you said that during the eighties, full-time housewives felt that they were in a tough spot. They felt that they had to escape, but nowadays women like you don't feel that you're caught in a tough spot.

MM: Not tough at all. Since we don't feel stuck, there is no need to struggle.

JLM: Why have things become so easy?

MM: The biggest reason is that the way society sees women has changed. There are laws now requiring equal treatment of men and women. Men are entitled to parental leave just like women. For women the system has thus become much easier to live with. Another reason may be, I'm not really sure, that as it became easier for women to leave home and find jobs during the Bubble, women started having more fun than men. There were all sorts of good things – brands, overseas travel, the good life, good wine – that women got more of than men. That may be why we got so selfish. Before women's worlds were small; we found happiness within very limited boundaries. Then our world got much bigger. Now we could say that, 'I want this' and see a lot of new possibilities.

JLM: You said that the way that society sees women has changed. In what other ways has it changed?

MM: There are many different situations, but inside companies, for example, when working women my age found jobs the Equal Employment Opportunities Law said that we should be treated on an equal footing with men. Before, when we did get a chance to work, we would hear people saying things like, 'You're just a girl. You can't do this'. We would think, 'It can't be helped', and just give up. Why was that, we'd wonder? It was easy to say, 'Yes, that's discrimination!' Sexual harassment was the same sort of thing, something you just put up with.

JLM: Have things changed since the Bubble collapsed?

MM: It's become much harder for women to win full-time jobs at major companies than it was when I did. The official line says that this isn't so. Companies now say that women have the same chances as men, but men have more ability. Even so, that's a big change from 'You are a girl. You can't do that', which gave women no chance at all. Now women are officially equal, so we have no right to complain. We aren't being oppressed. We've had our chance.

JLM: I've heard older people say that during the Bubble, women had their chance but they blew it.

MM: I've also heard that, and I think it's true.

JLM: Really?

MM: I don't know about other countries, but when Japanese women were urged to become more like American women and to assert themselves more strongly, the response was half-hearted. American women, or at least the ones involved in women's liberation, worked really hard. In Japan that kind of woman was rare.

152

The system changed, we had our chance, but many women weren't willing to suffer to take advantage of it. When people said, 'OK, go for it, see if you've got the ability' too many of us, compared to men, didn't have the strength for the hard slog. We were too sweetly dependent (*amaete iru*). That is why so many women have quit their jobs and why we find more interest in having children now.

JLM: How has all this affected male-female relationships?

MM: Inside companies, it is the women who have changed. Men haven't changed that much. Officially, we are equal, but when someone says, 'Let's do this', what we hear next is 'We have to include a girl, don't we'. 'Girl' (*onna no ko*), that is the word they use. They've loosened up just a bit, to the point that they are willing to say, 'Let's get a girl's opinion on this'. But basically things haven't changed at all.

JLM: What about in society at large?

MM: In the family, the position of the wife and mother is much higher than it was ten years ago. For a long time now, women have controlled the family finances. Still, in the past, they would pay attention to their husband's opinions and ask permission before buying something big. Now they don't bother to negotiate with their husbands. Wives now have the right to make decisions on their own. Inside the family, women have become more powerful.

JLM: How about social life outside the family? Dating? That kind of thing?

MM: I don't know about the early eighties, but by 1986 or 1987, women had become much stronger. There were tribute boys (*mitsugukun*) who gave girls presents, leg boys (*ashikun*) who drove them where they wanted to go, and chow boys (*meshikun*) who took them to dinner. It hasn't changed much since then.

JLM: Changing the subject a bit, you've been married now for almost two years. How do you see the ideal marriage?

MM: My marriage is ideal. I can live just the way I want to. The real ideal, of course, would be to cook meals for my husband but to still be able to work and to go out drinking with other women. But that's impossible. If I go out drinking with my girlfriends, I can't make supper. If something has to go, it's my cooking supper. For me, that is what I like. For him it is probably less than ideal.

JLM: But doesn't he go out with his friends after work?

MM: Japanese men have believed for a long time that the ideal wife stays home, has supper prepared, and is ready to welcome them when they get home. If they get home and there is no rice to eat, something's missing. I understand that, but the life I lead is better for me.

153

JLM: In HILL reports and other sources I've discovered three models for ideal relationships. Let's see what you think. First is the 'Couple' model described by HILL in 'Husband-Wife Holons'.

MM: Intellectually speaking it looks ideal. But if I had to live that way, I would be exhausted. If both husband and wife have qualities like passion and leadership, the result is a household in which everyone has to work too hard. In my case, passion and leadership are what I bring to my job. At home I want to take it easy. I want things to be more natural. 'Leadership? If you want it, take it'. I think he probably feels the same way. I want a place where I can take it easy and relax.

JLM: That suggests the second model I wanted to ask you about. I've heard people say that the ideal relationship is like the air we breath (kūki mitai).

MM: It's what you most take for granted, but it is, after all, the most important thing. I understand people who think this way. For a recent survey, I was interviewing families, and found that the older people are the more likely they are to describe their relationships in this way. It seems very comfortable, but for someone like me, there isn't enough air. I'd like a place with more oxygen, more nourishment, where I can be more relaxed and feel really good.

JLM: There is also the possibility that we've talked about before, women treating their husbands like pets.

MM: It's a possibility, but it's not for me. To have a pet, you have to have power. If you aren't in firm control of yourself, you can't raise a pet properly. Me? I want to be the pet.

But, talking about views of marriage, it wasn't very long ago that the ideal husband was a 'three highs' (sankō: highly educated, high-income, and tall) type. If you ask now, the answer is different. It varies depending on a woman's character, but what most women are looking for now is someone gentle. If you think of men as pets, they should be the kind of pets who won't bite, not the type that drags you off somewhere, but the type who snuggles in with you. We haven't got it down to three words, but it's someone who loves you, someone healthy, the exact opposite of someone who jerks you around. We might say that he's like warm air. That's the modern woman's ideal.

JLM: Could you spell that out a bit more?

MM: The 'three highs' man was vigorous and active, so the woman could be the pet. Then, strong women began to treat men like pets. Now nobody wants to be the owner.

6

WHAT'S HAPPENING TO THE CHILDREN?

Worries about the younger generation are a universal phenomenon. Anxieties about Japanese youth do seem, however, to have a special intensity. In the *Nikkei Shimbun's* 'Warning Bell from the Year 2020' series, we find them likened to the characters described in the late Meiji novels of Natsume Sōseki. Sunaga Ichizō, the protagonist of *Until After the Equinox* (*Higansugi made*) says, 'Since graduating from school last year, I haven't spent a single day thinking about getting a job' (1997:46–47). Like Sunaga, Japan's younger generation feel polluted by making too big a fuss over work. They resemble those Japanese who, shortly after Japan's victory in the Russo-Japanese War, found themselves strangely listless and unable to find a meaning in life.

Heisei idlers have appeared, says the *Nikkei*, fifty years after the end of World War II, at a time when Japan's economy seems to have passed its peak. A Meisei University student exemplifies the type. He has not enjoyed his university years. Nothing he has done – clubs, part time jobs, or studies – has been absorbing. His 50-year-old father, formerly employed by one of Japan's large corporations, has been forced to take early retirement. When his father says, 'Twenty years and this is what I get', the son despairs of finding his own dream job developing solar batteries.

The one time he has felt good about himself was after the Kobe Earthquake in 1995, when he worked as a volunteer helping to distribute emergency relief supplies. Then, he says, he felt of some use to others. Since returning to Tokyo, he hasn't found anything to equal this experience. While working part time, he sold a record number of personal computers. He was criticized for working too hard, and achieving record sales had no effect on his wages.

Another example is a girl with eating disorders. She, too, worked as a volunteer following the Kobe Earthquake. While she worked as a volunteer, her symptoms disappeared, only to reappear when she returned to Tokyo.

The authors assert that only in an emergency will Japan's young people find themselves. They quote Saitō Yukio, Chairman of the Japan Suicide Prevention Association: 'Because of the low birth rate, children have been overprotected; they have never experienced hardship. Their sickness is worse than that which appeared in Meiji. One symptom is refusal to go to school'.

The Pleasures and Perils of Affluence

The material circumstances in which Japanese children grow up have changed dramatically during recent decades. The following figures and comments are extracted from the Japanese government's 1996 *White Paper on Youth (Seishōnen Hakusho)* (Prime Minister's Office 1996). They make this point abundantly clear.

Increasing affluence

Between 1965 and 1995, clothing sales increased by a factor of 1.9. Retail sales of food products rose 2.5-fold; restaurant sales doubled. Having a wide choice of foods and frequently going out to eat are no longer seen as remarkable.

Between 1963 and 1993, home ownership declined from 64.3 per cent to 60.8 per cent. During the same period, however, the proportion of homes equipped with flush toilets rose from 9.2 per cent to 77.0 per cent and those equipped with their own baths rose from 59.1 per cent to 95.2 per cent.

From 1965 to 1995, refrigerator ownership rose from slightly more than 50 per cent of Japanese households to nearly 100 per cent. Automobile ownership increased from just over ten per cent to more than 70 per cent. As of 1995, more than 70 per cent of Japanese families owned room air conditioners, microwave ovens, and videocassette recorders. More than 50 per cent owned CD players.

From 1966 to 1994, sales of toys and entertainment equipment rose, in real terms, 10.7 times. A 1995 Prime Minister's Office survey revealed that 68.8 per cent of children aged nine to fourteen owned TV game machines, 59.4 per cent owned radio cassette/stereo players; 51.5 per cent had their own rooms; 18.7 per cent had their own TV sets; 12.4 per cent had their own video players. In the 15–23 category, the number with radio cassette players had risen to 87.4 per cent; 79.6 per cent had a room of their own; 49.9 per cent had their own TV set; 41.4 per cent had their own videocassette recorders; 21.7 per cent had their own word processors.

Deluged with information

In 1965, Japanese publishers released 14,238 new books. In 1994, that number had risen to 58,310. At the end of 1965, 2,172 magazines were published in Japan. By the end of 1994, there were 4,178. There were, in short, nearly four times as many books and twice as many magazines as there had been three decades earlier.

Figures for *manga*, comics that range from innocent fantasies targeting elementary school students to hard-core pornography, are staggering. In 1981, 223,240,000 volumes of comics were published in book form. In 1994, the number reached 783,500,000. During the same period, annual production of comics magazines increased from 955,450,000 copies to 1,594,750,000 copies.

As of 1995, radio broadcasts were available 23 hours and 9 minutes per day; TV broadcasts, twenty hours and 19 minutes per day.

The one medium that has shown declines in recent decades is the cinema. The number of movie theaters in Japan decreased from 4,659 in 1965 to 1,776 in 1995. During the same period, movie audiences shrank from 372,680,000 to 127,040,000. The number of feature films produced in Japan declined from 751 to 610. While films remained popular, film consumption had become an increasingly private experience. By November 1996, the number of video rental shops had reached approximately 12,000.

Another major change in the information environment surrounding Japanese youth was overseas travel. In 1965, the number of Japanese who traveled abroad was 159,000. By 1995, that figure had risen to 15,290,000.

For the White Paper's compilers, the critical issue is how the material affluence and superabundant information these figures represent are affecting Japanese youth. Having noted that there is relatively little reliable data spanning the whole thirty years from 1965 to 1995, they present instead a variety of suggestive studies.

Outdoor play declining

According to a 1994 NHK study of children's play habits, participation in outdoor activities such as baseball and softball, soccer, dodge ball, and hide and seek was down. (Only soccer had experienced a brief revival, owing to the creation of the J-League professional soccer league.) By contrast, time spent on such indoor activities as video games and playing cards had steadily increased. A Prime Minister's Office survey in 1995 reported that, during holidays, 57.2 per cent of children aged nine to fourteen watch TV or listen to music; 49.3 per cent read comics. Only 46.4 per cent play outdoors; 39.8 per cent play video games or cards.

The video games that are now so popular did not exist 30 years ago. According to the NHK study, 71.8 per cent of elementary school children now play these games. According to the Prime Minister's Office survey, 66 per cent of junior high and high school students play video games; 13.8 per cent do so every day.

Increased pressure to study

In 1965, about 70 per cent of Japanese children went to high schools or vocational schools after graduating from junior high school, the last level of compulsory education. By 1995, that figure had risen to 96.7 per cent. In 1965, 17 per cent went on to universities or junior colleges; by 1995, that figure had risen to 45.2 per cent.

As a growing proportion of Japanese children competed for slots at prestigious high schools and universities, the number attending cram schools also increased. According to a Ministry of Education study, from 1985 to 1993, the proportion of sixth year elementary school students attending cram schools rose from 29.6 per cent to 41.7 per cent; the comparable figures for third year junior high school students were 47.3 per cent and 67.1 per cent. Paying for extra education had become a major burden on household budgets. During these years, the average amount spent by Japanese households on tutors and cram schools increased 6.5-fold for elementary school students and 6-fold for junior high school students.

Sleep in short supply

In 1965, elementary school students slept on average nine hours and 22 minutes a night. By 1997 this figure had fallen to eight hours and 43 minutes. High school students got only six hours and 58 minutes of sleep per night.

As of 1995, the average total amount of time spent on such activities as sleeping, eating, personal care, study, commuting, and contact with media is 22 hours and 18 minutes per day for elementary school students and 23 hours and 15 minutes for junior high school students. Private time is rare.

Only 32.8 per cent of elementary school students and 24.2 per cent of junior high school students included household chores among their regular activities. Elementary school students spent an average of 38 minutes per day on chores; junior high school students 42 minutes. Comparable figures for socializing with friends are 48 minutes and 53 minutes. Only 4.1 per cent of elementary school students and 2.6 per cent of junior high school students reported involvement in community activities.

The White Paper's authors are concerned about the implications of all these figures for children's mental health. A Bennesse Institute of Education study shows that 57.6 per cent of elementary school students often feel tired; 48.0 per cent frequently feel like screaming; 42.7 per cent become irritated over little things; 33.6 per cent are unhappy because things aren't going well. Among junior high school students, 75.2 per cent say they have trouble getting up in the morning; 73.9 per cent describe themselves as tired; 57.4 per cent say that they lack energy; 43.8 per cent say that they often feel irritated. The White Paper's analysis of current youth lifestyles ends with the suggestion that, confronted with growing numbers of choices but confined by rigidly structured lives, 'Elementary and junior high school students are showing signs of exhaustion and stress'. (Prime Minister's Office 1996:65)

Yes, it is true that Japanese children now lead affluent lives. I wonder, however, as I read this conclusion, if the early maturity, detached perspectives, camaraderie, and sensitivity that HILL researchers find in Japanese children today might not have something in common with the battle fatigue of soldiers who have won the latest skirmish but face an endless war. No wonder they prefer comfort, peace and quiet, and being left alone.

What Has HILL Discovered?

This chapter includes translations of three HILL studies. Note as you read them that the first, 'Children After School', was published in 1982. Its subjects, children of the Baby Boomers, the Baby Boomer Juniors, were nine years old. In 1993, when 'Living as One Thirty-fourth' appeared, the cohort studied had reached the age of twenty. While the individuals studied were not the same, it is not hard to imagine the children of the 1982 study growing up to be the young people whose attitudes were the subject of study ten years later. The 'Children After School' and 'Amenbo Kids' studies, by contrast, look at children of about the same age, fifteen years apart. The subjects in 'Children After School' were fourth graders, while those in the 1997 study, 'Amenbo Kids', ranged from fourth grade to the second year of junior high school. What is striking, however, is the broad consistency in the trends these studies reveal, trends which, if we look back to earlier chapters, seem rooted in the habits and attitudes of 'Sneaker Middle' and later generations of Japanese parents.

Children After School
Lifestyle Times, July 1982

The Art: The cover, reproduced as Figure 6.1, is a child's drawing of children playing soccer. The face that catches our eye is the somber-looking boy with his arms outstretched as if on guard. The headline on the opening spread reads, 'School is over. The seventh hour of class begins. Our playgrounds are cram schools and practice fields'.

The Research Design: For this study, intensive interviews and drawing exercises were used to explore the lives of 22 boys and girls in the fourth grade of a Tokyo elementary school.

The Children

The children of the Baby Boomers (about 6.12 million of them) are now in third to fifth grade. How different is the world of these children, who are being raised by Sneaker Middles, from the worlds of previous generations? We interviewed 22 fourth-grade boys and girls to find out.

The seventh hour of class

These children are busy. They all have a seventh hour of class after school. Boys study such directly practical things as abacus, math, and swimming. Girls study piano, electric organ, tea ceremony, or puppetry – all connected with self-expression.

They no longer study in the dining room

At the Komon cram schools to which many of the boys go, students arrive whenever they like, do their drills, and then go home. 'The same method could be used at home. But their parents say that at home they wouldn't persevere. Even for swimming, parents seem to feel safer leaving instruction to experts. The kids like to come because they get to meet their friends. And every child wants to be able to do well in school' (Komon teacher, Mr. S).

The HILL researcher comments that, when she was young, she liked doing her homework in the dining room where her mother was knitting. Her mother would scold her: 'Your posture's bad! Don't suck your pencil!' Sometimes, however, her mother would also sharpen her pencil for her. Children who attend cram schools don't have these kinds of memories.

Figure 6.1 Cover, 'Kids After School'

Discipline was one reason children studied in dining rooms. A calligraphy instructor with twenty years experience says, 'It used to be that when mothers brought their children to me they said, "This child wants to learn to write. Please teach him, starting from zero". Now it's different. They say, "I think that if he does calligraphy, his manners may improve at little".' Discipline as well as instruction has been turned over to the experts.

Children and TV

'My life is divided into four parts: sleeping, school, TV, and play'. When we ask children how it would be to have no TV, they say they wouldn't like that at all. They would miss their favorite programs, and many want to grow up to become

161

professional baseball players or TV celebrities. If there was no TV, 'I couldn't become a star', they say. Still, we don't see them as TV addicts.

When parents say '30 minutes each day' or 'No TV today', they obey. They don't sneak a look or throw tantrums if they can't watch. Having been exposed to TV ever since they were born, they aren't excited by TV per se. When we mention programs that adults would call vulgar, they talk freely about what they enjoy and what they don't like. They don't seem brainwashed.

The ups and downs of being a child

'When I'm big I'd like to build a house'. 'If I had a million yen, I'd buy baseball equipment and model trains'. These are a boy's dreams. But there are also boys who say, 'When you become adult, you have to learn to drink and going to the company's a pain'. 'I don't want to grow up', they say. In contrast, girls are little adults. They talk about exchanging presents with friends and singing and dancing at parties. Some talk about wanting to marry early and be taken to Australia. If they had money, they would certainly save it. The boys are miniature salarymen; the girls are miniature wives.

Boys form teams; girls small groups of friends.

We asked what they do when alone, and also when there are two or three, five, ten, or twenty children playing together. Whatever the size of the group, boys play ball. Baseball is their favorite sport. If alone, they will toss a ball against a wall. If there are twenty boys, they choose sides and play a game. They sort things out so that everyone can play. If left to their own devices, many play with a game or put together a plastic model.

Girls don't play in large groups. When we asked how twenty girls would play together, one girl raised her hand and said, 'That would never happen'. While boys always play ball, even by themselves, girls play in smaller groups but do a wider range of things. Boys play in teams. Girls play with small groups of friends.

What do they want?

The owner of a stationery store says, 'Today's children are spendthrifts. They don't care if something is expensive or cheap. All that matters is whether they like it or not. If they want it, they'll buy it. Their parents come with them and will buy anything that seems pretty, cute, or new, regardless of price. Anything that is advertised on TV is sure to sell. In their manners and the way they behave, kids today act like small grown-ups. They aren't as cute as children used to be'.

That is an adult opinion. A typical kid's remark is, 'I'll stay a kid until I'm bored. Then I'll stay an adult until I'm bored. Then I'll be elderly until I'm bored. Then I'll die. Oh, well' (boy, 4th grade, Sakurada Elementary School, Kita-ward).

Tell Us About Your Teacher

Boys

- Teachers know if you goof off or deliberately throw a ball onto the roof of the gym.
- Some school clubs have too many members, so you have to draw lots to join them. I didn't get into the one I wanted. What a drag.
- Our teacher is interesting. He draws pictures of graves for us.
- My teacher is a man, but if I do something I couldn't do before on the horizontal bar, he kisses me on top of my head. Feels weird.
- He doesn't say anything if boys are fighting. He says that we have to settle it ourselves. He's a good teacher. I like him.
- I think he's irresponsible. He starts playing with the girls and doesn't pay attention to what we boys are doing.
- The homeroom teacher and the drawing teacher are strict. Still, they'll play with us. They have their soft sides.
- Last summer our teacher took the members of our class for a walk around the city. This year he has talked about going to a pool.
- If you joke around when the teacher is serious, he'll get angry. It doesn't hurt at all, but he'll whack you with a bamboo stick.
- I got whacked three times in one day.
- If you bully or betray someone, you'll be scolded. Doing these things is disgraceful for a man. It brings shame on 4th grade, class 2.

Girls

- I don't like the way the teacher does things. Everything is so competitive. Homework, essays, cleaning, exercise on the horizontal bar – we always have to compete in teams and be compared with other teams.
- Sometimes teachers are strict but still very popular.
- I love the music teacher. All the girls do. That's why I joined the music club.
- She gets angry so fast.
- Our teacher is a weakling. So sometimes he doesn't do gym class. Still, he works hard. He is really dedicated. But, I wish he'd think more about how we feel.
- There are things I just don't understand about him.
- A teacher with a sense of humor would be good.
- We have one student who is really good at music. He's the teacher's pet. That's why nobody likes that teacher.
- Being the teacher's pet is a pain, but you can't complain about it.
- We are always having these 'work-hard' meetings or 'too-bad' meetings where people compete to see who gets the most pluses or minuses.
- I always get pluses, so the other kids hate me.

- Our previous teacher understood our feelings. That was great, but she was maybe a little too soft. She wouldn't scold the bullies.
- Moms are happy when a teacher is strict. They'll say, 'I am so glad you have that teacher'.

What Will You Do When You Grow Up?

Boys

- I want to grow up. I want to try working.
- I'd like to have an audience. To be an actor (neat!) or a singer (I'd like to stick out) or a star.
- People are always getting mad at me. When I'm grown up, I'll do it to my own kids. (I guess I'm bad.)
- Grown-ups die sooner. I don't want to grow up.
- Doctors make mistakes, that's terrible.
- I want to be a pilot.
- What if you turn out like Captain Katagiri and crashed your plane in Tokyo Bay? That won't be so good.
- While I'm a kid, I can do what I want.
- It's tough being a grown-up. Kids get away with things, but if grown-ups do the same things, people talk about it.
- Me, absolutely, a baseball player. Or an umpire, or announcer.
- You stop getting gifts of money at New Year's. It's better to be a child.

Girls

- I'll run into people and make dates to go drinking.
- Now Mom does everything for me. If I grow up, I'll have to work and make money. That's tough. I don't want to grow up.
- I wonder who will be the most popular singer when I'm a grownup?
- If we formed a trio and put out a record together, we would have to divide the money we make three ways. Each of us would get less.
- I like a certain someone in the class. Because he's likely to have to change schools, I want to grow up and say 'yes' real fast.
- Mothers get to say 'Study now!' to their kids. Looks like fun.
- I want to marry a rich man and get him to take me to Australia for our honeymoon, so I can see koalas.
- When I was little, everyone called me 'little teacher Satchan'. I enjoyed the praise. Now that rarely happens. I want to be little again.
- I want to get married and have children.
- If you are grown up, you have do to things for yourself. Your mother won't tell you what to do. Grown-ups are fretting all the time. Looks really tough.

What Is a Good Kid? Or a Popular Kid?

Boys

- Tachie-kun. He always listens to what the teacher says, always gets 100 on tests, never gets below 70.
- He's sweet and popular, too.
- I'm bad. I had to stand in the corner today.
- Because I was always looking behind me, I was tied to my chair. Everyone said I was cute.
- I'm a swimmer. The girls all say I'm handsome.
- I look manly.
- Girls are always following him home.
- The best is being an athlete.
- Smart kids get liked a lot, too, you know. Don't have much to say, though.
- There is this one kid. Today he wrote that on his way home he will stop for a math lesson. Then even though he's done that, he'll still study when he gets home. When I saw what he wrote, it gave me a headache.
- The best is to be an athlete and smart, too. But if you have to choose, being an athlete is better.
- Bullies? There are some.
- I'm one. But I don't do anything. Don't say ugly things about me.
- I hate guys who show off for girls and act like they're big shots.
- Our bunch is stuck up because we're good at baseball. We won't let him be part of our group.
- There are good kids here, too. They are good at all sorts of sports and super popular with the girls. Popular with grown-ups, too.
- Can't be bullied, smart, gentle, can do sports. That's a good kid. Ah, yes, Yamashita-kun!
- We are just ordinary kids.

Girls

- If you listen to the teacher while posing like this (strikes a goody-goody pose).
- She is really smart!
- She listens even when everyone around her is rowdy, a really does-it-right kid.
- She's so smart, she can do anything. She's the class representative. But her handwriting's so rotten. It's not like her.
- Tomo-chan is the most popular. She is good at studies and good at sports.
- I am famous for the way I catch the ball when we're playing dodge ball. I've got stacks of erasers and notes from the boys who sit next to me.
- Sounds great. I've had nothing but bad luck with the boys who sit beside me.

- The athletes are the popular boys, but really, behind their backs, everybody hates them.
- I don't want to associate with them, but if you go against them, they will make you cry. So everyone goes out of their way to be their friends, even if it hurts.
- In our group the boys aren't strong. So the girls have to be tough, or we would be in trouble.
- Roll up my skirt. Still do it. Want to catch a popular boy.
- Popular kids. Most girls hate them. Everyone gossips about how they think that wearing high heels makes your legs look longer.
- They are so snotty.
- I don't pay any attention, but they won't listen to what you say. If you refuse to play, you'll get scolded at the 'self-criticism' sessions.

A Peek Inside Children's Worlds

How big are children's worlds? Who are the characters who appear there? What is the radius of the circle in which they move?

To find out we conducted a picture-drawing exercise in addition to our interviews, making use of mental mapping techniques. Instead of asking, 'How do you see your father, mother, and friends?' we asked, 'Could you draw for us the people around you?' The first response was 'Eeeh!' Then came the barrage of questions: 'How do you want us to do it?' 'Should we draw faces?' 'May we include names?' When we answered, 'Just draw whatever you like', the kids started drawing, chattering as they drew, and having a lot of fun. The drawings they produced were mental maps of human relations as seen through the eyes and the hearts of children.

When we analyzed the drawings, we realized that this exercise had turned out to be an effective way of doing research with children.

Assertive (draws self big)

We found two types of drawings, those in which the circle that represents the self was drawn very big and those in which it was no bigger than the others. In some examples, the self-circle is placed in the middle of the map and is also drawn larger than the others. We got the impression that these were self-assertive kids and, indeed, when we interviewed them, the kids who drew these maps were very active and aggressive.

Cooperative (draws self as one among others)

In other maps, there is no difference in size between the circle that represents the self and the circles that represent the others. We noticed, too, how one child first drew the other circles, then inserted herself at the end. We inferred that she belonged to the cooperative type. Both boys and girls who drew this kind of map tended to seem more adult. In the interviews they waited their turns to speak and seemed to think carefully about their answers.

Bossy-at-home, timid-in-public (draws self above family)

Did Yutchan forget to include her friends? First, she drew herself at the top, then she added her family and relatives. As a youngest child, she is used to being taken care of and may have become the *uchibenkei* (bossy at home, timid in public) type. She doesn't mind sticking out. During the interviews, however, she didn't compete with the more self-assertive children. She is very satisfied to be the focus of her family and runs away from situations where she isn't the focus of attention. We saw a warning signal here.

Miniature adults

We have already said that today's boys and girls are like miniature wives and miniature salarymen. In one map drawn by a girl, the gray fill represents friends, the green fill family and relatives and the white fill other adults. The cutie who drew this map is a girl whose way of talking and thinking are just like her mother's. 'I don't like my teacher that much. But, after all, she is our teacher. If I dislike her, it will ruin the whole year. I can put up with her. I think I'll do my best'. A special feature of her map is the way that she has written in the names of so many school and private teachers. It shows how strongly she wants to act like an adult. (Note, however, that the way that she has also drawn big circles for the crabs, parakeets, and parrot shows that she is still a child.)

What is distinctive about the boy we have placed in this category is the way in which he has included so many friends. Wanting to make friends is characteristic of all the elementary school boys in our sample. Still, the way that this boy includes relatives, father, mother, and lots of friends shows the broad range of human relations that make an outstanding student. Also, he lumps all his teachers together. While getting along well with adults, he doesn't pay too much attention to them.

She started with the one who feels closest

All the children's drawings were honest and straightforward, but the one who made us look most carefully at what she had drawn was Daifuku-chan. Daifuku-chan has older sisters who are now in their first and third years of high school. Daifuku-chan really likes the younger of her sisters. She wants to be as big as she is, so they can do things together. Her sister's was the first picture she drew, and as she drew it, she had a happy, gentle smile on her face. She even included her sister's socks. Next she drew herself, facing her favorite sister, jumping up and down beside her. Her third image was her father – undressed, wearing polka-

167

dotted underpants. But the father was laughing, too. Daifuku-chan also seems to like her father. Next came her older sister. Her face is pretty, but her hand is big. Perhaps she was trying to show us that they fight all the time and her sister uses that hand to hit her. Notice how the feet are all messed up, with a slapdash, forget-it, flavor. At the end, she erased them. Last was mama. Perhaps she had just completed her mother's face when her friends finished their drawings, so she, too, decided to stop and just dotted in her body.

There used to be vacant lots

We are looking at a map of where he plays drawn by a boy who lives in an apartment complex. He lives in Apartment Block No. 6. His school is located beside the apartments. After class, he plays baseball with his friends in the space in the center of the complex. This space, the biggest thing in his picture, is in reality only one-fourth the size of the schoolyard. We note, too, that he hasn't drawn the supermarket, gasoline stand, and restaurants that are also part of the complex. In children's mental maps, only places essential to their lives get drawn.

We turn, then, to a map drawn by a girl who lives in a house. Children like this girl, who don't live in the bounded spaces that apartment complexes provide, find it hard to draw the places where they play. The girl who drew this map tore up one piece of paper after another. Lacking a sense of the whole, she can't draw a map she is happy with. The places where these children play are usually the streets in front of the houses where they live. Other places are added as afterthoughts. We can see how rarely a child like this gets to play away from home.

When we ask ourselves if the difference between these two mental maps could be a difference between boys and girls or if where they live is more important, we realize that we need to do more research.

What the Editor Really Thinks

These children have no dreams. They aren't latchkey children, but still their lives are constricted. Between study and private lessons, they aren't able to play. Looking back on when I was growing up, I remember the evenings I used to spend at a nearby vacant lot. Today's children are pitiful. Yes, as times and adult values change, we expect to see change in children. Change is only natural. But our children's worlds are mirrors of the times in which we live. We should look at our world through children's eyes, shouldn't we, Dad?

Wanting to Live as One Thirty-Fourth
The In Thing is Silent Appeal
Lifestyle Times, March 1993

The Art: As shown in Figure 6.2, the cover of this issue of the *Lifestyle Times* is empty except for the headline. On page two we find the following data:

The Research Design: The data reported here come from a wide variety of sources including an informal survey of young people in their late teens and early twenties who were asked to talk about how they like to assert themselves.

- Average number of friends reported by those aged 15 to 19:   34.06

  (Lifestyle Annual 1992)

- Believe: 'The young are the central figures of the age'

	Males, 20–29	Females 20–29
1990	30.8 per cent	18.6 per cent
1992	18.0 per cent	9.3 per cent

  (Lifestyle Annual 1992)

- Agree: 'We often tell each other about new products'

	Male 18–29	Female 18–29
1988	52.0 per cent	44.9 per cent
1991	45.9 per cent	29.2 per cent

  (Nikkei Sangyō Consumer Research Institute,
  'Comprehensive Consumer Survey')

- Cases of bullying in elementary, junior high, and high schools

1985	155,066
1990	24,308

  (Ministry of Education)

- Consider keeping personal secrets 'extremely important'

1981	32.7 per cent
1990	43.8 per cent

  (Economic Planning Agency 'Survey of Citizen Preferences')

How Do You Feel?

Our themes are 'self-assertion' and 'self-expression', especially among young people who are now in their teens and twenties. In their fashions, interests, speech, and behavior, they seem very quiet. In their social relationships they

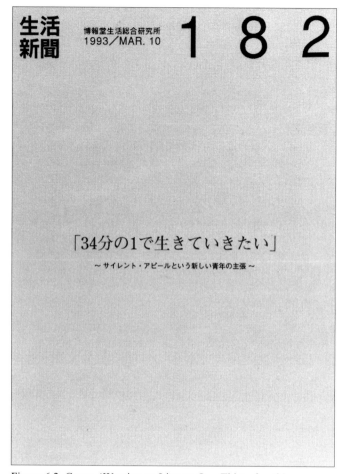

Figure 6.2 Cover, 'Wanting to Live as One Thirty-fourth'

prefer a certain distance, or, more precisely, not to interfere with each other. Self-assertion no longer seeks praise or to influence others' behavior. Self-expression no longer seeks to make a deep impression on others. College students we talked to put it this way, 'Not to say anything dangerous, to hold back; that is my way of asserting myself'. 'I want to communicate through my everyday speech, expression, and behavior, without going out of my way to show off'.

- 'See fashion as important as a means of self-expression'.
  Males, 18–29: 35.9 per cent
- 'Want to be judged by their hobbies and leisure activities'.
  Females, 18–29: 23.4 per cent
  (*Nikkei*, 'Comprehensive Consumer Survey', 1991)

To the youth of the 1960s and 1970s, self-assertion meant rebellion, a refusal to accept others' opinions. 'There is no music besides the Stones!' they'd say. Egos were slamming against one another. During the sixties, the Baby Boomers constructed themselves through self-assertion: 'If we don't shout, nothing will change!' The eighties were a time when uniqueness was a weapon in the battle to define a New Breed self. Now 'being myself' is detached from self-assertion. We hear young people say, 'Accept what others have to say, but don't be too interested in it' (Male, 19). 'Hold on to your own opinions. Talking of better and worse is like pissing in the face of a frog' (Male, 21).

In today's society, individuals no longer clash; instead, they accept each other's differences. They neither assimilate nor differentiate themselves. No one is interested any more either in filling in moats or in making new enemies. Some observers say that they have become more conservative, but we see something more transparent about them, something less guarded. Individuality is simply assumed. Each acts on behalf of himself or herself, secure in his or her individual character, without regard for others. The result is a very quiet world.

- 'Have confidence in social skills'
    Aged 15–19: 67.5 per cent
- 'Have confidence in ability to do well in a more competitive society'
    Aged 15–19: 24.6 per cent
    (HILL, *Survey Annual, 1991, The Confidence of the Japanese.*)

What we are seeing is not the older type of confidence that consists in feeling superior to others, but a new type, characteristic of young people who have confidence in simply being themselves. There are no complexes lurking behind the surface. The way they behave says clearly, 'I was born to be loved'.

Are today's young people monads? Do they lead a self-absorbed existence? The answer is no. They have a strong desire for social interaction. We are surprised, more than anything else, by the number of friends they claim. According to the most recent Lifestyle Annual survey, teenagers have on average 34.06 friends. Those aged twenty to twenty-nine have 22.83. What these numbers suggest is that the meaning of friendship has changed.

Responses to Self-Assertion Questionnaire, January, 1993

How do you assert yourself?

- I don't say much, but if asked about myself, I try to make my answer conform to everyone's expectations. (Male, 20)
- I like the words 'no resistance, no surrender'. What they mean to me is that there is no beauty or goodness in acting aggressively. To me self-assertion is not about pushing myself forward. I don't worry about how to express my ideas through words or through the fashions I wear. (Male, 21)

- I don't care if other people accept or reject what I say. It's enough to be able to say what I feel. (Female, 19)
- I don't want to assert myself in direct opposition to others. The way I like best is humor. (Male, 20)
- I want to live like the air. (Male, 23)

What forms of self-expression do you like?

- Not saying too much. Saying things that can't be understood unless you pay attention. (Male, 25)
- Inside you are very particular, but you don't impose your preferences on others. (Female, 22)
- Nonchalance. For example, in the way that you hold chopsticks, or the way you touch your hair. (Male, 19)
- Enjoyable. Light conversation for example. (Female, 22)
- When the timing is good. (Female, 21)
- When it's something only those in the know can understand. (Female, 21)
- It feels best when the person speaking seems unconscious of what he or she is saying. (Female, 22)

What forms of self-expression do you dislike?

- People who speak loudly and try to overwhelm you. (Female, 22)
- People who respond too quickly. (Female, 23)
- People who always perform in a minor key, as if trying to stress that they refuse to do what's popular, that they won't accept others' opinions. (Female, 20)
- It feels unpleasant when people strain to seem different. (Female, 19)
- I don't like the kind of assertiveness that exaggerates and makes it too easy to understand its intentions. (Male, 21)
- When something only a little different is presented as a breakthrough. (Female, 20)

How to you deal with unpleasant forms of self-expression?

The answer is to adopt an 'it's got nothing to do with me' attitude toward distasteful or unpleasant behavior. There are criteria for like, dislike, and ignore, but a huge gap between the first two and the third. It's better to ignore your friends' distasteful aspects or interests that you can't understand.

- I escape as fast as I can. (Male, 22)
- Since any response will play into the other's hands, act as if you don't notice. Pretend to be stupid. (Female, 22)
- Even if I don't like it, it's their way of expressing themselves. You accept the other as an individual. (Female, 21)

- Neither approve nor reject. (Male, 21)
- Just go 'hmmm' and keep your mouth shut. Sometimes murmur 'I don't understand'. (Female, 22)
- In sumo you'd call it side-stepping (to evade the opponent's thrusts). (Male, 21)
- Smile. Accept only that this is what he thinks. There is no need to think that you have to change someone else. Whatever happens, don't let yourself be drawn in. Stand firmly on your own feet. (Male, 21)

Why don't you want to influence others?

We are seeing a new type of rudeness. Compared to motorcycle gangs or middle-aged 'Mrs. Monster' *(obatarian)* women who deliberately make trouble for others, these young people have no interest in how what they do affects anything outside their selves. They will buy a hamburger at McDonald's and eat it at the Kentucky Fried Chicken shop. They will refuse to do work that they don't want to do. They aren't conscious of breaking rules. Because they act destructively but not aggressively, they are harder to control.

- I want to be like the character Snufkin who appears in the Moomin books. (Male, 21)
- I think that it's pushy or affected to say that you want to share an opinion. (Male, 25)
- Self-assertion should only be an appeal for recognition, nothing more. If somebody remembers you when they are old, that is enough. (Female, 22)
- Self-expression is a way to get the other to understand and accept you; you shouldn't seek admiration or make others envious. (Female, 21)
- It is OK to accept some influence. (Female, 19)

Silent Appeal

What surprised us most was that all of the 120 opinions we collected seemed so similar. Everyone we talked to seemed to share the same character. What all our subjects had in common was feeling they don't want to be special. They want to live quietly as one thirty-fourth of the group. Still, they don't want to lose their uniqueness as one of the 34. They favor the quiet self-assertion that we have labeled 'silent appeal'. In the questionnaire mentioned above, we included the question, 'Why don't you work harder, so that people will really like you?' One answer was, 'I don't want everything to be what I like. If I like something, it might not be right for someone else'. (Male, 21) Here's another: 'I don't tell people what my favorite book or movie is. That would reveal too much about the real me'. (Female, 20)

What puzzles us is whether these one thirty-fourth attitudes represent only a change in mood or a fundamental change in society? They could be just a fad. If, however, today's young people are truly different from previous generations, a more profound transformation could be underway. Take friendship, for example.

Average Number of Friends by Generation
Teens: 34.06   Twenties: 22.83   Thirties: 13.15
Forties: 12.04 Fifties: 12.16   Sixties: 13.60

(Lifestyle Annual 1992)

'What does "friend" mean to you?'
'Eh? Someone to whom I give my phone number'.

When the number of people counted as friends is divided by the number of those included in a person's personal list of telephone numbers, the younger the generation, the closer the result approaches one. While we don't know whether this is a fad or a true transformation, we are sure that what is going on is not a deliberate attempt to create a new culture. It doesn't have any particular purpose. There is no reason to be angry about it. We, too, should focus on taking care of ourselves.

The Appeal of Simply Being

In the TV drama 'Family Court', the character Tsuru Tarō is strange. In his conversations with plants, he never attempts to persuade. Like the plants, he is just there. 'Here, now, just existing', that is all he does. It is, however, precisely his passivity that melts your heart and moves you. It shows the stupidity of trying to control others.

In *Lifestyle Times* No. 179, which looked at high school students, we reported a statement from one who said, 'I want to live by photosynthesis'. What he says he wants is a plant-like existence. But would he be really happy?

Let's think about advertising. For a long time I've been attracted by ads without copy. In European posters, it's the ones without copy that stand out. Advertising copy is mostly used to persuade, and American ads are especially likely to speak clearly about what they are aiming at. Pictures, however, are polymorphous. A person can read into them whatever he likes. They have a presence; that's advertising.

This form of communication may be becoming more popular. Instead of acting like a carnivore and attacking head-on, it depends on a vegetable-like feeling of presence. While self-sufficient, it reaches out to its surroundings. The artifice involved in TV is worrying. The hand of the director is always there. A better technique might be to behave like a plant and to focus on simply being there.

Amenbo Kids
Lifestyle Times, September 1997

The Art: The cover of this issue of the *Lifestyle Times* (Figure 6.3) shows Japan's population pyramid. Inside, on page three we find a photo of an *amenbo*, the insect called a water strider (Figure 6.4) that inspired the title of this report. The text on the following page explains the rationale for another study of Japan's children. On the page opposite the photo is a chart (Figure 6.5) that resonates with the image of the insect but also recalls the representation of the five trends affecting silver aristocrats (see Figure 7.5 in Chapter 7).

The Research Design: The data for this study were taken from a survey of 1,500 children. Details are included in the text.

Fewer and Fewer Kids

People have been talking for a long time about the shrinking numbers of Japan's children. As a glance at the population pyramid reveals, when the ten- to fourteen-year-old children who are the subjects of this study were born, the transition to smaller generations was just beginning. This trend is correlated with the increase in unmarried adults and the tendency to later marriage, but the small size of their parents' generation (father's average age is 44; mother's 41) has also had an impact.

If we compare the proportions of the population in the young (14 and under) and elderly (65 and older) segments, the changes in Japan's population structure in the last twenty years are astonishing. During the 1970s and 1980s, the young were two to three times more numerous than the elderly. Now, however, because of the shrinking number of children, they account for only 15.46 per cent of Japan's population, while the elderly account for 15.50 per cent. The old outnumber the young.

If we look at trends in the ten- to fourteen-year-old segment, we see that its numbers peaked with the Baby Boomer Juniors in 1985 and have been declining ever since. In 1996, there were only 7.343 million kids in the ten-to-fourteen segment, 2.7 million fewer than at the peak. In terms of market scale, this segment is now 27 per cent smaller than it was in 1985. In only a decade, this market segment has shrunk to three-fourths its former size.

A decrease in the number of children will also have a major impact on the production side of Japan's economy. It will not be a temporary issue that disappears when these children enter their teens. In the twenty-first century,

Figure 6.3 Cover, 'Amenbo Kids'

when these children become the core of Japan's labor force, they will pose an even larger problem for industry.

How should one address the market they represent? It is vital to understand this generation's behavior and attitudes and to grasp its values now. This 1997 research annual report is basic information for anyone thinking about the future of consumption in the twenty-first century.

Survey Details:

- Area: Within 40 kilometer radius of the center of Tokyo.
- Subjects: Male and female students who, as of March 31, 1997, were in grades ranging from fourth grade elementary to second year junior high school (priority given to year of entry into school; unrestricted by actual age).
- Sample Size: 1,500.

176

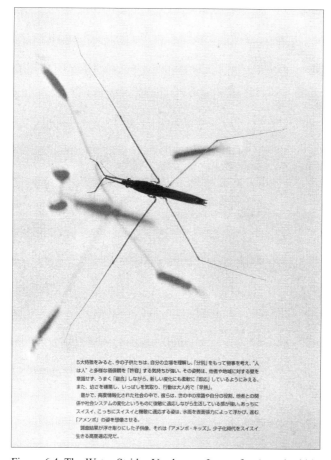

Figure 6.4 The Water Strider Used as an Image for Amenbo kids.

- Sample Composition: 150 boys and 150 girls in each of the fourth, fifth, and sixth years of elementary school and the first and second years of junior high school.
- Sampling Method: Random selection from 150 randomly selected areas.
- Survey Method: Interview with questionnaire left behind (direct interview concerning basic attributes).
- Survey Period: March 7 to March 31, 1997.

Basic Facts Concerning Heisei Kids

The questions put to these children covered a wide range of topics. We asked them about their clothing, diet, and housing; study at school and at cram schools. We also asked about how much time they have for play and how much they

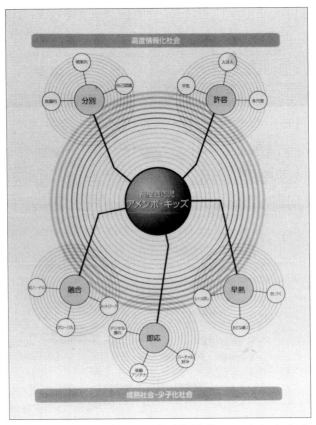

Figure 6.5 Graph Showing Amenbo Kids' Characteristic Attitudes.

would like to have. We examined relationships with friends and family members; contact with media and interest in sources of information; plus, of course, their consumption behavior and wants. We tried to look closely at their attitudes and behavior in each of these areas.

Listed below are a number of key points about the lives of these 1,500 children. What kinds of activities and experiences fill their days? How much money do these children who are growing up in an age of affluence command? What sorts of things do they own? To answer these questions, we've assembled the figures in this 'Getting to know the realities of being a Heisei kid'.

Environment

- They typically wake up at 7:01 a.m. They go to bed at 10:38 p.m.
- 24 per cent eat breakfast by themselves.
- 42 per cent of their mothers are full-time housewives.

- 84 per cent have rooms not shared with their parents; 43 per cent have a room to themselves.
- 8 per cent have no brothers or sisters.

Daily activities

- 44 per cent attend cram schools. They get home at 8:09 p.m.
- 56 per cent take lessons (piano, calligraphy, English, etc.).
- 44 per cent have participated in volunteer activities.
- 26 per cent have been bullied; 16 per cent have been bullies.
- 19 per cent have been hit by teachers.

Economic situation

- Average monthly allowance is ¥1,930.
- 49 per cent feel that their allowance is too small.
- Average gift of money received at the New Year is ¥29,900.
- 77 per cent have savings accounts.
- Average savings are ¥108,300.

Personal property

- 90 per cent own video games; the average number owned is 22.
- 37 per cent have their own headphone stereo sets.
- 47 per cent have their own radio cassette players; the average number of CDs owned is 12.
- 26 per cent have their own cameras.
- 83 per cent have their own bicycles.

Five Major Characteristics

To discover the distinctive characteristics of this generation, we analyzed our data and compared these results to the results of our 1989 survey of 10- to 14-year-old children and our 1996 *Lifestyle Annual* study of 20- to 69-year-old adults. Five major characteristics appeared. These children are

(1) pragmatic;
(2) tolerant;
(3) able to mix with others;
(4) sensitive, and, in effect;
(5) miniature adults.

Pragmatic

Their thinking is pragmatic, based on precise understanding of where they currently stand. Keeping their distance, they coolly analyze their own position and the world around them. Their powers of discrimination are much higher than expected from among elementary and junior high students.

Morally sensitive

61.8 per cent consider making a contribution to the world more important than benefiting Japan alone (compared with 60.2 per cent of adults in the 1996 *Lifestyle Annual*).

Pessimistic

40.1 per cent believe that the world will get worse (compared with 29.5 per cent in the 1989 survey).

Self-aware

77.6 per cent see themselves as happy (compared with 77.7 per cent of adults in the 1996 *Lifestyle Annual*).

Tolerant

They don't worry about seeming different from others. They say that 'people are people' and accept others' values. More than half of these children will not oppose another's opinion; this trend has become the mainstream. They don't think of formal education as the only measure of worth; they accept a variety of standards.

Difference is no problem

57 per cent are not disturbed by seeming different from others (compared with 44.5 per cent in the 1989 survey).

People are people

74.8 per cent are unconcerned when they see friends who don't go to cram school.

Multiple standards

Only 36.5 per cent now say that study is more important than play (compared with 50.9 per cent in the 1989 survey).

Able to Mix

These children are often said to be poor at playing together with friends, preferring to stay at home by themselves. That isn't what we discovered. Also, even among the older children there is no resistance to associating with non-Japanese; that hurdle is low. They seem to mix easily with all sorts of people. Especially among the girls, network building through exchanging presents, print club photos, and letters is flourishing.

Low hurdles

68.9 per cent say that they can make friends with anyone.

Global

64.4 per cent want to make friends with non-Japanese (compared with 47.3 per cent in the 1989 survey).

Networks

60.2 per cent would give birthday presents to friends made during the current school year.

Sensitive

They always have their antennae extended, searching with acute sensitivity to changes in the world around them. They respond quickly to new waves of digital and virtual technologies. More than 40 per cent of these children are interested in *Tamagotchi* and other portable mini games. More than 30 per cent regard video games as friends.

Comfortable with digital technologies

70.3 per cent have used a personal computer.

Sensitive to trends

65.7 per cent are sensitive to trends (compared with 56.3 per cent in the 1989 Children's Survey).

Prefer the virtual

81.2 per cent like video games.

Miniature Adults

They hate being seen as childish. They are interested in the opposite sex and their own appearance. They seem to mature very quickly but without having to strain or push very hard. They appear to grow up rapidly by responding naturally to currents in the world that surrounds them.

Full-fledged

48.2 per cent want to become adult as quickly as possible (compared with 38.1 per cent in the 1989 survey).

Dislike the infantile

71.8 per cent say no when asked if they like it when children appear in ads.

Reaching puberty

38.9 per cent want to be popular with the opposite sex (compared with 35.0 per cent in the 1989 Children's Survey).

Conclusion

Today's children understand their own position. They are discriminating in the way that they think about things. They say that people are people and accept diversity in values. Because of these attitudes, they feel no barriers between themselves and other people or places. Able to mix easily, they also have the flexibility to respond quickly to change. They hate being seen as childish and are proud of seeming grown-up.

Living in an affluent, information-saturated society, these kids are highly responsive to changes in public opinion, in their own role and relations with friends and other social systems. We see them as water striders (*amenbo*), supported by surface tension as they skitter here and there. They are children suited to the fluid lifestyles of an age in which the number of children is shrinking.

Conversation with Shimamoto Tatsushi
September 1998

Shimamoto is 38, married, with one daughter, aged seven. A member of the New Breed generation, he joined Hakuhodo in 1983 and moved to HILL in 1990. Before moving to HILL, he worked as a marketing planner.

JLM: What is your favorite research topic?

ST: It's a little ambitious, but I'm working on a new lifestyle model, a new model of happiness.

JLM: Can you say a bit more?

ST: One important issue is whether it will be one lifestyle or many. That is, whether person A will have his model A and person B will have her model B, or whether everyone will share the same model.

JLM: How are these two possibilities different?

ST: For example, A might decide to leave Tokyo, while B chooses to stay and seek happiness in the city. There may be several options.

JLM: Turning, however, to children, how would you explain the difference, if any, between the children described in 'Kids After School' (1982) and young people and children described in more recent studies. For example, both those in 'Kids After School' and those in 'Amenbo Kids' (1997) are described as 'small adults'.

ST: In the 1980s, children were already growing up in an affluent society and becoming like miniature adults. That is one similarity. The difference is that kids now are much less worried about seeming different from other people.

JLM: Back then kids were still worried about being different?

ST: Yes, but now the idea of changing your behavior to go along with others' expectations has disappeared.

JLM: What about 'Living as One Thirty-Fourth' (1993).

ST: I did that study.

JLM: In 1982, the children in 'Kids After School' were nine years old. The ones in 'Living as One Thirty-Fourth' were in their late teens and twenties.

ST: Exactly ten years later.

JLM: Could we say, then that the kids in the earlier study grew up to be the ones in the later study? Was there any change in that ten years?

ST: Some things changed and some things didn't. In the later study they are ten years older, at a different life stage. Nobody gets to be nineteen with no changes since they were nine. Still, inside them, there were things that didn't change.

JLM: For example?

ST: Their lack of the feeling that something is missing. That feeling wasn't there at nine and it still wasn't there at nineteen. That's what it means to say that they were already small adults. They weren't hungry. There wasn't anything they wanted that they couldn't have. They didn't have to struggle to achieve an affluent life.

JLM: Even in 1982, when they were nine?

ST: That's right.

JLM: What had changed, then?

ST: The volume of information to which they were exposed in the mass media had changed dramatically. With so much information to choose from, they could have found a lot of different lifestyles. In the last ten years, however, kids have become very similar to each other. In their language, the way that they talk, the way they dress.

JLM: I've heard people say that you are a member of the New Breed. How do you see yourself as different from these kids?

ST: The biggest difference is this: When I was young there were still subcultures. For kids today there is nothing but 'main culture'. We had our own clothes, music, and habits. The differences might have seemed minor, but they were our own, not just what everyone else was doing. These kids don't have that.

JLM: I've been told that the Baby Boomers and Boomer Juniors are very similar.

ST: Parents and children get along well. Is that what you mean?

JLM: Conversely, I've heard that the New Breed and their parents didn't get along so well.

ST: For us getting along well was something to be embarrassed about.

JLM: Why embarrassed?

ST: To resemble the old generation, not to be a new generation, not to have a distinctive lifestyle. Today's kids don't have this attitude. In a very real sense they have all become consumers. They aren't people who make things. They are people who buy things. They consume culture; they don't make it.

JLM: Boomers resemble Boomer Juniors, but what about the New Breed and their kids. Is your daughter similar to you?

ST: She is very different. Kids now don't have subcultures, not at all. My daughter resembles the 'Amenbo Kids'. Here's another thing, when I was a kid the range of children's choices was small. Now they are much broader. As a result, children today are very 'neutral'. The psychological distance between themselves and product A or product B is the same. In contrast, when I was a kid, there were things I really liked and things I just didn't care for. For kids now, everything is at the same distance. Things aren't as differentiated.

JLM: Can we say then that the Amenbo kids are continuing the same trends as the Boomer Juniors?

ST: The trends are continuing, but the kids now have even less interest in other people.

JLM: Please tell me more.

ST: For example, we described the Boomer Juniors as one thirty-fourth (one of 34 friends). There are kids now who have 300 'pager friends'.

JLM: Three hundred?

ST: Putting pagers, PHS phones, cell phones, and the Internet together. Not everyone has 300, but, while in the one thirty-fourth groups there were still distinct clusters, these kids have spread their relationships so widely that, while they may say that they have 300 friends, they can't know each other's personalities and characters.

JLM: If these kids are the future, what will happen to Japan?

ST: As more and more information is provided, it will become harder and harder to make or create anything unique. We will enter an 'everybody's elite' era in which everyone is choosing and editing. Japan will become the world's editor. Everyone here will have editor-like attitudes. Traditional Japanese craftsmanship will disappear with the older generation.

JLM: Will Japan's international competitiveness decline?

ST: No, functions will become more differentiated. Really creative people are scattered everywhere, in every country. It will be all right if Japan can edit what they produce. But if creating is what we are talking about, Japan will be very weak. Isn't this what has already happened, with production moving overseas more and more?

JLM: What about Sakaiya Taichi's idea that Japan has changed radically before – from Edo to Meiji – and can do it again?

ST: In any era there are only about three per cent who are real geniuses and able to create something new. That three per cent are here, even in Japan (laughs). But if we look at people who are now in their forties and fifties, it is hard to believe that ordinary salarymen are suddenly going to become creative. That is even more true of these kids. In the countryside there are still people who practice traditional crafts. The people who gather to learn from them are all Europeans. There are places that specialize in making knives or scissors or Japanese-style paper. The disciples are all Germans. The next ones to do that won't be Japanese. The Japanese will all be salarymen.

7

GROWING OLD IN
AN AGING JAPAN

No issue is more disturbing to those who think about Japan's future than the aging of Japan's population. The burden of paying for the Baby Boomers' retirement as the number of tax-paying citizens declines will strain the nation's finances; demand for health and nursing care will rise. But where will the workers come from to fill that demand if the number of young people is shrinking? Who will care for the elderly when interest in nursing's daily grind is low? What, too, of other industries that depend on energetic youth to staff their offices, factories, and shops?

The material issues are real; but over and above them a mood of gloom has spread. As the nation's population ages, its vitality seems to be ebbing. After a brief moment of glory, the Japan that was hailed as No. 1 now seems fated to lead a lonely existence. Isolated from a younger, more vigorous Asia, it has, it seems, no real friends among its OECD partners, who, while they share its problems, seem all too ready to cheer its comeuppance.

Or is there another possibility, that Japan's elderly can cast off the traditional definition of old age as a second childhood, with its implications that the aged return to a state of helpless dependency, and find for themselves 'a second active life' with positive contributions to make? A Ministry of Health White Paper describes this possible future:

> Freed from the responsibilities and tensions of being on society's front lines, the elderly will have a second active life; they will take advantage of their freedom to live, to work, to enjoy and contribute to local communities through a wide variety of activities. This kind of life will not be exceptional. It will, instead, become the usual pattern for elderly lives.
>
> (Kōseishō 1997:102)

The White Paper's authors are conscious that a reason to live *(ikigai)* contributes to good health and will help to lower the costs of health care. They take hopeful note of the growing number of older Japanese who set their own goals and take steps to achieve them. Lifelong learning programs may be one sign of that trend.

What Happens When Workaholics Retire?

In 'Retirement Shock', HILL researchers begin with a test-yourself game (Figure 7.2) whose winners are those who experience little or no shock at retirement and wind up on Optimist Island. There, retirement is entertainment. Retirees enjoy leisure, find interesting part-time jobs, and become politically active. Some move to foreign countries, where Japanese pensions will support more luxurious lifestyles.

The losers experience shocks that range from severe to catastrophic. On Pessimist Island, they pass their retirement years playing gateball, a form of croquet associated with the elderly. While waiting to retire, they have given up; they contribute nothing to their companies. A retirement bonus followed by divorce is seen as a real possibility. When their business cards are taken away, they find themselves reduced to ciphers.

If these fears seem overly dramatic, we may want to remember that in Japan retirement has meant something very like a return to powerless childhood. Only recently have things begun to change.

The Changing Image of the Japanese Elderly

In *The Chrysanthemum and the Sword*, Ruth Benedict writes,

> The arc of life in Japan is plotted in opposite fashion to that in the United States. It is a great shallow U-curve with maximum freedom and indulgence allowed to babies and to the old. Restrictions are slowly increased after babyhood till having one's own way reaches a low just before and after marriage. This low line continues many years during the prime of life, but the arc gradually ascends again until after the age of sixty men and women are almost as unhampered by shame as little children are.
>
> (Benedict 1946:254)

In 'Mixed-Bathing Generations', the second issue of the *Lifestyle Times* translated for this chapter, we find evidence that elements of the pattern described by Benedict persisted well into the 1980s. In 1986, a measure of indulgence and freedom from shame were still characteristic of both the young and very old. So were physical and financial weakness and participation in group activities organized and run by others. To be infantile was not only to be indulged; it was also to be dependent and subject to others' whims.

In 'Silvers Ten Years Later', older Japanese appear far more adult than they do in 'Mixed-Bathing Generations'. The subtitle proclaims boldly, 'The elderly are becoming lifestyle aristocrats'. The title is a take-off on 'single aristocrats' *(dokushin kizoku)*, a term that refers to singles, who, being free from family responsibilities, have the disposable income to lead more lavish lifestyles.

188

The meaning of 'lifestyle aristocrat' is summed up in five major trends. First, there is the personal: what elderly Japanese now want is private space and time to do things by themselves instead of in groups. Second is a leisurely pace: those who have ample time and money prefer freedom from bothersome social demands. It should, however, include 'an enjoyable life and position'. Desire for work as a source of identity remains undimmed.

A third trend is to hate being old. A minority of the elderly dress in styles they admit are regarded as more suitable for younger people, worry about how they are dressed, and turn to health foods as a way of staying young. Fourth is a growing desire to enjoy a more refined life. Refinement can mean either self-cultivation through art or classical music or surrounding oneself with tasteful possessions. Most striking of all is the fifth trend, the growing numbers, over 40 per cent, who say that they live for leisure instead of for work.

And, Finally

After that long retirement, where does it all end? How do Japanese visualize death and dying? What would a good death and that final retirement look like? These are the questions posed in 'Final Identity'. So far in this book we have seen only one death, Mishima Yukio's dramatic suicide in 1970. Mishima's death marked, I argued, the triumph of the salaryman, the white-collar worker who prefers a safe and stable career cocooned in a large corporation to the high romance and virile glory that Mishima sought to epitomize. In 'Final Identity', a study published in 1994, all trace of that high romance is gone. But so, for that matter, is the group-orientation epitomized by the salaryman and said to be the very core of Japanese values. Instead we find a preference for a quiet, easy death, alone or at most in the company of a single loved one. Neither dying for one's lord nor working oneself to death for the sake of the company, this death is strikingly asocial.

Retirement Shock
Lifestyle Times, February 1982

The *Art:* On the cover, reproduced in Figure 7.1, is a cartoon of an aging man who is shaking violently as the earth yawns under his feet. Figure 7.2 shows the opening spread, the test-yourself game described above.

The Research Design: The data reported here are taken from a study whose 300 subjects were male, aged 53–57, plus 200 women of the right age to be their wives, all living in Tokyo.

The Retirement Generation – What Husbands Say, What Wives Say

For this study our subjects were 300 men aged 53–57 and 200 women with husbands about that age. The data reported here are early results from a subset of 200 men and 100 women. The analysis examines six factors (the six Hs) that affect the lives of retirees, displayed as a six-sided mandala.

The first three are (1) Health, (2) Harvest, that is, economic well-being, and (3) Home, a sense of wholeness. According to the *Asahi Shimbun,* these are the top three topics of calls received by the counseling hot line Maturity 110. We added three additional topics: (4) Housework, the ability to do for oneself, (5) Heart, emotional self-sufficiency, and (6) Hobby, personal interests.

Overall impression

Retirement is not a happy thing, but the outlook is relatively bright. While uncertain about their marriages and how well off they will be, our subjects score high on self-sufficiency and hobbies. Concern about health is low, although it is likely to increase as they get older. Men's ability to do for themselves is low – that is, indeed, an issue.

Retirement lights and shadows

At retirement one is suddenly stripped naked and confronted with the question, 'What is the meaning of life?' Optimists answer one way, pessimists another. There are islands of optimists and islands of pessimists. This survey's results may seem optimistic because only 9.3 per cent of our subjects are already retired.

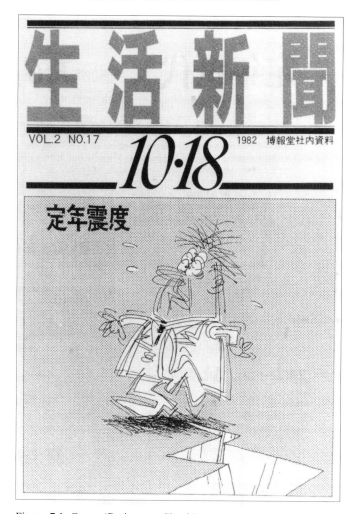

Figure 7.1 Cover, 'Retirement Shock'

What is retirement?

In letters to the *Asahi Shimbun*'s editors, we find descriptions of retired husbands who still set off as if to work each morning. One day it's a class on baking cakes, the next it's bonsai. Every day the husband comes home with something he's made. For the wife who sees him off, it's hard to watch him leave. In one of our subjects' own words, 'What he's doing isn't a human retirement; it's only leaving one workplace for another'.

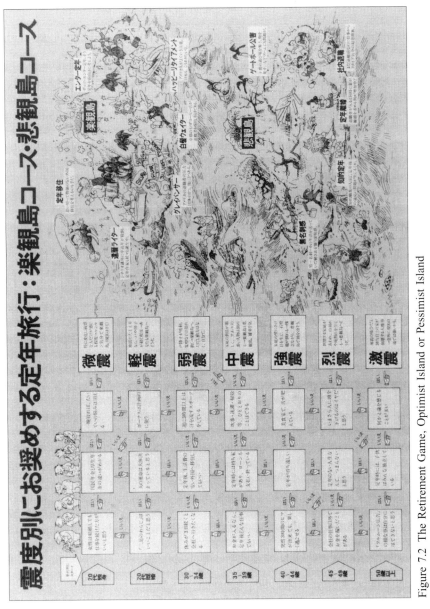

Figure 7.2 The Retirement Game, Optimist Island or Pessimist Island

Financial worries

When asked to forecast their family finances, fewer than 50 per cent of the men said, 'We will be well off'. Fewer than 40 per cent of the wives agreed. Over 60 per cent of both said that decisions on how to use separation-from-work bonuses would be made after retirement. Overall, the financial outlook was not too rosy, with wives less sanguine than their husbands. They disagreed with husbands who believed that the family had sufficient savings and that after retirement the couple could get by on ¥50,000 a month. When it comes to household budgets, men are ignoramuses.

Husbands and wives differ a bit in what they would like to do after the husband retires. Most men said that they wanted to go on working; 32 per cent (and only 21 per cent of the wives) said that they would go on working after the age of 66. The wives preferred a more relaxed retirement; 63 per cent (but only 49 per cent of their husbands) wanted to be able to live on their pensions after the age of 66.

Men need to be more independent

We asked politely if our subjects were willing and able to do household chores. Wives scored 100 per cent, but husbands lagged far behind. Only 30 per cent of husbands were confident of being able to live by themselves; 50 per cent could manage for a while (from 2 to 90 days). Twenty per cent had no confidence that they could cope at all. Chores men found especially difficult included ironing (59.5 per cent), sewing on a button (56.0 per cent), laundry (45.4 per cent), and cooking (38.5 per cent). All are tasks it would be expensive to hire someone else to do, and there is no guarantee that old men left by themselves will have the financial resources required. They are in for a more severe shock than the women are.

My body, my capital

When people talk about retirement, it makes you feel old. But retirement can also be an elixir. One man says that he doesn't feel inferior to young people in either body or spirit. Most men still enjoy good health and are able to go on working. Make no mistake about it, however, fear of illness is the biggest worry of all. According to a Prime Minister's Office survey, health is retired people's greatest concern (40 per cent). Most retirees are worried about their health, and 28 per cent of husbands and 32 per cent of wives are thinking about taking up a sport.

Serious hobbyists

Only two of the 200 men we talked to identified work as their hobby. Forty-six per cent of men and 52 per cent of women said they have five or more interests.

The majority of both men and women are thinking about new hobbies and getting new qualifications to make post-retirement life more enjoyable. Interests they would like to pursue travel, fishing, and calligraphy. The majority would also like to have a driver's license. These trends reflect the growing number of retired people with time on their hands.

Burning issues

In retirement planning guides, 'Have a reason to live' is a phrase that we often encounter. Still, behind this positive attitude, we sense loss and confusion. Both men (22.5 per cent) and women (24.0 per cent) say 'When I think of how long I have to live, I feel depressed'.

Danger! Mature marriage ahead!

On average, husbands and wives talk with each other 83 minutes per day on weekdays, 147 on holidays. For people who will be spending long days together, these figures seem low. On holidays, there is wide variation by couple, from ten minutes to ten hours. One wife in four says, 'I hate the idea of spending all day having to look at my husband's face'; 15.5 per cent of husbands reciprocate this sentiment. More women than men say that they can understand the feelings involved when retired couples get divorced. Relatively high proportions of parents talk with their children every day (67.6 per cent of fathers, 88 per cent of mothers). Obviously, the husband – or wife – may be a problem.

Mixed-Bathing Generations
Lifestyle Times, May 1986

The Art: Figure 7.3 shows the cover, an outdoor bath where old people and children of both sexes are bathing together. Note their relaxed air and how they all face inward, toward each other. The contrast with the middle-aged couple wearing traditional Japanese lounging robes *(yukata)* who stand apart with their backs to each other is striking. Inside, the first spread is built around two group photos (not reproduced here) showing old people and school children, respectively. In these posed 'class photo' style pictures, they look, except for their ages, very much alike.

Figure 7.3 Cover, 'Mixed-Bathing Generations'

The Research Design: The data reported here are taken from a street interview survey of tourists at twelve locations around Tokyo. The subjects were male and female individuals, 200 in their twenties, 200 in their sixties, for a total n = 400.

Old People and Children Look Like the Same Generation

You might imagine that the aged and children have different lifestyles, but look at parks in the afternoon. They are filled with old people and children. The tour groups assembled by bus guides in front of the Imperial Palace grounds to see the double bridges are almost all old people and children. In the outdoor baths at hot spring resorts, make no mistake, the ones who enjoy mixed bathing – once again, it's old people and children.

If we look at their behavior and at how they spend their leisure, there are many ways in which children and the elderly resemble each other. We labeled them 'the mixed-bathing generations' and looked for the points they have in common.

Shared Characteristics of the Mixed-Bathing Generations

The Elderly
- Relaxed in mixed baths
- Like group travel
- Thoroughly enjoy their hobbies
- Don't have much money
- Have lots of time
- Innocent emotions
- Weak interest in sex
- Unconcerned about fashion
- Need help getting around
- Consumers, no longer involved in production
- Weak physically

Children
- Horsing around in mixed baths
- Feel safe traveling in groups
- Totally absorbed in their hobbies
- Don't have money
- Have free time set apart
- Strong emotions
- No interest in sex
- Not fashionable
- Their behavior must be controlled
- Consumers, not producers
- Physically weaker than adults

These two generations are very similar in the attitudes and assumptions that underlie their behavior as well as in their behavior itself. Indifference to sex explains why neither feels shy about mixed bathing. Group travel reflects the widespread attitude that, for both the old and young, travel managed by others is safe. Chatting is another interest they share. Both have little money to spend but time they are free to use as they like.

Tour buses are filled with them

We asked both people in their twenties and people in their sixties where they would take old people from the countryside who were visiting Tokyo. The Imperial Palace and Asakusa are favorites by far. Groups wait in lines to have

196

souvenir pictures taken at the double bridges in front of the Imperial Palace. Nakamise street in Asakusa remains, as always, jammed with visitors. The Hato Bus Company provides tours that visit these and other favorite places. As soon as you board one of their buses, you realize that most of the people around you are old. Bus tours allow them to see all the main spots in one day. The elderly also like these tours because they don't have to worry about their legs giving out.

School outings follow the same routes. The souvenir stores in Asakusa and at Tokyo Tower are filled with herds of children as well as flocks of old people. If one of the members of a group enters a store, the others all follow.

Time yes, money no

Both the elderly and small children seem to have lots of free time, but neither has much money to spend. So, they can't be active consumers.

The Azabu Jūban Spa, a health club and gymnasium in central Tokyo, has recently become an 'in' spot for the young. In the middle of day on weekdays, however, it's an urban resort for grandpas and grandmas. The entrance fee of ¥1,000 entitles you to stay the whole day. The folk singers and dancers on the stage perform free of charge. Some old people bring along their portable tape recorders (the ones that were popular before the advent of radio-cassette players) and play music to which they dance. They have to spend a bit on food and drink, but that would be true elsewhere as well. Besides the security of knowing that they will find their friends there, for those who fear that the price will go up, the facility offers a fixed-term discount ticket, usable for a month, for ¥13,000. Many old people take advantage of this offer.

Children live in a different world from that of hot springs and folk songs, but, like the elderly, they lack money. For them the equivalent of spas are public parks. Instead of singing folksongs, they gather in front of computer stores. That is where they know they will find their friends. Their ability to stop work and start playing instantly is another trait that they and the elderly share. Whether in the park or playing with PCs or game machines, children compete to show off their skills, just like old people with their singing and dancing.

Lacking money to spend, what both look for is places where a single fixed payment (or, for children, no payment at all) allows them to spend as much time as they like. At long-established health resorts, there is always an area where you can warm yourself very cheaply. At Sangayu, a spa in Aomori Prefecture that is famous for being the very first government-sponsored national health resort, you can spend the whole day for only ¥600. You can leave your futon spread out all day long and spend your time chatting. When you're tired of talking, you can take a bath. The shops provide food and other daily necessities. Many old people spend a lot of time in places like this.

The 'Health Centers' that have recently become so popular provide many of the same facilities. You can spend the whole day using the baths, the athletic facilities and the swimming pool. These places are now attracting not only the elderly but many young people as well. For the older crowd there are even indoor gateball courts. Being able to pay a single fee to enter and spend as much time as you like: for today's busy people that's real luxury.

Relaxed, smiling and fresh

'Wow! Smiling and refreshed' *(Hō, nikkori, sappari)* describes the behavior of old people making the circuit of famous tourist attractions. As they follow the bus guide's flag, we hear them saying 'Oh, wow!' when something catches their interest. They smile for the group photos. Then off they go to the toilets to freshen up before boarding their buses again. This cycle is virtually identical with that of school trips for elementary school students. The only difference is that the children say *'Waaa!'* Instead of *'Hō'* when they're impressed.

Because their destinations, the spots where photographs are taken, even the toilets they use are all determined in advance, these trips would be suffocating for more experienced travelers. But we shouldn't simply dismiss these tours as old-fashioned. They are just what many older people are looking for. There is a feeling of security. Not having to worry about the arrangements is more comfortable than traveling alone. That is also why group travel, with all the arrangements made and help always close at hand, is better for elementary school excursions.

Spontaneous and recorded

'That mountain is wonderful!' 'Look, look, there's snow'. 'An amazing waterfall'. How long has it been since we responded to each and everything we saw in such terms? Elementary school children's exclamations are full of feeling. Compared to older teens with their fixed, apathetic expressions, these children still know how to feel.

Old people share that capacity to be moved. You see them intently taking photographs, discovering rare and unusual things, searching for something to stir them. We are impressed not only by their having the time to enjoy these emotions but also the spontaneity with which they express them.

Some elderly people sketch instead of producing snapshots as souvenirs. Others are intent on finding just the right word to express what they feel. There are grannies intently noting down every word the guide says in their notebooks. Old men who are eager not to miss a thing use tape recorders. Children might do the same, but the elderly will keep using their aids to expression and recollection all day long.

More than anything else, though, it's in conversation that the feelings they want to share with others blossom. Love of chatting is another characteristic shared by old people and children. Both often seek to communicate what they think and feel. At tourist spots, in the streets, too, when we note the innocence with which these generations express their feelings, we are forced to ask ourselves when it was that we ourselves lost that unaffected simplicity of spirit (*sunao no kokoro*).

Places that provide excuses to talk

The salons of the elderly are public baths, parks, senior clubs, special interest groups, clubs for players of the game of go, and theaters. At spas we find some dancing on the stage, while others watch sleepily from the audience, eating the lunches they've brought from home or enjoying a drink after getting out of the bath. Most aren't looking at the stage, though. The grannies lost in conversation are saying things like, 'That fishmonger's daughter, she's got a job at some company, and now she's got her fingernails painted red'. Those on the stage are absorbed in 'Tomi-san, move with the music, curl your hands, and hold your head like this'. It's all a muddle. Still, it's the chance to meet people and have these kinds of conversations that brings the elderly to places like this. Even at go clubs, more than winning or losing the game, it's the chance to get together and chat that keeps them filled with elderly players.

The salons of early elementary school students are after-school classes and children's reading rooms in public libraries. Of course, they do go to classes to study, so they can't be chatting all the time. But while waiting for class and on the way home, many children spend their time happily chatting about their favorite games or gossiping about their friends. Viewed from this perspective, the salons of the elderly and those of the children both provide excuses for getting together. It can be hard to assemble a group just to play and chat. But dancing, playing go, learning the abacus, or reading books are all good excuses.

The Silvers Ten Years Later
Lifestyle Times, June 1996

The Art: The cover (Figure 7.4) is plain text, laid out in a simple graphic design. The paragraph above the title summarizes some of the differences between retired Japanese in 1996 and those studied ten years earlier. The art inside this issue of the *Lifestyle Times* consists only of charts and icons. One example is Figure 7.5, which shows five trends affecting 'silver aristocrats', The contrast with the lively illustrations and photos used in earlier issues is striking.

The Research Design: The data reported here come from a large sample survey of three distinct groups, conducted in January, 1996. The design of this study replicates that of an earlier study conducted ten years earlier in 1986. Details are included in the text.

Becoming Lifestyle Aristocrats

A decade ago, 12.3 per cent of the elderly played gateball. Now, in 1996, that figure has fallen to 2.4 per cent. In contrast, the proportion of retired people who swim has increased during the same ten-year period from 2.5 per cent to 7.8 per cent. Of women in the 60–74 age group, 69.5 per cent still like to be called cute. That's compared to 59.4 per cent a decade earlier. During the last ten years the proportion of old people who hold a passport has increased to 27.9 per cent. Japan's silver generation is changing.

1986

A decade ago, HILL conducted a quantitative study of silver attitudes and behavior. That study was published as 'The New Silver Tide'. In that year, 10.6 per cent of Japanese were 65 or older.

- Tokyo Silvers, male and female, aged 60–74, living within a 40 kilometre radius of Tokyo. N = 1650.
- Takamatsu Silvers, male and female, aged 60–74, living in Takamatsu, the capital of Kagawa Prefecture, on Shikoku. N = 300.
- Tokyo 40s, male and female, aged 40–49. N = 300.
  Area sampling, home interviews with questionnaires left behind, August 1986.

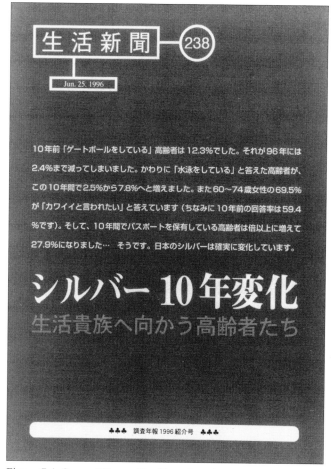

生活新聞 — 238

Jun. 25. 1996

10年前「ゲートボールをしている」高齢者は12.3%でした。それが96年には2.4%まで減ってしまいました。かわりに「水泳をしている」と答えた高齢者が、この10年間で2.5%から7.8%へと増えました。また60～74歳女性の69.5%が「カワイイと言われたい」と答えています（ちなみに10年前の回答率は59.4%です）。そして、10年間でパスポートを保有している高齢者は倍以上に増えて27.9%になりました… そうです。日本のシルバーは確実に変化しています。

シルバー10年変化
生活貴族へ向かう高齢者たち

♣♣♣ 調査年報1996紹介号 ♣♣♣

Figure 7.4 Cover, 'Silvers, Ten Years Later'

1996

On July 1, HILL published *Silvers Ten Years Later*, a follow-up to our 1986 study. As of 1995, the proportion of those 65 and older in Japan's population had reached 14.5 per cent.

- Tokyo Silvers, male and female, aged 60–74, living within a 40 kilometre radius of Tokyo. N = 1650.
- Takamatsu Silvers, male and female, aged 60–74. N = 300.
- Tokyo 40s, male and female, aged 40–49. N = 300.
  Area sampling, home interviews with questionnaires left behind, January 1996.

Figure 7.5 Graph Showing Trends Affecting Silver Aristocrats.

2020

According to Ministry of Health and Welfare estimates, by the year 2020, persons aged 65 and older will account for 25.5 per cent of Japan's population. We will be a society in which one person in four will be in the silver category.

Five Major Currents That Pull on Silver Hearts

The personal

- Personal standards: 'I want to choose fashions that are both distinctive and reflect my own tastes' (15.6 per cent in 1986, 24.5 per cent in 1996).

- Personal world: 'I like do things by myself instead of with friends' (48.7 per cent in 1986, 53.5 per cent in 1996).
- Personal use: 'I absolutely have to have my own private room or space' (29.9 per cent in 1986, 34.4 per cent in 1996).

Greater respect for the individual is a trend that over-65s share with other Japanese. The number of those who see time with the family as important and are eager to give money to their children or grandchildren is down. It may seem like a lonely existence when we see the elderly living by themselves, but it makes a great difference if this is what you yourself want to do. When it comes to making choices, the members of the silver generation assign great importance to their personal standards. Their desire for private rooms, TVs, stereo equipment, and telephones is also strong. This trend is especially clear among those who live in Tokyo and among women overall.

The leisured

- Satisfied with the status quo: 'I am satisfied with the things I have' (61.2 per cent in 1986, 64.2 per cent in 1996).
- Simple and unassuming: 'I want to age appropriately' (48.6 per cent in 1986, 53.1 per cent in 1996).
- Detached: 'I want an enjoyable job and position' (70.9 per cent in 1986, 76.2 per cent in 1996).

These orientations are for the affluent, those who have ample time and money. More than 70 per cent see themselves as better off than their parents' generation. The number whose favorite country is Japan has increased. Their preferred way of life is simple and unassuming. Few desire a longer life or to leave a famous name to later generations. Members of this category are strongly inclined to detachment, more practical than romantic. They are thankful for things as they are, don't overdo, and live at their own pace. Theirs is a leisurely life.

Refusing to grow old

- Hate aging: 'I like to dress younger than my real age' (12.4 per cent in 1986, 16.3 per cent in 1996).
- Stylish: 'I absolutely want to be stylish' (11.6 per cent in 1986, 18.0 per cent in 1996).
- See body as capital: 'I would like to try natural foods and health foods' (24.7 per cent in 1986, 27.8 per cent in 1996)

The members of this category want to remain eternally youthful. The number of those who like to spend money on health check-ups and medical treatments and of those whose favorite sport is swimming have both increased. These silvers see their bodies as capital. Interest in stylish hair, interest in dieting to keep in shape, and the greatly reduced numbers of those who play gateball all suggest their hatred of aging. The desire to be stylish is correlated with the greatly increased proportions of both men and women who worry about losing their sexual prowess. The desire to remain sexually active to the end of their lives is strong.

Wanting to be more refined.

- Self-cultivation: 'I would like to have more time for study' (17.2 per cent in 1986, 25.0 per cent in 1996).
- Refinement: 'My current interest is art appreciation' (11.2 per cent in 1986, 17.8 per cent in 1996).
- Discriminating taste: 'I want curtains, bed, and lighting fixtures that match my interior' (12.8 per cent in 1986, 15.4 per cent in 1996).

Among silvers, interest in art and classical music is rising. Preferences for original art and traditional Japanese cuisine are up. They are particular about the things they choose to have around them; more now insist on matching accessories or tableware. This desire for a high-status life style also includes self-improvement. Some want more time for study and reading or to learn to use a computer so as not to fall behind in an increasingly information-oriented society. These silvers don't drive themselves hard, but see self-cultivation as another aspect of a high-status way of life.

Becoming more playful

- Work evaders: 'I live for play instead of work' (36.5 per cent in 1986, 42.5 per cent in 1996).
- Other directed: 'I am interested in trends' (36.6 per cent in 1986, 42.6 per cent in 1996).
- Full of life: 'I don't participate in sports' (34.0 per cent in 1986, 26.2 per cent in 1996).

We used to say that Japanese lost their will to live once they had stopped working, but that is no longer true. Many want to escape from work, and fewer want to go on working forever. Conversely, the number for whom the meaning of life is found in play instead of work has risen. That group is lively and full of life; karaoke is their way of relieving stress. The proportion of silvers who traveled overseas within the last year is now higher than for those in their forties. The number of those who pay attention to trends is growing. Outgoing, lively, energetic, and playful, the members of this group will enjoy a happy retirement.

Summing Up

If we examine these five currents, we find that where they converge a certain image appears: a figure who lives as he or she likes, is eternally young, enjoys leisure, is absorbed in hobbies and is aiming at an elegant and refined life. This way of life resembles that of aristocrats whose position frees them from practical concerns. Japan's elderly worked hard in an era of radical change. Now they are 'Silver Aristocrats'. The currents shaping their lives may hold the key to responding effectively to a rapidly aging society.

Last Identity
Lifestyle Times, July 1994

The Art: Figure 7.6 features two illustrations. One shows a tiny female figure at the end of a long tunnel with grass and flowers in the foreground at the end of the tunnel. The other shows a male figure asleep at the foot of a tree. Nature and a peaceful tone are prominent themes in both. The captions describe the feelings of the individuals who drew them.

> *The Afterlife* (60-year-old woman)
> 'I don't know what the world after death will be like. But there could be something. I want to believe there's something'.

> *An Ideal Death* (22-year-old man)
> 'Lying against the roots of a tree, thinking back over all the happy moments I've had. Then to die with a smile on my face, after just a moment of pain. Then, in that moment, to turn into earth'.

The copy on the upper right below the headline reads,

> We live in a time when individuals want things uniquely their own. We wondered if that desire might extend to having a unique death. Or, to put it another way, a life uniquely one's own to the very last. We collected a wide variety of thoughts on the theme of death.

The Research Design: Life's Exit Survey, May, 1994.
Subjects are male and female, 18-69; n = 351 (134 male, 217 female). The method was a mailed questionnaire.

Final Questions

Are you afraid of death? If so, why?

Yes, said 70 per cent of our subjects; more often by women than men and most often by those in their thirties and forties. The most frequent reason is still having things they want to do or worry about their families, for example, 'I'm not yet ready to leave this world'. The second is anxiety at the disappearance of the self or at going to an unknown world. The words of one 30-year-old man are typical, 'Because I don't understand what death is, I am afraid of being nothing'. Fear of pain in dying ranked third.

Figure 7.6 Cover, 'Last Identity'

On the other hand, if we look at reasons for not being afraid, first is the view that dying is a natural process. The second is that you never know how long you will live. Third is the fatalistic view expressed by one twenty-year-old man, 'How long your life will be is decided when you are born'.

An Ideal Death (54-year-old woman)
'It's spring when the trees are just leafing out. I'm on the veranda of a small cottage in the mountains, with a view of the mountains and a lake. I'm talking to the one I love the most'.

207

Have you ever thought about your own death before? What was going on?

Over 70 per cent of our subjects had thought about their own deaths; 10 per cent more women than men said 'Yes' to this question. There was no significant difference by age.

If we look at what they said about when they had thought about their own death, the most common answer was when someone close to them had died. The second most frequent was upon hearing news about random killings or airplane accidents. Third was feeling in danger when boarding an airplane. Fourth was finding themselves in bad health and being worried about cancer.

Nearly 80 per cent of those who have thought about their own death want to be conscious at their deaths; 66 per cent say that they want to leave the timing of their death to fate.

Those who want to think and talk more about death account for 52.6 per cent of our sample. There is, however, a wide range of variation by age, falling from 63.7 per cent for those in their twenties to 44.3 per cent for those in their thirties and forties and 40.6 per cent for those in their fifties and sixties. Death becomes more real as we get older.

Which of the following statements is closest to your view of life and death?

The sample is almost evenly split between 'This world is all that there is' and 'There is something more besides this world'. But men and women tend to answer differently. Of the men, 60 per cent prefer the former statement, 60 per cent of the women the latter.

These responses parallel the trend we saw in contrasting the 'It is the end' group and the 'Continuity' group, with 58.2 per cent of men preferring the former and 58.1 per cent of women preferring the latter. When it comes to talk of another world, it's women who are the romantics.

Men's pragmatism also appeared in their answers to the next item: 'After death I want to live on in people's hearts' (women, 83 per cent; men, 68.7 per cent). Over 30 per cent of men preferred 'After death it doesn't matter what people think'.

Men were slightly more likely than women to choose 'When I die I want to leave some evidence that I lived'. Here, however, the largest gap divided generations, with scores ranging from 64.9 per cent for those in their twenties to 47.2 per cent for those in their fifties and sixties. The desire to leave evidence of one's life seems to grow weaker with age.

About one person in two in our sample wants to know the time of his or her death. The score for men is higher, which may reflect their having more practical affairs to wind up. In the highest age group more than half do not want to know when they will die. It does seem that they feel the pressure of death's reality more.

However, when we compared the 'leave it up to fate' group and the 'want to be conscious' group, we found that 58.9 per cent of the sample belong to the former. There are more women than men in the 'want to be conscious' group (men, 35.8 per cent; women, 46.1 per cent). We will see a similar difference in later items dealing with living wills and hospices. The 'want to be conscious' group includes 47.6 per cent of those in their twenties, 37.1 per cent of those in their thirties and forties, and only 32 per cent of those in their fifties and sixties. Once again we see a falling off with age.

Forty per cent of our subjects say that 'You can't avoid dying for your ideals'. More men than women agree with this statement, and 50 per cent of those in their twenties agree. Among those in their thirties and forties, however, over 70 per cent find the idea of dying for one's ideals repugnant. This result seems only natural if we think of the practical realities of this stage of life.

We might also note that when we asked how people would respond if ordered by their companies to work in dangerous countries, the percentage of those who would agree to go rose from 14.3 per cent for those in their twenties and 14.6 per cent for those in their thirties to forties, to 29 per cent for those in their fifties and sixties.

When we asked how people would respond if required to do work that would put children in mortal danger, 70 per cent said that they would be opposed. At 76.5 per cent, women scored 15 per cent higher than men on this measure. When the results are broken down by age, we find that 90 per cent of those in their fifties and sixties would oppose this request.

When we asked how people would respond if asked to volunteer for work that would put children in mortal danger, we found the same trends. One difference was the higher proportion of men who, now having a choice, would, they say, reject the request (men, 67 per cent; women, 76 per cent).

The Afterlife (42-year-old woman)
'Death is the color of ashes. Life after death is pink'.

When you hear the word 'death', what color do you associate with it? What about the word 'afterlife'?

Black is the color most often associated with death; white is the color most often associated with the afterlife. Black ranks fourth overall in association with the afterlife. Colorless transparency is second. *Mushoku* (the 'colorless' in 'colorless transparency) may be associated with *mu* (nothingness).

When we compare the results of those who fear death and those who are not afraid, white is the color both associate most often with the afterlife. We note the appearance of pink at fourth for those who do not fear death.

How do you feel about living wills?

More than 60 per cent of men and slightly less than 70 per cent of women say that they would like to have a living will.

As one 22-year-old man puts it, 'The right to die is part of the right to live and thus a basic human right'.

A 21-year-old woman says, 'Prolonging life in a vegetable state is hard on those around you'.

A 55-year-old woman comments, 'If I communicate clearly, the family won't be confused about what to do'.

Another woman, 59, says, 'Because I've seen a person half-naked hooked up to a machine'.

While 93.8 per cent say that if they were unconscious (unable to preserve their dignity), they wouldn't want to live, whether or not they would actually state that is another matter. Just under 30 per cent say that while they approve of living wills, they wouldn't have one for themselves.

A 39-year-old man says, 'I can't stand the idea of throwing away one's own life'.

A 61-year-old man says, 'I can't make up my mind to that'.

A woman, 63, comments, 'I have an 88-year-old mother. I approve of living wills, but I couldn't write one'.

Overall, 69 per cent of our subjects say that in the case of a spouse they wouldn't want to see excessive effort to prolong life (men, 64.9 per cent; women, 73.3 per cent). Overall, 31 per cent say that they would want a spouse to live a little longer no matter what (men 35.1 per cent; women, 26.7 per cent).

How do you feel about hospices? *

More women than men welcome the idea of approaching the end in a hospice. Most who find the idea attractive add as their reason that they want to die in their own way. One man in three approves of the idea of hospice programs but wouldn't want to enter one himself. Most say that they would prefer to die at home in the care of their families.

A 26-year-old man says, 'Because in Japan we don't have the kind of religions to rely on that people do in other countries, this is worth thinking about'.

A 23-year-old man remarks that, 'It would be OK if you were 100 per cent sure of dying. If there is even a one per cent chance of living, you should fight on'.

Another man, 22, comments, 'If I had the money for that kind of thing, there are other things I would rather spend it on'.

---

* A hospice is a program to assist people in completing their lives in a human manner. When death is near, comfort and relief from pain are given priority over prolonging life. Meals and visits are at the dying patient's discretion. Please think of a place where the focus is on making the dying comfortable.

Suppose that the god who controls length of life told you, 'Your life on earth has one year to go. During that time your health will remain unchanged. We have put aside ¥30 million for you to use however you like. Also, on your last day you can have whatever you wish for.

IF YOU KNEW THAT YOU HAD ONLY ONE YEAR TO LIVE, WHO WOULD YOU TELL? WHO WOULD YOU NOT TELL?

We found little difference between single and married people in who they would tell if they had only a year to live. The unmarried would most want to tell a lover. For the married, the lover is replaced by the spouse. In either case, we are talking about the person who is closest, the one with whom you would like to spend that last year together.

Both married and single people agree on who not to tell: their parents. They fear what the shock would do to the parents. They would also not tell friends or colleagues, because they would find it unpleasant to receive special treatment.

HOW WOULD YOUR LIFE CHANGE?

More than half those now working, including two out of three married men, would quit their jobs.

Close to 40 per cent of students would continue with what they are doing now. There is, however, a strong contrast between males and females. Male students were more likely to quit school (38.5 per cent), and less than 20 per cent would work harder than they do at present. Among female students, those who would work harder (29 per cent) outnumber those who would quit school (22 per cent).

Housewives are the most likely of all to continue with what they are doing, and more than 30 per cent would work even harder. This group includes more than 40 per cent of housewives in their thirties.

Fewer than ten per cent in each category would give up their present hobbies. Nearly half of those in their twenties would work harder at them. More than 60 per cent of those in their fifties and sixties would continue doing what they now do. They have, perhaps, already achieved a satisfying lifestyle.

HOW WOULD YOU SPEND THE YEAR? HOW WOULD YOU SPEND THE 30 MILLION?

When we asked how people would spend their last year, far and away the most frequent answer was 'Travel'. The number of those who would stop holding back on spending was also striking.

A 23-year-old man says, 'I'd pour the whole 30 million into my dream and, if I could, create a foundation to support people who pursue that dream'.

A 31-year-old man says, 'I'd quit my job and build a house near my parents in the country. There I would spend the year living surrounded by nature with my wife and children'.

A 24-year-old woman says, 'I'd fall passionately in love and have a child. The ¥30 million would be to raise him'.

A 29-year-old woman describes her dream, 'I'd rent a cottage on an Italian island, take vacations in southern France, gamble at the casinos in Monaco, learn oil painting, and paint the beautiful scenery I can see from the cottage. I'd send the painting to my mother so she could see it too'.

A women, 41, says, 'Because I have children in the second year of junior high school and the fifth grade of elementary school, I'd like to write letters for them to read, to guide them each step of the way when they graduate from junior high and high school, become adult, get married, and have children. The ¥30 million? I'd leave it to my husband and children'.

A woman, 52, writes, 'I'd like to visit all the people I've gotten to know and find out what they have thought of me. I'd work hard to leave a good impression'.

What would your last wish be? (It can't be to go on living!)

A 39-year-old man says, 'I'd like to become a guardian spirit'.

A man, 61, says, 'I'd like to go to the highest heaven and be free of suffering'.

A man, 62, says, 'I'd like to have sex however I like with a gentle young woman'.

A 20-year-old woman says, 'I'd like to have my lover's memory of me completely erased'.

A woman, 46, says, 'I'd like to go to paradise and be free of the wheel of rebirth'. A woman, 47, wants, 'As much as possible, to have my dead face to be beautiful'. A 61-year-old woman wants, 'Only the strength to say "Thank-you" to the one by my side'.

The Afterlife (Man, 56)

No words here, but the picture shows a young couple as angels dressed to play golf, accompanied by a puppy with a halo.

Last words (Woman, 33)

'I decided a long time ago how I want my dying moment to be. I really believe this. For me, anything else would be impossible ... "Ah ... I enjoyed myself".'

People Can Only Die as They Have Lived

Her fingers still moved. What were they doing, my mother-in-law's fingers that moved in her sleep? When she woke, we talked about her dreams. While she slept, she said, she was arranging flowers. 'I must be ready for the flower show', she suddenly said to the nurse. To the very last she clung to her identity as a teacher of Japanese flower arranging.

Perhaps because she had worked in the office of a Buddhist temple when she was young, she was unselfish. She spoke of refusing efforts to prolong her life. However, when faced with the actual question, when asked where to draw the line, she understood how difficult it was. If you do something to ease the suffering or to take nourishment intravenously, isn't that unnatural? And what about oxygen? Reading a book on terminal care written for physicians, she became confused.

Even when you can't swallow food, you can still be kept alive for several months. Would it, then, be acceptable to refuse the drip? Many hospices overseas don't provide intravenous feeding.

There are religions that reject blood transfusions. You may think it strange, but you realize it's a matter of degree. If you've only got a few weeks to go, you may find stopping the intravenous feeding acceptable. But if it's a few months, you hesitate. You may refuse an artificial respirator but think it's all right to receive oxygen through your nose. When you think of your last identity, heavy decisions come crowding in, one after the other.

We were in her hospital room watching a TV broadcast from the scene of an airplane crash. She said, 'That's the way, to go in an accident, how enviable'. 'But in that case it is terribly hard on those who are left behind, who haven't had time to compose themselves', I replied. 'Well, yes, there is that to think about. But it is less hard on the one most directly concerned'.

We see a lot of life insurance commercials these days with the message that what you do at the end of your life is something that you yourself should decide. It seems to be the way things are going. Still, one wonders, are people really intelligent enough to make that decision?

Conversation with Sekizawa Hidehiko
September 22, 1998

JLM: What has been the biggest change in the lives of Japan's elderly since HILL was founded in 1981?

SH: HILL did large-scale surveys of the lifestyles of the elderly in 1986 and 1996. For both, our subjects ranged in age from 65 to 75. In 1986 we found that people had plenty of time left for long retirements and suggested that they should relax and enjoy themselves. The retired people with whom we talked understood what we were saying, but some didn't like the idea. Many of their friends had died in World War II. They knew war and, in many cases, had been soldiers. Their friends had been killed but they had survived to grow old and have time on their hands. Talk about relaxing made them feel guilty.

By 1996, very few of those people were left. More than fifty years had passed since the end of the war. Retirees had experienced the war but only as children, as victims. That is the cohort whose support made high growth possible. They were the ones people called worker bees, and they were ready to taste the honey. When we talked about how they planned to relax, there was no guilt involved.

The biggest difference, then, may be that the asceticism characteristic of traditional Japanese culture has weakened. Today's older people have an active interest in recreation and leisure.

The other big difference, of course, is that the proportion of older people in Japan's population is larger.

JLM: Thinking ahead, then, to 2006, what kind of changes would you expect?

SH: The Baby Boomers will be retired. If the trend we saw in the difference between 1986 and 1996 continues, people will be more concerned about what they will do with their lives and be more skilful in their choices. In 1986, the American style of 'happy retirement' didn't make sense to Japan's retirees. Retirement was sad and lonely, because they didn't have work to do. By 1996, the percentage of people who wanted to retire early and were looking forward to retirement had increased. That same trend will continue. Still, however, the proportion of Japanese who would prefer to go on working will probably be high compared to other parts of the world. There will be many people in their seventies who still want some kind of job.

A big difference may be that by 2006, retired people the world over will become more similar. They will all have listened to the Beatles. The subculture

214

of the elderly will be the same the world over. In that sense, their lifestyles are likely to resemble one another.

JLM: The retirees you studied in 1996 belong to the 'Greying Corporate Warrior' generation. In other HILL studies, especially those of salarymen, it seems like there's a big gap between this generation and those that follow it. Also, it seems like these people have been the most successful of Japan's postwar generations.

SH: Their pensions are quite good, even on a global scale. Also, they bought their homes before the economy overheated. Even though the value of their real estate fell after the Bubble, it is still higher than when they bought it. In many different senses, they are the best off of the postwar, or prewar, generations. When the Baby Boomers retire, their pensions will be relatively smaller. They will inherit some property from their parents, but overall they will have fewer assets.

JLM: What about psychologically speaking?

SH: Today's retirees still have a 'fight on' *(gambaru)* spirit. They were the ones who, during the high-growth period, worked a lot of overtime. They are the generation for whom the image of Japanese as worker bees and workaholics fits best. They are the people who worked their way up the consumption ladder, from a refrigerator to a car.

JLM: When I was talking with Shimamoto, he said that what today's kids find hardest is being asked to set their own goals. I wonder if it isn't related to something that HILL noticed as early as the 'Sneaker Middle' study, that Japanese were becoming consumers instead of the makers the Greying Corporate Warriors had been.

SH: In that generation, they were working to achieve the nation's and society's goals. As a result, their income increased and they were able to buy those refrigerators and cars. They didn't need to decide what they themselves were going to do. If they worked hard they would make more money, and with the money they could buy a TV set and begin to relax a bit at home with their families. The Oil Shock in 1973 may have made them think a bit, but, compared to today's youth, they didn't have to worry about what their personal goals would be.

It was an era when national, corporate, and personal goals were all the same. The personalization of goals hadn't happened yet. Since public and personal goals were fused, people were happy. But now those people are retired. Japan's economy isn't doing very well. Their connection with corporate goals has been severed. Now they are asking themselves 'what's it all about?', for them personally.

JLM: I'm still a bit confused. Reading the 1996 'Silvers Ten Years Later' study, the attitudes of the elderly seem very similar to those of the 'Amenbo Kids'. But in other studies that same generation seems very different from the 'Sneaker Middles'. What's going on? Has the gap disappeared?

SH: The gap may have disappeared. But think of it this way. There may be a gap but the two groups are moving in parallel. Among young people 'me-ism', is very strong. Compared to the young, the elderly may seem more society-oriented. But compared to earlier retirees they may look like they, too, are moving in the same direction as the young.

JLM: Shindō has suggested that Japan is a country where the older generation tends to follow the lead of the young. How does that sound to you?

SH: Could be. A movement starts among the young, and then the older generations tag along.

JLM: It reminds me of what people say all the time about Japanese organizations: that they tend to operate more from the bottom up than top down. But changing the subject, you told me the other day that you are working on a book?

SH: It's done. But it's not just me, it's a group effort. The publisher is Iwanami Shoten, and the title is *Discourses on the Culture of the Aged* (*Rōnen Bunka Ron*). People always talk about youth culture. This book is a reaction to that. It's said that young people have the time to be innovative. Especially in Japan, I think, people become too busy with work and families in middle age. Private life becomes very thin. The young, though, get money from their parents and can do whatever they like. That's how they produce different subcultures. In middle-age, people have to worry about making money.

Now elderly people, who didn't have much time for private life in middle age, are climbing mountains, riding Harleys, enjoying themselves in all sorts of ways. They're enjoying a second moratorium (*laughs*) before going on to the next stage. People are reading novels, watching movies, listening to music, and thinking about the meaning of their lives. Like the young, this group is freed from work and has the time to think about that question. They are looking for a personal identity, a sense of who they are as individuals.

8

REAL PLACES,
IMAGINARY SPACES

What is it to know a place? A world? A country? A city? A neighborhood? Or a self? One partial answer is that we carry mental maps in our heads. On these maps are the paths we have traveled, the locations we have visited, the landmarks by which we orient ourselves. Other parts of a map are secondhand, sketched from information provided by teachers, friends, family, co-workers, and, of course, the media. One thing is always sure: the map is never the territory. There are gaps, additions, distortions; one thinks of the notice 'there be monsters' on medieval maps of the world. Emotions are at work in shaping our maps. Some places are vivid, gleaming with promise and aspiration. Others are dark and threatening – or off the map altogether.

Issue No. 7 of the *Lifestyle Times* was entitled 'Mental Maps'. In it HILL researchers began to explore how Japanese mental maps are formed. Their inspiration was research by Japanese geographers that drew on the classic *Image of the City* by American geographer Kevin Lynch (1960). Lynch's studies of mental images of Boston, Los Angeles, and Jersey City had focused attention on the paths, edges, districts, nodes and landmarks that make up mental maps and challenged urban planners to consider the ease with which cities can be visualized as a vital element in the quality of life they offer.

'Mental Maps' launched two lines of research for HILL. One points outward, returning us once again to the changing material conditions that shape life in Japan. Pursuing this line, HILL researchers have explored real places, examining economic factors, pedestrian traffic flows, and the information intensity of different types of businesses for explanations of how the urban centers in which so much of Japanese life now takes place have changed. Here we examine one example: the study reported in '600-Meter Shops' develops a theory of how centers grow up around train stations, which play a role in Japan not unlike that of major highway interchanges in the United States, becoming the foci around which commercial development takes place.

The HILL researchers report that a station area starts as undifferentiated space in which shops and residences are jumbled together; it may, if strategically located, eventually become a major center divided into 'Parfait', 'Pub', and

'Parking' zones and sometimes abutting a fourth 'Park' zone defined by the presence of a large public park. The term '600-Meter Shops' refers to a new type of business that in 1983 was springing up around the edges of major centers and appealing to the trendy young women the researchers label '3C' (counter, cigarette and Campari) girls.

While one line of HILL research explored real places, another was devoted to analyzing imaginary spaces. From that group, this chapter presents 'Dream House'. Published in 1987, this issue of the *Lifestyle Times* reports on a study in which subjects were first shown slides of several types of houses and architectural details and then asked to draw their own dream houses. What I find striking here is the prominence of two themes seen in other studies. The first is the mournful observation that the subjects who participated in this study seem lacking in imagination. Having a big house on a big plot of land seems almost unthinkable, a dream within a dream. Instead we find the recurrent image of a small, bright space of one's own, a space in which to be alone. 'Brightly autistic' is the way HILL researchers describe it. While the theme of a deprived imagination echoes the fear of what might happen to children deprived of empty spaces in which to play in 'Children After School' (Chapter 6), the theme of a very personal space evokes an image similar to the good deaths sketched in 'Last Identity' (Chapter 7).

HILL also addressed the quality of urban life in Japan as the population ages and youthful vitality ebbs. Japan's political and economic leaders take such questions seriously, and so, perhaps, should marketers with products to sell in Japan. What becomes of Japan when the aged outnumber the young? Whole industries depend on the young consumers who drink soft drinks, eat fast foods, shop in convenience stores, spend lavishly on trendy fashions, are the first to try the latest entertainment technology, and, yes, fill cram school and university classrooms. The young, who are still shopping around and have not yet developed fixed buying habits, are the darlings of advertisers the world over, and Japan is no exception. Manufacturers can shift to robots or offshore production, but without hordes of young people, who will their customers be?

In 'A Society of Regulars', HILL researchers propose an answer: Japan may become a less frenetic, more 'European' place. The urban landscape may settle into the kind of pleasing vistas found in paintings of old Edo, where residential neighborhoods have the patina that comes from a long, settled history. Restaurants, bars and other neighborhood businesses will no longer need to spend heavily on neon and glitz to attract new customers. Their clienteles will be groups of regulars with familiar tastes. When they say, 'the usual', or perhaps say nothing at all, the shop's staff will know their needs and provide just what they want. The implicit contrast here is with the 'American' model of youthful exuberance, hard sell, and fleeting, arms-length relationships between merchants and customers.

If the external model for an aging Japan is Europe, the local model might be a well-run hostess bar, where, in a quasi-Western setting, a tired salaryman enjoys a kind of pampering he cannot find at home (Allison 1994). These pleasures, however, are expensive. What happens when the Baby Boomers retire and no longer have expense accounts? What happens to those who never climb the corporate ladder beyond the first rungs?

Thoughts like these may point to why the opening image in the text of this *Lifestyle Times* isn't a hostess bar, but a simple noodle shop like the one made famous in Itami Jūzō's film *Tampopo*. Pursuing this thought, I recall the men of Miyamoto-chō, the middle-class Tokyo neighborhood studied by Theodore Bestor. These men, writes Bestor, 'prefer places that are smaller and more intimate, where they know and are known by the owners, and where the fuss made over them is more genuine than the synthetic, effusive greetings indiscriminately offered everyone in the Otani [a nearby station area] nightspots' (1989:42). Will the future of Japan be more like this peaceful scene than the Bladerunner glitz that cyberpunk – for example the image of Chiba in William Gibson's *Neuromancer* (1995) – suggests?

Before we examine these studies, however, let us return once more to the research that laid the foundations on which much subsequent HILL research was based.

The City in the Mind's Eye

To residents of Tokyo, where the research for 'Mental Maps' was conducted, imagining the city is not easy. Cliché calls Tokyo 'a city of villages' and suggests the confusion that greets departure from familiar paths. Sheer size and repetitiveness make Tokyo one of the world's great examples of urban sprawl – 'the quintessential urban desert' (Jinnai 1995:8)

In the daily lives of Tokyo residents, the Imperial Palace in the center of the city is a vacuum. The action and the crowds are at subcenters, nodes located at intersections of rail lines that bend around the Palace before shooting off to the suburbs. Each subcenter has a distinctive character, but none is the focus around which the city as a whole revolves. There is no all-encompassing grid, like that imposed on ancient Chinese capitals or, in the nineteenth century, on cities in Europe and America.

There is, however, a sense of place and direction with deep roots in Japanese history. In the cover illustration for 'Mental Maps' (Figure 8.1), we see two trains. The one on the left is bound for Zushi, a resort and upscale residential area southwest of Tokyo and Yokohama, in Kanagawa Prefecture. That train is bright and shiny, and the images associated with it include the waterfront, a palm tree, automobiles, a cruise ship, seagulls. The train on the right is bound for Chiba, northeast of Tokyo. The landscape beside it is rural, with fields, and hills dotted with the torii gates that signify shrines. The tree is a pine, a distinguished motif in Japanese art that here seems only to suggest 'old-fashioned'. The birds are black, unlucky crows, one of whom is crapping on the dirty, battered train. The poster that floats between the trains says, 'Say no to linking the lines!' The note below it reads,

Figure 8.1 Cover, 'Mental Maps'

A resident of Kanagawa Prefecture is unhappy about the extension of the Yokosuka line to Chiba. His mental map may look like this.

(HILL 1981:1)

In the real world, the tracks the two trains are running on lie roughly on a line connecting the southwest and northeast quadrants of the greater Tokyo metropolitan area, directions that conjure up a wealth of associations.

Traditionally the northeast is labeled the 'devil's gate', the direction from which danger and pollution come. There is, however, more to the story than that. When the first Tokugawa shogun, Tokugawa Ieyasu, moved his capital to the place that was then called Edo and is now called Tokyo, he was part of the process by which Japanese civilization, with its roots in the southwest, expanded toward the northeast. Edo's topography conspired with history to sustain the prejudice that makes the southwest sections of the city more prestigious places to live and the northeast unlucky and uncivilized. Edo Castle, its site now the grounds of the Imperial Palace, was located on the high ground at the tip of the Musashino Plain, overlooking Tokyo Bay. Commoners were settled on the flats east of the castle. In the southwest, the terrain is more dissected. There the numerous hills became the favored sites for daimyo, the lords of the semi-independent domains outside the direct control of the Tokugawa, to build their Edo residences. To this day, the southwest retains a certain cachet, while the northeast, toward which the train to Chiba on the 'Mental Maps' cover is running, remains, somehow, the wrong side of town.

Tokyo in the 1980s and 1990s

When HILL was founded in 1981, Tokyo was, as it is today, the capital that dominates Japan. Osaka businessmen may still take pride in their city's history as a center of commerce, and Kyoto retains a special position as the center of Japanese tradition; but Tokyo, to use American imagery, is Washington, D.C., New York, Chicago, and Los Angeles, all in one.

During the 1980s, corporate competition for centrally located real estate drove land prices to levels where, at one point during the peak of the Bubble, Tokyo land was said to be equal in value to all of the land in the United States of America. The land reserved for the Imperial Palace alone was equal in value to California. In 1990, the ratio of daytime to nighttime population was 139.4 per cent for the 27 wards that constitute the core of the Tokyo metropolitan region (Ōtomo 1996:30). In the three most central wards, the ratio was 2,637.3 per cent for Chiyoda Ward, 1,106 per cent for Chuo Ward, and 565.5 per cent for Minato Ward (Ōtomo 1996:32). Between five and twenty-five times as many people worked there as lived there. Commuting had become a way of life for those who worked in these wards, and even where they lived in less central parts of the city and the suburbs, real estate prices were staggering.

In a statement that could serve as a charter for much HILL research, Mike Douglas, for example, writes that Tokyo is

a habitat where land ownership is increasingly concentrated, where more and more people are renters of apartments of diminishing size, where fathers and their children meet only on Sundays, where neighborhoods have lost their social fabric, and where offices have begun converting desks into nighttime sleeping capsules as a gesture of kindness to workers facing two-to-three hour one-way commuting times. In this milieu, association and communication even among family members are diminishing, and such trends as the demise of the public bath and the inability of government to construct new parks and other amenities have led to the 'collapse of meaning of public space'.

(Douglas 1993: 113)

This, then, was the environment in which HILL researchers began to examine how middle-class Japanese form mental maps of the spaces in which they live – or, if given a choice, imagine they would rather live.

By Foot or by Train? That Is the Question

'Mental Maps' reviews a variety of previous studies on mental mapping and reports on two new pieces of research. In one, subjects were asked to draw maps of train lines in and around Tokyo. For the other, a map of Tokyo and neighboring prefectures (Saitama, Kanagawa, and Chiba) was divided into blocks, each representing four square kilometres. Subjects were asked to color in the locations of their elementary, junior high, and high schools, their universities and workplaces, original and current place of residence, friends' homes, and other places they go for shopping or entertainment. (The choice of train lines instead of roads and highways as the focus of the first study reflects both the overwhelming importance of trains as the primary means of transportation for commuting within and in or out of the city and the role of the shopping and recreation complexes located at major stations as urban subcenters. The second study's focus on schools and workplaces, shopping, and entertainment mirrors the importance of these topics in the lives of city residents.)

What these and previous studies showed is that for most elementary and middle school students, the paths they walk to school define a small but densely meaningful world. With high school comes commuting, traveling by train instead of on foot. Mental maps expand in scale but also become more abstract, losing the sounds and smells that together with visual detail fill the memories of those who walk to school. In contrast to high school, when life is rigidly structured, a student's university years are a time of maximum freedom to explore what the city has to offer. Now mental maps not only expand; they also begin to include places off the commuter's well-beaten paths.

Graduation and finding a permanent job transforms mental maps, without doing much to enlarge or enrich them. Business trips may provide opportunities to travel to new places. Only a fortunate few, however, get to travel to places that they would choose to visit themselves.

There is more at stake here than size and diagrammatic features, for mental maps are structures of feeling as well as cognition. Thus, for example, the authors of 'Mental Maps' point out that when elementary and middle school students walk to school, they form mental maps permeated with memories of sounds and smells as well as familiar sights. Mental maps remembered from this period in people's lives may carry a heavy charge of nostalgia. Think back, for example, to the way in which the author of the 'Kids After School' study reported in the *Lifestyle Times* and translated in Chapter 6 recalls his childhood playgrounds.

I find myself thinking of my own experience; memories created by commuting are largely confined to crowded trains, the stations where commuters get on or off, and the names and brief glimpses of stations passed on the way. Wandering on foot through the entertainment districts that cluster around the stations where commuters board or leave their trains is a sensory experience that contrasts sharply with those of the classroom, office or train. The contribution of night life to mental maps is a subject that needs exploring.

Variations in Mental Maps

Mental maps vary depending on the lives that shape them. In 'Mental Maps', HILL researchers identify three patterns. One is characteristic of those who travel frequently within a contiguous region. It tends to be both broad and continuous, connected by frequently traveled routes. A second pattern is discontinuous and characteristic of those who, for work-related or personal reasons, have lived in a series of widely separated locations but do not travel widely in everyday life. In both these cases, the largest mental maps are those of individuals who have traveled or lived overseas. In contrast, the third pattern, the smallest, most densely textured maps, are those of long-term residents for whom both life and work are largely confined to the neighborhoods in which they grew up. (But not always confined there; they may be like my barber, a local man who has taken a package tour to Southeast Asia.)

Besides direct, personal experience, the other important factor in shaping Japanese mental maps is, of course, the media. In media-saturated Japan, images of places beyond the daily commute and occasional excursions for business or pleasure are shaped by what is seen in newspapers and magazines, billboards and transit ads, heard about on radio, or seen and heard on TV. In 'Mental Maps', HILL researchers note, for example, how differently various parts of the world are treated in Japanese newspapers. In data on the number of column inches devoted to different regions collected in a four-month period in 1981, the USA, China, and the USSR loom large. There was also substantial coverage of Poland and the Middle East, because crises in both regions had been important news stories. Coverage of other parts of Europe was less extensive, and Latin America and Africa were barely covered at all.

600-Meter Shops
Lifestyle Times, March 31, 1983

The Art: Figure 8.2 shows a woman walking up stairs into a new kind of store, a trendy bar-boutique. The contrast with the man who is ducking out of a traditional public bath is marked. Figure 8.3 shows the woman sitting alone at the bar. If the image represents an imagined self, what kind of self is this? It seems very odd, indeed, that she doesn't have at least one friend, probably another woman, sitting at the counter and chatting with her. The contrast with the intimacy enjoyed by the archetypically male 'regular' who hangs out at a neighborhood pub is striking.

The Research Design: Desk research and direct observation of eight urban subcenters in the Tokyo metropolitan region.

Where Crowds Gather, Places Display a 3P Structure Within a 600 Meter Radius

Six hundred meters is the usual radius of the catchment zone of liquor shops and drug stores. (Perhaps because people won't walk any further?) Now this zone is taking on a clear and definite structure. For example, from the famous meeting spot in the center of the Ginza, under the Wako clock, to one end of the Ginza, Shimbashi Station, is 600 meters. The Ginza's other end, at Nihombashi, is the same 600 meters away in the opposite direction. Couples can stroll that distance in about ten minutes. Like other, similar, areas, it contains three zones.

The Parfait Zone (1P = the shopping and eating area)

Contains (1) places to shop and eat (*Sun Town*); (2) department stores, boutiques, coffee shops; individual women shopping alone; (3) parfaits, elaborate ice cream confections sold at coffee and sweets shops catering to such women. These are its symbol. Typical images include McDonalds, families, crepes, crowds, people waiting, school uniforms, big book stores, banks, fortunetellers, fruit stores, pedestrian malls, record shops, Renoir coffee shops.

The Pub Zone (2P = the area for play and drinking)

Contains (1) an area with places where people go to play and drink (*Moon Town*); it is filled (2) with pachinko parlors, mahjong rooms, pubs and cabarets;

Figure 8.2 Front Cover, '600m Shops'

it was formerly (3) an area exclusively for men. Typical images include cheap bars marked by red lanterns, neon, noise, groups of friends, discos, drunks, game centers, the sound of Japanese ballads, trashcans, shills, saunas, coffee shops, narrow alleys.

The Parking Zone (3P = the boundary area)

Here (1) business and residential areas are jumbled together; (2) there are parking lots and hotels (indicators of a crowded center) together with beancurd makers, public baths, and rice stores (factors that make them residential). Typical images include dogs, dog droppings, open spaces, telephone poles, rent-a-car dealers, Yamazaki Bread stores, vending machines, liquor stores, small

Figure 8.3 Back Cover, '600m Shops'

parks for kids, quick print shops, small bookshops, launderettes, and hot lunchbox shops.

A fourth P is introduced as a small circle tangential to the others.

Park Zone (4P = peripheral zone)

Here we find the large parks that in Tokyo often abut 3P zones. Examples include Harajuku (Yoyogi Park), Ginza (Hibiya Park), Shinjuku (Shinjuku Gyōen), Shibuya (Yoyogi Park), Kichijōji (Inokashira Park). It's pleasant to think about all the different things there are in the areas covered by the 4Ps (especially if you are part of a couple).

How Centers Mature

Economic laws are at work in the way that centers develop. As a center becomes lively and noisy, peace and quiet are lost. People who once lived there move away. Shops whose business was supplying the daily needs of the residents are also pushed away from the center. Big capital with an eye on large crowds of customers moves in. Real estate prices soar. Except for stubborn old men, landowners are happy to sell.

The four stages of growth

If we look once again at the bull's eye chart on the previous page from a different perspective, we find that it represents a whole series of images. First, there is the undifferentiated town. Shimokitazawa, a small station a few stops out from Shibuya, is one example: many different functions are jumbled together within 200 meters of the station. This most basic type of center is simply an enlarged version of the shopping streets found at all train stations. Its edges are blurred, blending into the residential areas that surround it. Its businesses include stylish coffee houses, restaurants, and boutiques.

As centers grow a little larger, 1P and 2P zones become differentiated. As the center expands, large shopping complexes emerge. The radius of the area where crowds gather expands to 400 meters. The shopping and eating zone becomes differentiated from the play and drinking zone. The Parfait zone and Pub zone appear. Kichijōji is an example.

The 2P centers, still surrounded by residential areas, are clearly differentiated from 3P centers like Ikebukuro. The latter displays the mature form of an urban center. Everyday shops are now completely absent from the area within 600 meters of the station. Massage parlors, love hotels where couples can rent rooms for brief periods of time, and other sex-related businesses appear next to the 2P zone.

Recently, however, the appearance of 600-meter shops around the edges denotes centers that display a new stage of maturity. These shops may also spring up along streets that link centers. Kōen Dōri, the street that links Shibuya, a transportation nexus and major shopping area, with Harajuku, the quintessential youth zone, is one example.

Historically, three-zone centers were the crowded places where rail lines converged. The area around the station would be filled with high-rise buildings. Then in the Parking (3P) zone, large stores requiring heavy investments would appear. Recently, however, restrictive laws and regulations and a sluggish economy have blunted the straightforward expansion of 1P and 2P zones. There are fewer examples of major construction projects totally transforming the urban scene.

Instead, we are seeing the appearance of small, radical businesses that break old taboos and require only a small investment. These small-scale businesses try to find niches away from the centers or on top of hills where real estate is cheap. These adventurous shops employ strategies that make them confident that customers will be willing to walk a long way. These are what we call '600-meter shops'.

600-Meter Shops Are Filled with 3C Girls

To visit a 600-meter shop, you have to stroll about ten minutes away from the station. The neon will disappear; the street will seem lonely. There you will find the 600-meter shops, up two flights of steps or downstairs in the basement. When you open the door and go in, the first thing to catch your eye is the gleaming brass pillars and rails. Next you will notice the coldly shining marble counter and floors. There will always be uncovered pipes running across the ceiling. Girls pose at the counter, where they sit smoking their cigarettes and sipping Campari. That's why we call them the 3C (counter, cigarette, Campari) girls. When you turn your head, you will see a table on which accessories and sweaters are displayed. It's a modern technique, this fusion of pub with boutique. The JVC speakers that every pub used to have are gone. Now the Sony Profeel monitor lets you spend a quiet night at a 600-meter shop, absorbed in watching the latest in video art.

Dream House
Lifestyle Times, July 1987

The Art: A caption describes the cover illustration (Figure 8.4) as follows: N, a salaryman, aged 24, says, 'It's a grand residence, but the garden is small. The land and the building each cost about the same. When Japanese talk about a dream house, this is the most we can hope for'.

Notes scribbled on the illustration highlight some key features of this 'Dream House'.

Fashionable Moto-Azabu in Minato Ward, Tokyo; lot size, 1,000 m^2, structure 400 m^2; tiled roof with gable ornaments in the shape of a mythical animal with the head of a tiger and the body of a fish; family crest; pine tree; Japanese cypress construction; top quality tiles on roof; *no* aluminum window frames; decorative stones in the garden; a Mercedes-Benz.

A small note at the bottom reads, 'A grand residence built in pure Japanese style with a pond, rocks, plants, and fence'.

The Research Design: Asking several groups of subjects primed with visual imagery to sketch their own dream houses. The details are described in the text.

Dreams Expand 'Internal Demand'

It is International Housing Year. Interest in housing, the key to expanding domestic demand, is rising. Our question is, 'How do consumers feel about housing?' To explore more how consumers visualize their 'dream house', we conducted three surveys. Survey A had several elements. To groups composed of forty housewives (30–49 years old), twenty men who are household heads, and 38 men and women in their twenties, we showed slides of different kinds of houses and asked them to fill out a self-administered questionnaire. Afterwards, we asked them to sketch their dream houses for us.

Architects and pre-fabricated housing

For his recent book, *Stubborn Thoughts on Urban Housing* (*Iji no Toshi Jūtaku*), Nakahara Yoshi presents a wide range of information. 'More than the fact that residences are small', he writes, 'the problem is that Japanese have forgotten the variety of ways to use a small space seen in the traditional tea house'. Nakahara

Figure 8.4 Cover, 'Dream House'

hopes that producers of factory-built housing will learn from what the architects who are struggling to revive such interesting uses of spaces are trying to do.

Impoverished images

Housing is an issue postponed for so long that our images of what our homes might be are impoverished. Even drawing the house of our dreams is difficult. One middle-aged man spoke aptly when he criticized himself: 'Not being able to draw this kind of image is deplorable'. One housewife had to think for 30 minutes before, at last, she began to sketch a house plan.

Our dreams show us giving up

Only one of our 98 subjects, a man of 35, drew a broad expanse of land. Others drew tiny gardens, with a pool, or pond, or an artificial mountain at most. Stretching themselves as far as they could, some managed to draw a row of cherry trees. Just having a large house was as much as they could dream of. Having a lot of land as well? That is a dream within a dream these days.

Brightly autistic

We didn't expect so many of our subjects to draw only a private space for themselves. Why was it, we wondered, that a 44-year-old housewife put only a single chair in the room that she drew? A 37-year-old housewife included only a single pair of slippers. A 21-year-old man's dream house consisted only of a room of his own. There was, we found, a strong tendency to draw an enclosed world of one's own. But the images weren't dark. They seemed, instead, to be bright but autistic.

From quantity to quality

We have passed the stage of simply wanting to own a house. The desire to have a place with a living room, kitchen, dining room, children's room, and separate bedrooms seems to be satisfied. What people now complain about is how cut up and small the rooms they inhabit are. From simply wanting more rooms, they have advanced to wanting larger rooms. They are also replacing existing kitchen and bathroom fixtures with higher quality system kitchens and unit baths.

Japanese ethnic

People are putting more effort into what they do with the spaces they live in. We see a rising tide of interest in adding Japanese touches to a Western-style base. The dominant element is Western, with the Japanese touches mixed in to create a fresh impression.

Lovable nature

There is a lively interest in having trees or water beside the house. This is not nature in the wild; it's nature under control that people like. The trees must have attractive foliage, pets are fish in a pond or birds in a cage. Dogs are preferred to cats. The wild side of nature is kept at a distance.

Satisfaction with Current Home

When we asked our subjects to rate the homes in which they now live, on a scale of 100, their answers fell between 50 and 60. 'Even if you make an extra effort, what you get is bad. There's nothing you can show off, nothing really functional; I've given up', says one 41 year-old housewife. Still, many are renovating. And they speak freely about their discontents.

Points of dissatisfaction

When our subjects were asked to assess the quality of individual rooms, kitchens drew the most complaints, followed by living rooms and bedrooms. Complaints about bedrooms were a new trend. Next, we asked them to write down freely what they don't like about the places in which they live.

The biggest complaint was, 'Too small'. Here we see a change from wanting more rooms to wanting more space in each room. 'A six-tatami living room feels dreadfully cramped; it's so inconvenient when guests come', sighs one 38 year-old housewife.

Second is equipment. People want something that feels luxurious. 'A toilet on the second floor', 'a mini-kitchen on the second floor', a new entry way, kitchen, or bath were all among the things listed. What's new and notable in this list is the desire to renovate the entrance.

Third is 'hard to live in', dissatisfaction with the basic floor plan. 'You can't get to one room without walking through another', says a 22-year-old woman. 'The kitchen and living room are stuck together', says a 35 year-old housewife. 'Since the rooms aren't really separate, I'd rather just have one big room' observes a 37-year-old housewife. A 22-year-old woman complains, 'With only paper *shoji* and *fusuma* sliding doors to divide them, rooms aren't really independent'. Another 38-year-old housewife doesn't like 'seeing the kitchen from the entry way'.

Fourth is 'dark'. There's a strong desire for light. Here we sense new needs emerging for more natural and healthy places to live. Other complaints worth noting include 'noise' and 'lack of good taste', especially from young people. 'Wooden construction is old-fashioned', says one twenty-year-old man. Women complain about 'lack of storage space'.

Lifestyle and Housing

We asked our subjects to choose among four possible lifestyles: 'nuclear living' (in a nuclear family), 'mixed living' (with two generations sharing the same facilities), 'separate living' (two or more generations living together but having separate facilities), and 'joint living' (space shared by a group of families who are friends). More than half the middle-aged group would prefer 'separate living'. The majority of the young group choose 'nuclear living'. Both want to avoid 'mixed living', and the truth seems to be that 'joint living' is virtually unthinkable.

New Housing Needs

There is strong demand for solar-energy systems, duplexes, and houses that break away from the combined living room-dining room-kitchen pattern. Both our middle-aged group and our housewife group would like at least two connected Japanese-style rooms. Among young people, demand for a hiding place of their own and for custom-designed houses is high.

Becoming a Society of Regulars
Lifestyle Times, July 1993

The Art: The cover, reproduced in Figure 8.5, is an abstract design of spheres connected by a ribbon-like path. On the sphere in the lower right-hand corner there stands the figure of a man. There are chairs on all of the other spheres. Who is this man we wonder, and where will he decide to sit?

The Research Design: Data were collected in a survey conducted in July, 1993, whose subjects included 88 university students, 48 unmarried working adults, 91 married salarymen, 118 housewives, and 26 retired individuals. Total n = 371.

Plain and Simple

On a TV program that features ramen noodle shops we see a certain kind of place. From the outside it looks like it's gone out of business. The simple wooden structure is covered with something that looks like black vinyl. We see no sign, not even a name. The owner tells us why. 'It is only when those who make the food and those who consume it are both satisfied that we share the right feeling. That's why at our place, we only serve those who already know about us. We don't need a sign or a fancy décor'.

Places with regular customers and places that serve drop-ins are different. They differ in how they interact with customers, in their communication activities, in the way they present themselves.

In today's Tokyo, however, few places seem aware of this difference. Take, for example, the stores along the shopping street in an ordinary residential neighborhood. That's right, just think of the place where you live. Most of the stores depend on a neighborhood clientele for customers. Even so, we see them working hard, in both their architecture and signage, to attract new customers, transient drop-in customers who are and remain strangers.

Drop-ins and regulars are different. In contrast to the scattershot attempt to attract we find in stores that target drop-ins, shops that target regulars offer more depth. In contrast to the young, lively, energetic image of places that target drop-ins, the places that target regulars require a certain maturity that only comes with the passage of time. Shops that target drop-ins work at being exciting. Those that target regulars aim at a feeling of security instead. Drop-ins are the kind of customers who only come occasionally; to catch them, you must always keep your nets spread. Regulars make an effort to come, so even the need to be in an easy-to-find location is small. Since drop-ins only come once or twice, you might as well

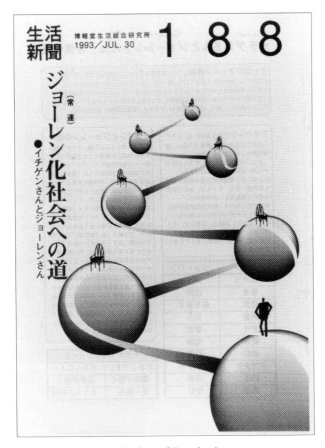

Figure 8.5 Cover, 'A Society of Regulars'

cheat them. (There are places like this in the center of Tokyo, aren't there?) Cheating regular customers would destroy a business. Low prices, though, are important for attracting drop-ins. To regulars, price matters less than quality.

Drop-ins	*Regulars*
Breadth	Depth
Youth	Maturity
Lively	Quiet
Exciting	Safe
Changing	Stable
Newly opened	Old established
Impulse	Planning
Persuasion	Empathy
Confused	Orderly

235

Drop-ins	Regulars
Easy to cheat	Not easy to cheat
Price-conscious	Quality-conscious
Detailed explanations	Anticipating needs

An example: computer bulletin boards. Here is a place dominated by regulars. They have their special language, expressions, tools, atmosphere; they are the ones who rule this space. Try it for yourself, sign up for a new personal computer network. You will find yourself drowning in the warm but hard-for-an-outsider-to-understand expressions the regulars use.

Another example: the outdoor life. Here is another domain dominated by regulars. When novices, who know nothing about outdoor life, go to places frequented by veteran outdoorsmen, they will find themselves welcomed by a whirlwind of advice (and, yes, sometimes preaching) about habits, tools, values, and behavior.

To those who think that regulars must be monomaniacs, we would note that an obsessive nut can be a nut all on his own. A regular requires a place where there are fellow regulars. It's a place in which the atmosphere is familiar, where the regulars understand one another's feelings and don't have to speak up to be understood.

As a bit of extra service to our own regulars, we have added a table of contrasts between drop-ins and regulars broken down by genre. These include both the ways in which streets and shops are constructed and characteristics of conversation, advertising, and marketing.

A society of drop-ins is one in which strangers are always meeting other strangers. A society of regulars is one in which old friends are constantly seeing familiar faces. These two societies differ in the ways in which people relate to other people, to stores, to products, to service. Even when people first meet as drop-ins, there is a tendency to shift toward becoming more familiar and thus becoming regulars. The joy we felt while living in a developing country where something new was always happening will soon come to an end. Japan is on the road to becoming a society of regulars, with a richer, fuller, more settled life.

Genre	Drop-ins	Regulars
Urban spaces	Confused, lively	Orderly, quiet
Stores	Friendly but shallow	Exclusive but have a special flavor
Products	To be consumed quickly	To be savored
Service	Everyone is treated the same	Individuals get special treatment
Feelings	Curiosity, novelty, difference	Safety, relaxation, subtlety
Conversation	Politeness	Frankness
Advertising	Name recognition	Understanding, depth, persuasiveness
Communication	Clear, verbal	Heart-to-heart

Cities Filled with Regulars Will Be More Sedate

The stores on major shopping streets compete for the attention of large, undifferentiated masses of customers and emit high volumes of information. Without comprehensive city planning, the shapes of buildings, signage, and billboards become chaotic.

As cities mature, however, markets become more fixed. The volume of information declines. Another way to describe this process is to say that the stores acquire a clientele of regulars. Now the signs, displays, and posters required to attract new customers disappear. Mirroring this process, the landscape of the city becomes more settled and sedate.

Hong Kong, for example, is typical of many Southeast Asian cities, flooded with signs, disorderly, overflowing with energy and vitality. In contrast the cities of Europe have long histories. Outside of tourist-oriented areas, signs are very small. With the orderliness there is also a quiet, relaxed feeling. What we see here is, of course, more than history and maturity alone; it is also closely connected to wealth and ethnicity.

If we look at pictures of Edo, what we see is a largely homogeneous landscape. Edo began as the smallest of villages, then grew to maturity during the 300 years of Tokugawa rule. When Tokyo was rebuilt after the war, however, explosive growth was continuous; order disappeared.

There are those who argue that new residential areas are almost too orderly. What they sense, however, is sterility, not order. In newly developed areas, the sense of human presence is thin. We sense a lack of humanity. In the orderliness of streets populated by regulars, the scent of shared values is strong.

The Furukawa district still has a tenement that was built in 1927. The first floor is mostly shops. The second floor is residences. The building is old and worn-out, but its basic design shows an overall unity of concept. If urban development were to move in this more mature direction, the result might be a landscape more like those in Edo-period paintings. It's a pity that everything later is chaos, that the careless rush to build has made Tokyo a concrete jungle.

At present, most shopping streets in Japan are caught up in a building boom labeled redevelopment. We wish that someone would stop and think for a moment. We would like to see redevelopment that is not simply putting up something new. It would, instead, skillfully incorporate existing structures and preserve, in a true and authentic sense, the uniqueness of place. If all we do is tear down the old and put up the new, mature neighborhoods will never appear.

Becoming a Regular

We presented our subjects with a list of sixty types of business and asked them if they always go to the same place. We found 24 types of businesses, from dentists to cosmetics shops, where regulars make up 50 per cent or more of the customers. These types of businesses are usually found close to residential neighborhoods. Businesses with fewer regulars are found in major shopping areas close to business districts. When shopping in the neighborhood, customers stick with the same shops. When shopping in major shopping complexes, they go to a wider variety of stores.

The process by which customers become regulars moves through certain stages. When we asked what made people feel like regulars, we heard five types of answers. 'Being greeted by the staff'. 'Having one's name remembered and being addressed by name'. 'Having one's preferences remembered and thus being given the usual thing without having to say anything'. 'Talking freely or enjoying recreation together outside the store'. ' And, finally, 'Feeling like part of the family, able to talk about private matters'.

We find a series of steps here that reflects the depth of relationships. The order of these stages may, however, vary. Having one's needs understood, before being known by name, for example, is characteristic of bars and coffeehouses. Everyone has had the experience of saying 'the usual' and getting it from someone who doesn't know his name.

On smaller shopping streets, most shops have regular customers. There is no need, then, for a chaotic jungle of signs. Store architecture can have a quiet, unified feeling that expresses the street's uniqueness instead of calling attention to the individual business. Instead of background music that prevents your hearing anything else, the street can have its own refreshing sound.

These streets make it easy for tacit understandings to form between customers and shops. We are not talking here about tacky little shopping streets with names like Something-or-Other Ginza. Truly mature cities are those where small, quiet shopping streets convey a feeling of history.

From this perspective, it doesn't matter if the streets we are talking about are central or out of the way and hard to find. You step out of a suburban station and, somehow, sense the uniqueness of the place. The nearby shopping streets have a special flavor.

Interview with Ōta Masakazu
September 8, 1998

Ōta is 42, married, with no children. He joined Hakuhodo in 1979 and was a TV and radio commercial planner before moving to HILL in 1983. He is responsible for several HILL studies of how the shopping and entertainment centers built around railway stations develop.

JLM: During the early eighties, HILL did many studies of urban spaces. '600 Meter Shops' was one example.

OM: I did all those studies.

JLM: Why was the theme of change in urban spaces so interesting?

OM: Things were very different then. Streets were changing in a law-like way, following economic principles. During the Bubble, though, development became mechanical, with no relation to economic laws. People were opening new stores and developing out-of-the-way places with no economic rhyme or reason. But back in the early eighties, places like Shibuya seemed to be growing naturally. One type of shop would fail, another would take its place. Since what was happening was law-like, you could predict what would happen next.

As a student, I studied botany. The field called plant ecology lets us understand why a willow tree was growing on a certain place on a mountain. A deciduous tree would replace it, a beech, for example. Then the beech would give way to an evergreen, a pine or a cypress. You could understand the succession of different kinds of plants and why some plants would flourish in places that others couldn't enter. I continued to study plant ecology in graduate school. So, then, when I looked at places like Shibuya, I found myself asking why some businesses did well while others went out of business. Or why certain businesses appeared in residential areas. That made them very interesting to me. Looking at Tokyo from an ecological point of view led me to the kinds of research reported in '600 Meter Shops'.

JLM: But, then, you say, the Bubble era was different?

OM: Completely different. Before then, shops set up away from stations had been at a disadvantage. Conversely, land was cheap, so that people with only a little capital could try out new types of business. During the Bubble, everything came down to money. People with money didn't set up small, experimental businesses. Instead they would rush in and throw up a whole new shopping complex. Small shops with only one or two rooms were suddenly replaced by tall

239

buildings. The power of money changed the face of the city. It had nothing to do with ecological processes. If we go back to the mountain, it was like a bulldozer, chewing up everything in its path.

JLM: So, can we say that while in the early eighties the changes were natural, during the Bubble they were unnatural?

OM: Completely unnatural and artificial. For that reason, the city ceased to be meaningful as a topic for research.

JLM: Your research was focused on station areas. How did it relate to the 'Dream House' study?

OM: What I did mostly was focus on how businesses developed. It was a concern with how urban landscapes were changing that led to 'Dream House'. Salarymen were buying new houses in the upscale areas along the Tokyū Den'entoshi railway line. 'Dream house' looked into what they were hoping for when they bought those new houses.

JLM: I wonder why you weren't doing studies of workplaces (offices or factories) or condominium complexes.

OM: We might have looked at them, but in the housing field in particular, real estate companies had already done a lot of research. Without having the same resources, our own studies wouldn't amount to anything. That is why, instead of existing housing, we decided to focus on not-yet-existing housing; on dream houses instead of real houses. The construction companies had already thought about things like how people would arrange and furnish space in existing apartments and houses. We thought that by looking at dream houses, we might see something that they had missed.

JLM: I had thought, perhaps, that a condominium unit wasn't the stuff of which dreams are made.

OM: In the early eighties, Japanese housing was still cramped, dirty, and cheap. It was more fun to play around in the city than it was to go home. It was only in the late eighties, when people began to have more money, that housing became a serious issue. Until then, housing was so poor that it didn't seem worth doing research on.

JLM: What about offices or factories? Isn't that where people spend most of every day?

OM: In the second half of the seventies, offices and factory environments improved dramatically. Housing lagged behind by about ten years. It was during the second half of the eighties that housing began to improve. In the early eighties the office was a better environment than the home; that's why people worked so much. Going home wasn't interesting at all. Then housing gradually improved. Now people care more about where they live. That's a big change.

JLM: Is that why, even in the 1987 'Dream House' study, the dreams were still so small? In the new study you've just released this year, you say that people's dreams are bigger now. The images they draw show big lots with trees as well as larger houses.

OM: During the Bubble, housing became a hot topic. Even if people couldn't afford them, they saw pictures in magazines and on TV and dreamed about what they would like. That is why their dreams are bigger now. Ten years ago, we lived in a two rooms plus dinette-kitchen – 2DK – culture.

JLM: In a 2DK culture, a 3DK (with three rooms in addition to the dinette-kitchen) was about all that people could dream of owning. I imagine that as the Bubble took off and land prices went out of sight, people's dreams were crushed.

OM: Prices were rising too fast, but people's dreams were getting bigger at the same time. There was, of course, a difference between people who could buy and people who couldn't, depending on price. But good housing became more and more luxurious. People's dreams were expanding. The 'Dream House' research was done just before that expansion began.

JLM: In the 'Dream House' study we find the word 'autistic'. The theme of having a small, bright space for oneself seemed very prominent in the responses to that survey. Has this disappeared?

OM: At that time, a house was seen as a place from which you could shut others out. As houses and apartments got bigger, they ceased to be places from which you excluded others and became instead places that others could enter.

JLM: Psychologically speaking, 'Dream House' seemed to me to be a continuation of the theme of feeling small and cramped that was prominent in other studies in the eighties, 'Kids After School', for example, or 'Sneaker Middles'.

OM: Back then, making a space for oneself was a major theme.

JLM: Now things have changed?

OM: During that period one-room, efficiency apartments had just become popular. Many young people wanted a room of their own where they could hide. Previously, young people had lived in dormitories. Instead of living together, they wanted a place they could be by themselves. It was during the eighties that neighbours stopped knowing what one another were doing.

JLM: Why have things changed?

OM: Once you have a house of a certain size, you have enough space to invite guests. In the 2DK era, it was very rare to invite friends to come over. As housing became more spacious, people began to think about houses as places for social life. That began about the middle of the Bubble. That was when the custom of having parties at home began to take root in Japan. Before then, you might have had a barbecue in the garden once a year; relatives might get together, but you wouldn't invite anyone else into your home.

JLM: It still seems very much that way.

OM: Not everyone has the kind of place to which you can invite people. Not everybody can have parties at home. But compared to ten years ago, the desire to have such parties is stronger. People who can't host parties go to parties at other people's places.

JLM: What is happening now? Sekizawa has written that real estate ads and overseas travel are the reasons why people's dreams have expanded. What do you think?

OM: Dreams are bigger, but incomes haven't been growing as quickly. Dreams and realities have diverged.

JLM: What happened to the efficiency apartments that were once so popular in the eighties?

OM: There are many of them around, but their popularity is way down. They aren't good places to live. People live in them because the cost is very low, but that is all they offer.

JLM: Where do people in their twenties live now?

OM: There are many possibilities ... to share a larger space with others ... to decide to live in a place that isn't close to the city, moving farther out to get more space. Another factor is that, since there are fewer children, parental support has increased. That is why some can afford bigger places. Twenty years ago, at the beginning of the eighties, families still had a lot of children. Parents weren't able to provide the kind of help they can now. That limited the places that people could live. If we look at today's students, first of all, their parents' salaries are higher. Families are smaller, too. So parents can afford to supplement their children's income.

JLM: That doesn't mean living with the parents, does it?

OM: No, they get money from their parents, but live separately.

JLM: In the original 'Dream House' study, there was talk of three-generation houses. Have they disappeared?

OM: Three-generation houses are becoming more numerous, simply because buying land and building a new house has become very difficult. Instead, people are rebuilding on land that the parents already own. Also, real estate developers have begun marketing three-generation houses that are easier to live in. They have separate entrances, for example. So people can live in the same house without interfering with one another. It's the same house, but people actually are living separately.

JLM: You mentioned the possibility of sharing a space. According to the original 'Dream House' study, very few people wanted to share space with non-relatives.

OM: The way that places are constructed has changed. The old 2DK style provides no privacy. Now developers are offering places in which, for example, rooms are separated, making them easier to share. There's been a great increase in that type of housing, especially in wards near the center of the city.

JLM: Returning to an earlier subject, what do you think about the Bubble period megaprojects that tried to create new urban centers out of whole cloth, like the Makuhari conference and business center in Chiba? Or Yokohama's Minato Mirai 21, with its skyscraper, hotels, and office buildings?

OM: They have a lot of entertainment value, but they aren't the kind of places you go to every day. They are different from the places that people usually go, like Shibuya or Shinjuku. I once did a study of how people use them, called 'After-Five Resorts'. The title captures the spirit in which people go to these places.

9

PUTTING JAPAN IN PERSPECTIVE

Friends who read early drafts of this book commented on how lucky I was to have worked with the HILL researchers. How exciting it must be, they said, to work with those who develop new cultural categories to describe changes in Japanese society. It is, I admit, appealing to imagine that one has stepped backstage in a major example of the Japanese culture industries, where master manipulators study and shape how the Japanese public sees itself. To be seen as able to explain how the trick is done would be even more delightful. But any such pretence is unsustainable.

The research and interviews presented here offer little support for the view that captains of consciousness armed with scientific techniques are discovering precisely what is going on in Japan. Neither do they validate claims that advertising agencies come up with arbitrary ideas that are then made so seductive that they swiftly come to be seen as part of the natural order of things. They give little comfort indeed to those who see the essential Japan as unchanging, albeit hard to understand for non-Japanese who lack the proper native feeling for what is going on. But neither do they offer support to those who believe that deep down the Japanese are just like 'us', where 'us' is understood to mean rational individualists eager to embrace the endless growth the free market promises.

In the conversations with Sekizawa (Introduction), Kobayashi (Chapter 4) and Shōji (at the end of this chapter), we discover that HILL was created with a purpose, to provide new insights by taking a broader look at Japanese consumers' lives. Rephrasing that purpose, we might say that the institute's research was deliberately designed to promote lateral thinking. Thinking outside the boxes imposed by specific marketing goals would become an edge for Hakuhodo in its efforts to sell its services to its clients.

HILL researchers strive both to provide genuine insights and to find compelling ways to describe them. Having sat in on their brainstorming sessions, I can testify to how seriously they take both objectives. Producing the research that is published in the *Lifestyle Times* is never merely a matter of collecting and analyzing data; nor is it creating ideas out of whole cloth. Insight feeds inspiration and vice-versa, in what are often highly particular ways.

Descending from purpose to practice, we discover that HILL began with only a handful of researchers. Today they still only number about a dozen. They are, as a matter of policy, not experts with specialized academic training. Instead they are 'high amateurs' chosen for their curiosity and ability to adopt a consumer's-eye view of what is going on around them.

Sekizawa tells us that when HILL was founded in 1981, the Japanese market was in transition. Homogeneous demand for durable goods was giving way to pursuit of distinctive lifestyles. In the 1980s, he says, 'consumption became, how shall we say it, more symbolic, more meaningful, not just consuming but a way of constructing a personal identity'. So much was going on that HILL researchers found it simple to notice what was new, identify and label it, and publish the results. Kobayashi says, 'At the beginning, it was great. We did whatever popped into our minds. It was enough to discover one new key word. We didn't have to have a lot of data to back up what we talked about, so coming up with a new idea or a new word was enough to have impact'.

Times changed. Early entrants in the market for trend spotters, HILL researchers would soon find themselves competing with journalists writing for magazines like *ACROS, Nikkei Trendy,* and *Dime.* Sekizawa remarks that, 'While HILL is still an antenna, what our audience looks for now is judgement, new thinking, and what it all means'. Kobayashi observes that the freewheeling style of the early days gave way during the Bubble era to use of large-sample surveys, in an effort to match the data produced by other research institutes.

Neither omniscient observers nor calculating manipulators, HILL researchers are individuals given the remarkable opportunity to study what seems most interesting to them in changes in their own society. As guerrilla ethnographers, they search for insight and inspiration concerning topics that, more often than not, are of special personal relevance to themselves.

Personal Insights

Rereading the interviews with HILL researchers, I discover that Shindō Kazuma's interest in salarymen is rooted in his work for Hakuhodo's company union in the early 1980s. Oota Masakazu's research on urban spaces reflects his training in plant ecology with its focus on natural succession as ecosystems change. Both are men in their forties who embrace a scientific approach to research that focuses on accurate description.

Shimamoto Tatsushi is in his late thirties, not all that much younger chronologically but perceived by himself and others as a member of a different generation, the New Breed. His ambition to create 'a new model of happiness' seems part and parcel of his generation's rejection of parental models and search for distinct self-definitions.

In contrast to these male researchers who focus on the workplace, cityscapes, and new models of happiness conceived in terms of whether to live in the city or country, Kobayashi Yoshiko and Masuko Miki both focus on themes of particular salience for women. Both are concerned with women's roles at home as well as in the workplace, what it means for a modern woman to be a mother and a wife as well as having a career of her own.

But here, too, we see a generation gap. While both agree that women's interest in pursuing careers has slackened, Kobayashi's comments on younger women's dropping out after less than a year with good jobs suggest a moral flaw, a failure in the eyes of her own generation of career women. In contrast, Masuko sees job and family as equally pleasant alternatives, to be mixed and matched in whatever way a woman finds personally satisfying. She is, however, curious about the impact of motherhood and whether having children will transform Japan's 'selfish girls' and restore a moral weight that now seems lacking in both work and private life.

Sekizawa's remarks are those of a Baby Boomer but also those of someone who began his career as a copywriter. The playfulness of the language found in the *Lifestyle Times,* with its wordplay and personal asides, is due in large part, one suspects, to his influence. The last words in this chapter, in the interview that ends the book, are, however, those of Shōji Takahashi, the President and CEO of Hakuhodo who, while serving on the company's Board of Directors, championed HILL's founding. In his voice we hear the authentic tones of a graying corporate warrior's reflections on what Japan has become – proud of Japan's accomplishments, anxious that the younger generation has been too protected and become too soft, but convinced that change is inevitable.

Careful readers will by now have long since discovered the tensions of gender, generation, and personality that resurface repeatedly in the topics that HILL researchers choose to study and the ways in which they present the results of their studies. It is then all the more remarkable that if we step back to review those results we discover a remarkably consistent vision of how Japanese lives have changed.

The History We Share

When HILL researchers note in 'Sneaker Middles' that soldiers returned home from World War II, men and women met, and large numbers of babies were born, the experience they describe was one shared by all the nations that fought in the war. Having those babies grow up as an age cohort so large that it strained social systems unequipped to handle so many new students, so many career-hungry workers, and then so many retirees has caused a continuing wave of problems with which these nations are still coping. Women entering the labor force just as new technologies disrupted the comfortable certainties and the clear division of labor typical of the modern industrial state has made the future of marriage, family, and child-rearing highly fraught issues wherever these processes have occurred. Birth rates slipping below zero population growth while the average life span has increased have turned many of the advanced industrial nations into aging societies worried about how to finance health-care and retirement for growing numbers of longer-lived elderly.

Not all Baby Boomers or members of later generations would find employment as salaried workers who sought security and a sense of belonging in large organizations. Those who did, however, became the icons of their time. Their 'typical' middle-class lifestyles were idealized and criticized as the norm for ordinary lives in the second half of the twentieth century. For the typical middle-class man, his job would be his primary source of identity. For the typical middle-class woman, marriage, a family, and guiding her children through the schooling that qualified them for corporate careers or successful marriages would serve the same function.

In Japan, the ideal to which middle-class families have aspired since the war has not been the traditional *ie*, the extended patriarchal household in which father was king. To the Baby Boomers, the ideal has been a nuclear family in which husband and wife are separate but equal powers and friends to their children as well as each other. But now that family, too, seems threatened by the growing number of singles who live alone and by changes that promote singles-like attitudes among those who belong to families but lead largely separate lives. As in other parts of the world, ideals that took root in the 1950s have been radically challenged by the impact of consumerism on the home as well as the marketplace.

In Japan as elsewhere, the roles of husband and wife associated with the new-model nuclear family popularized in the fifties were the products of modern, industrial economies shaped to meet the needs of mass production for national and then global markets. The newness of these economies, what we call their modernity, lay in insistence on clear functional divisions of space, time, and labor. The model is explicit: Work is work, home is home; both are distinct from leisure. The office or factory is separated from the home; resorts and shopping areas are separated from both. The contrast with the 'traditional' family farm or shop where work, life, and leisure share the same space is marked.

We have noted, too, that in Japan as elsewhere the corporations and government offices in which the middle-class, salaried worker found employment were organized on military lines. The lesson of the wars of the first half of the century was clear. If you have a big idea, if you want to do big business, the way to succeed is to create an industrial army. The soldiers who returned home from World War II and the younger men educated before and during the war brought to their new jobs the habits of loyalty, hard work, and self-sacrifice that made them ideal recruits.

Then, however, in Japan as in other parts of the world, stimulating consumer demand led directly to habits and values at odds with the disciplines that industry demands of its workers. Self-sacrifice and willing obedience validated by a sense of belonging have been challenged by advertising messages offering instant gratification and encouraging consumers to seek satisfaction of their own uniquely personal desires. The idea that, if happiness can't be bought, the next best thing is readily available to those who can pay the price has eroded the core values of modern, industrial, middle-class life. Delayed gratification, hard work, perseverance, and strong group loyalties no longer seem both desirable and inevitable. The HILL research collected here shows us some of the consequences as they work themselves out in Japanese lives.

Workers Becoming Consumers

As early as the 1950s, Ezra Vogel (1963:9) had noted the growing preference in Japan for the salaryman's safe and secure career, a choice that implied conscious rejection of both the risks and rewards of professional or entrepreneurial alternatives. When, in 'Sneaker Middles', HILL researchers describe a generation unlikely to produce new heroes, they are talking about people who had fully embraced this new ideal.

Squeezed since birth through a system too small for their numbers, the Baby Boomers started corporate careers at a time when the years of rapid economic growth were coming to an end. They learned, it seems, all too well that 'The nail which sticks up gets hammered down'. As consumers they enjoyed novelty. But instead of personal creativity, they preferred the stance of connoisseurs. They would cultivate personal taste and skillfully choose the products and lifestyles that suited them best from the cornucopia that industry provided. An education built around the multiple-choice test legitimated the correct choice as the ultimate value toward which to strive.

In 1982 the oldest Baby Boomers were thirty-five. In 1999, they are in their early fifties. They retain their preference for casual clothes and quiet, safe, laid-back lives. As predicted, they have not, says Sekizawa, produced many heroes. Neither, he says with a edge of disappointment in his voice, have they had the impact on society that their numbers made possible.

By the time that the 'New Breed' came of age in the 1980s, Japanese consumerism had become the envy and the marvel of the world. A smaller generation in a nation whose wealth and economic prowess seemed destined to be No. 1, the New Breed could afford to be self-indulgent. Their jeans would be designer jeans, their handbags made by Vuitton and Gucci. Their *Something Crystal* lives were said to be postmodern.

In a labor market where demand was outstripping supply, New Breed men felt free to demand more time for themselves and even to consider leaving the security of lifetime employment for better jobs. Then, however, as they entered their thirties, started families, and reached critical plateaus in their corporate careers, the collapse of the Bubble left them frustrated. They were feeling the pressure. They were disappointed and angry. But theirs were not the only lives that had seen radical change.

Nowhere, perhaps, has the impact of consumerism been stronger than on the traditional roles of women. With male producers confined to their desks and assembly lines, the modern division of labor assigns the role of consumer to woman. For women, however, becoming consumers was only a first step. Growing demand for consumer goods and the education that would, it was hoped, enable children to get good jobs (if sons) or find good job-holding husbands (if daughters) put pressure on family budgets. More and more women have found themselves seeking at least part-time jobs to supplement family incomes.

As growing numbers of women entered the workforce, advertising's insistence on instant gratification and personal fulfillment attacked the very heart of the self-immolation that 'traditional' female roles require. Yes, there were pressures on mothers to ensure that their children succeeded in school. But unmarried women and women whose children were old enough to go to school learned to use their free time in ways that challenged not only the older values of the *ie* but also the separate but equal, mother stays home, nuclear family. As described in 'The Era of Women, Highlights and Shadows', the possibility of new roles for women was exciting but also anxiety-provoking. Even successful career women might be caught in a 'Cleopatra Complex', fearful of losing the glamour and position they struggled to achieve.

As the meaning of life became increasingly centered on the role of consumer and lives split between work and consumption left little time for anything else, marriage and children ceased to be social imperatives or even attractive goals for many young Japanese. Marriage was delayed or avoided. The number staying single increased, and divorce rates – while still low compared with other advanced industrial nations – began to climb. With singles attitudes spreading even to those who did marry, the birth rate plummeted.

What, then, becomes of the children that Japan needs to reproduce itself? If, on the one hand, they find themselves under constant pressure to conform, they also learn that conformity has rich, material rewards. The lessons of an over-scheduled but also affluent life are to keep your head down, go along with the crowd, and keep personal and private matters to yourself. Food, shelter, entertainment – all will be provided. In a world where everyone is busy and self-centered, stay loose. Enjoy companionship, collect acquaintances, but don't let anyone get too close. Intensity can be dangerous. It is better to slip by.

It is striking, moreover, how closely the results of HILL studies of the elderly parallel those of children and youth. As recently as the early 1980s, retirement meant a return to childlike dependency. In contrast, the 'new silvers' seem to this American reader to have stepped straight from the pages of *Modern Maturity*. Financially independent, they are socially independent as well. They have reaped the rewards of participation in the one of the longest, strongest periods of economic growth in history and as 'silver aristocrats' are ready to sample the pleasures of travel, self-cultivation, or quietly cultivating their gardens. Some are still reluctant to relinquish the style and excitement of youth, but interest in collective action or even in living together with their children is low.

The question for the Baby Boomers who themselves will soon retire is whether their own retirement can possibly be this luxurious. Now the nation to which they belong and the organizations that provided their jobs say that they may not have the money to pay back the Boomer who thought he was trading loyalty for security. He reads his daily newspaper, and the news from the future looks grim. His wife looks at her mother-in-law, who seems likely to live forever. She wonders who will care for me when I am old?

The Organization Man and His Japanese Counterparts

The issues described above are not uniquely Japanese. As Ezra Vogel completed his study of Japan's new middle class, in America critics were sounding the alarm about the mass-marketed, 'other-directed' society that life in the suburbs epitomized. One of the first and most notable was William H. Whyte, whose classic *The Organization Man* provides a detailed portrait of a new way of life that seemed to mark a radical departure from the Protestant Ethic's rugged individualism.

The organization man, says Whyte, adheres to a Social Ethic. Two of its central principles are, first, that human beings need above all a sense of 'belongingness' and, second, that the group is the source of creativity. It is only through members of groups working together that great things are achieved. One is struck by how similar this seems to the group orientation said to be typically Japanese.

Other details strengthen this impression. Consider, for example, Whyte's statement that the organization man's duty is

> Not so much to the community in a broad sense but to the actual, physical one about him, and the idea that in isolation from it – or active rebellion against it – he might eventually discharge the greater service is little considered.
>
> (Whyte 1961:12)

In *Japanese Society* (1970), Nakane Chie makes precisely these points about the greater emphasis on *frame* instead of *attribute* in Japanese social organization. A frame is a concrete group of individuals united by some common purpose. It is, as Robert J. Smith remarks (1983:52–53), a group that lives and works together. In contrast, an attribute is an abstract category: gender, occupation, age, for example. It denotes a set of people whose members may, in fact, have little or nothing to do with each other. When behavior is constrained by frame, ethics are situational and more concerned with immediate issues confronting the group than with their long-term implications. Relations outside the group are thin and evanescent compared to those between its members.

I am also struck by Whyte's remark that for the organization man, 'The upward path toward the rainbow of achievement leads smack through the conference room' (Whyte 1961:21). How Japanese it sounds when I read,

> Not for lack of ambition do the younger men dream so moderately; what they lack is the illusion that they will carry on in the great entrepreneurial spirit. . . . The man of the future, as junior executives see him, is not the individualist but the man who works through others for others.
>
> (Whyte 1961:22)

And Yet

Contrasting Naperville, Illinois, the 'edge city' in which she conducted her research on the lives of American women in the 1990s, with Park Forest, the Chicago suburb where William Whyte collected data for *The Organization Man* in the 1950s, Sally Helgesen observes three radical changes. The first, she writes, is, 'The absolute, almost unquestioning faith and trust in large organizations that so obviously prevailed [in Park Forest]' (1998:20). Residents of Park Forest trusted the companies that employed the men, the developers who built the community, the churches to which they belonged, and the governments they elected, whose officials oversaw the building of the highways they traveled and the schools their children attended. In contrast, says Helgesen, today's Americans are skeptical and combative. Trust in large organizations is low.

A second difference is the Park Foresters' apparent homogeneity. They seem content with generic interests and ambitions. They like to blend into the crowd, 'shunning the display of any individual taste or aspiration that might distinguish them from their neighbors' (Helgesen 1998:20). In contrast, few Americans today can assume that their neighbors will share their values, tastes, interests, or ambitions. In Japan, the Baby Boomer Juniors and the new generation of Amenbo Kids may be more tolerant of individual differences than previous Japanese generations. Their tolerance is rarely stretched, however, by the kinds of racial and ethnic tensions that Americans encounter every day.

A third major change is the loss of predictability in life cycles. In Park Forest, people of the same age had children of about the same age. Husbands' careers were at the same stage and income levels were similar. Their lives were as regimented as those described in charts of typical Japanese life cycles. Now a group of women in their forties may include a new mother, a woman whose children have recently graduated from college, a woman whose marriage has lasted two decades, a woman who has married, divorced and remarried several times, and a woman who has never married at all. One is a successful career woman; another has never held a job. Demographics alone have ceased to be a strong predictor of individual lifestyles.

Feeling Cramped

One often hears from Japanese friends how spacious the United States seems. The houses are big, the vistas are big, and the highways are huge. In contrast, Japanese homes, highways, and vistas all seem cramped to them.

As we read the HILL research on Japanese consumers, it is precisely the lack of spaciousness that returns as a leitmotif or major theme in study after study. It lurks in descriptions of Baby Boomers grinding their way through a system that lacks first classrooms and then space for building successful careers. It surfaces in nostalgic memories of empty lots where children could escape from adult supervision and play as they liked, possibilities no longer available in crowded

251

urban neighborhoods and days filled with study, practice, and video games. One sees it most clearly, perhaps, in 'Dream House', where even dreams seem very small. It returns inverted in dreams of escaping to the sea or the forest, away from social pressures and, ultimately, in 'Last Identity', in the hope of dying in a quiet, natural setting, surrounded by open space.

It is tempting to relate these images directly to material realities. The small size of Japanese homes cannot be denied. The majority of urban Japanese have lived in cramped, modular, 'tenement-style' housing for as long as there have been large cities in Japan. The postwar rebuilding of Japan's cities and suburbs and the proliferation of nuclear families were, indeed, extremely rapid, and providing merely adequate housing was the immediate goal. With much of the original urban housing stock destroyed by wartime bombing, developers were under no pressure to create larger, more livable places to live.

Consider, however, the difference between Naperville in the 1990s and Park Forest in the 1950s. One notices, writes Helgesen,

> The sense of leisure and unhurried ease that pervades the lives of Whyte's suburbanites. The men, like commuters in a John Cheever novel, arrive home regularly by 5:30, so that evening ballgames and family barbecues are a regular event. They rarely travel for business, so there are none of the 5 a.m. departures for the airport or midnight returns that are so familiar a feature of corporate life in our era. The women seem to have unlimited hours for informal visiting, for the kaffee klatches and Tupperware parties that have become a proverbial feature of early suburban lore. The children, when not in school, seem always to be off amusing themselves, playing on front lawns or riding bicycles around the neighborhood, their activities rarely giving their parents cause for second thoughts. The sheer sense of the *spaciousness* in people's lives is like the remembrance of summer in childhood. Life today seems anxious, frantic, and overscheduled by contrast
>
> (Helgesen 1998:21).

The salarymen described by HILL have never had the option of leaving work to get home by 5:30 after commutes of an hour or more. Indeed, Japan's absent fathers are almost never home, except perhaps on weekends.

Long hours spent at work and commuting also account for the limited involvement of Japanese men in school and other community activities. Something like the vigorous local politics that Whyte found in Park Forest may be found in the Japanese lives of small business people whose routines keep them closely tied to the shopping streets where their businesses are located (see, for example, Bestor 1989). To the salaryman, however, who leaves early in the morning and returns late at night to what is for him, in a strict sense, a bedroom community, the ties that would lead to involvement are thin.

Ironically, the residents of Naperville in the nineties also lack both the leisure and the feeling of community that made life in Park Forest attractive. It is true that they live in homes with far more physical space than either the residents of Park Forest or the members of the Japanese middle-class described by HILL in 'Dream House'. The lack of 'spaciousness' in Naperville lives is not a lack of physical space but lack of time and social space.

In Naperville, time is consumed by a ceaseless grind of overscheduled activity. Families where both spouses work are increasingly common, and children are under pressure to succeed academically or, alternatively, as either performers or athletes. When children are not in school or at after-school classes, they are found at home playing by themselves. Fear of strangers and lack of comfortable outdoor spaces for unsupervised play are given as reasons.

This all seems very Japanese, until, that is, one pauses to reflect that what Helgesen is describing may simply be the normal condition of life in a late twentieth century, free-market-dominated, postmodern industrial economy. Neither middle-class Japanese nor middle-class Americans can find enough time for the family, children, and local community that both recall in memories with a warm, nostalgic glow. Middle-class members of both societies worry about absent fathers and overprotective mothers and what will happen if mother, too, leaves home for a job. People in both feel increasing pressure to lose themselves in work. Both wistfully dream of getting away to find their true selves in a place and a time they can call their own.

What Does It Mean to Belong?

Mission, group, self. The words that military organizations use to describe their ethics are a fair description of the group-frames in which Japanese situate themselves in a manner strangely similar to Whyte's organization men. What happens, however, when a group of this kind loses its purpose, not because it has been defeated but instead because its purpose has been achieved? So long as self-sacrifice is justified by the mission and supported by rich rewards, the group remains vibrant. When the battle is won, the mission over, the demands that the group makes on its members may suddenly seem arbitrary, no longer deeply meaningful. When loyalty ceases to reap an economic reward, the group may fall apart. Even if it stays together, it will be but a specter of its former self, its members reduced to watching out for themselves instead of for each other.

As I read the HILL studies translated for this book, that is the image that comes to mind. Corporate warriors determined to recover from defeat and overtake their rivals created what were, for their time, arguably the world's most perfect industrial armies. In efficiency, *esprit de corps*, and ability to work together they were, in their time, unsurpassed. But their very success would undermine them. The endless strain, the long commute, the lack of time for leisure, family, self – as high-growth slowed and the battle to dominate global markets seemed won, what, after all, did it all mean?

New generations of peacetime soldiers lack their generals' dedication. The generals themselves, whether corporate executives or government leaders, become more rigid as they grow older, convinced that the tactics that won the last war will win the next one as well. But there's the rub. The world has changed. It has changed at home, where the women who tended the home fires and raised the next generation have heard the siren call of advertising, first becoming consumers and then going to work to be able to afford the lives that marketers promise. It has changed in a global economy where, as Sakaiya Taichi points out, the intelligence captured in software now accounts for more value than the hardware produced on assembly lines and innovation earns more than dogged persistence and quality control (1997:23–24).

What most disturbs the last of the corporate warriors is worry about the next generation. Schooled and drilled to be good soldiers, they have, it seems, no fire in the belly. They are, as former Hakuhodo executive Ikari Tomohiko, put it to me, 'too polite'. In his generation, says Ikari, young men 'trampled into each others hearts with their shoes on', eager to get at the real feelings behind the superficial politeness that Japanese civility demands. Members of the current younger generation keep their distance, avoiding conflict at all costs. They are, says Hakuhodo's president Shōji Takahashi, like hothouse plants. The hothouse may have to be torn down to see which young people have what it takes to survive.

The Baby Boomers, whose children Shōji is talking about, may find their children disturbing. They can, however, sense the appeal of the new generation's attitudes. In summing up the results of 'Living as One Thirty-Fourth', Sekizawa describes a TV drama in which a character talks to plants. In his conversations with his plants, this character is never pushy, never attempts to persuade. 'It is, however', writes Sekizawa, 'precisely that passivity that melts your heart and moves you. It shows the stupidity of trying to control others'. I wonder, however, how far this process of distancing oneself from the group and relying on 'silent appeal' to attract a network of friends can go.

The Disappearing *Ie*

It is virtually impossible to read an account of Japanese social structure that does not enshrine the *ie*, the 'traditional' patriarchal household defined in Meiji law and assumed to be the root metaphor for social organization in Japan – from families to firms to the Japanese state as a whole. As we have seen, however, the *ie* model has not gone unchallenged. The American-style nuclear family in which relationships are supposed to be free, open, and egalitarian has been an attractive alternative for nearly a half century. The 'Husband-Wife Holon' envisioned by HILL researchers can be seen as an attempt to balance the claims of these two models in a 'Couple' as they define it, in which patriarchal authority is only a powerless shadow.

The impact of modern technology makes even this compromise seem very fragile indeed. In 'Tractors, Television, and Telephones: Reach Out and Touch Someone in Rural Japan', William Kelly describes the impact of TV on

254

traditional household organization. In traditional households in rural Japan, he writes, the center of family life was the *chanoma* or family room. Family and household hierarchy were clearly delineated by the seating arrangements around the open rectangular where the family shared its evening meals and entertained its guests. The place of honor was the seat with its back to the *tokonoma*, the ceremonial alcove where seasonal flowers and paintings might be displayed.

Traditionally, that was the seat of the senior male, the household head. When TV was introduced, however, the *tokonoma* provided a convenient place for the set. To be able to watch TV, the household head shifted his seat to one side, disrupting the traditional hierarchy of places. The voice of the TV newscaster began to compete with the household head as a source of authoritative pronouncements (Kelly 1992:84).

The June 1997 issue of *Brain,* one of Japan's leading marketing trade periodicals, carries a report that seems to carry Kelly's argument to a new extreme. It begins,

> One family, one TV has now become one person, one TV. One family, one telephone has become one person, one telephone. The living room where the telephone and the TV were the center of the household is buried in dust. The household's members are in their own rooms each watching their own TVs. They communicate with the outside world using their portable phones. To begin the day, each gets up when he or she has to, heats up some ready-to-eat food or stops by a fast-food restaurant to eat a 'breakfast set'. The family core of the household is now fragmented in time and space to a shocking degree
>
> (Tomiie and Ōzawa 1997:5)

There is, to be sure, an element of dramatic overstatement here. The analysis following this introduction reports that most Japanese still have warm and fuzzy feelings about what they see as traditional families. In their summary, however, the researchers write,

> As the family dissolves into individuals, we are groping for a new form of family. This group will be constituted in ways that turn a fragmented family into a family after all. There will be no feeling of constriction. Relationships will be like powder [not 'wet' and sticky like traditional relationships]. Its members won't be pushy, they will treat each other gently. New forms of consumption will be the tools by which these families are formed.
>
> (Tomiie and Ōzawa 1997:7)

Those used to reading and thinking about traditional Japanese family ideals may be shocked by the final sentences.

> No longer will families be the 'fated' families we have had until now. Family relationships will involve different kinds of friendship and love. In

the movie *Leon*, the assassin who is the main character always takes his plants with him wherever he moves. When asked if he likes potted plants, he replies, 'They are my friends. They are healthy, and they keep their mouths shut'. He and his plants form a household based on gentle, non-binding, relationships.

(Tomiie and Ōzawa 1997:7)

If Japanese identities are group-oriented and families and other groups are reconstituted along these lines, what then becomes of the Japanese self? The corporate warriors are almost gone. Their soldierly virtues and passionate identification with the groups that framed their lives seem to be disappearing. The Baby Boomers who embraced the Ozzie and Harriet ideal of a nuclear family whose members are friends and equals face an uncertain future. The lifestyles of the silver aristocrats studied in 1995 have strong appeal; whether later generations can afford them is an issue as yet unresolved. What will Japan's future be like when the children who skim society's surfaces like agile but fragile insects grow up? The future is literally hard to imagine.

Imagining the Japanese Consumer

What first caught my eye about the *Lifestyle Times* was each issue's unique design. I had, I thought, stumbled upon a new, postmodern form of knowledge. The issue-by-issue changes in covers and illustrations seemed evidence of a playful approach to 'knowing what's going on' that puts more stress on stimulation than piling up the data for ever more solid conclusions. It might, I thought, be the sort of knowledge recommended to young Japanese by Asada Akira, whose *Structure and Power: Beyond Semiotics* (*Kōzō to Chikara: Kigōron o koete*) became a surprise bestseller in 1983. Marilyn Ivy (1989:28) describes that knowledge as, 'a matter of style . . . a game suitable for the generation that has been labeled apathetic and superficial'. It represents a deliberate rejection of knowledge for knowledge's sake or for instrumental use.

While preparing the illustrations for this book, I noticed, however, a transformation that seems to correspond to the changes in Japanese society and the lives of Japanese consumers that HILL research documents.

The covers of issues produced in the early eighties make heavy use of vivid illustrations. Styles vary, but however they are drawn, the faces we see are highly expressive. The images are charged with energy, and whenever more than one figure appears, there is visible interaction between them. I think, for example, of Figure 4.1, where the cartoon woman flies out of her birdhouse with a big smile on her face. Another example is Figure 3.2, the classroom in which the salaryman schoolboys sit waiting for their teacher. In Figure 5.2, the cover for 'The Unmarried', the man and woman sit with their backs to each other. Her head is up, and she seems on the verge of speaking to someone. He looks depressed.

In Figure 5.1, the cover of 'Husband-Wife' Holons', we see a very different image. Here the figures are faceless. In Figure 8.5, the figure that exemplifies the 'Society of Regulars' has been reduced to a silhouette. In Figure 5.3, a typical member of the 'High Singles Society' is a faceless artist's mannikin. The wings suggest an escape from social norms, using the same artistic convention as in Figure 4.1. But the poem on 'High Singles' cover spells out the implications of the image's abstraction.

You

Me

We don't understand.

It is true, to be sure, that over the years the people in charge of producing particular issues have changed. The impact of desktop publishing software and a shift from more intuitive to more numerically grounded research cannot be dismissed as irrelevant. Still, when these and other *Lifestyle Times* covers are laid side-by-side, a pattern seems to emerge.

During the early eighties, HILL researchers felt confident when they visualized the subjects of their research. Salarymen, housewives, kids, the unmarried, the aged – each distinct social type evoked a vivid and well-defined image. As time passed and Japanese society changed, the researchers' confidence weakened. They found it increasingly difficult to imagine the features of the consumers whose lives they are trying to describe.

A similar trend can be seen, I suggest, in the style of analysis used. Kobayashi Yoshiko described a shift from the confident intuitions and big ideas of the early eighties to the more cautious, statistical analysis of the late eighties and nineties. What this reader notices is a shift from sociological ideal types to descriptions of psychological currents that are seen as pushing or pulling on all Japanese. We can see it clearly in the art selected to represent HILL researchers' conclusions. Contrast, for example, the illustrations of the salaryman's four faces (Figure 3.3) in the 'Guide to Salaryman Success' or the different types of housewives (Figures 4.2–4.6) in 'Housewives' Empty Nest Time' with the charts that describe forces converging on the lives of silver aristocrats (Figure 7.5) or attitudes of Amenbo Kids (Figure 6.5).

Masuko Miki suggests that what we are seeing is a shift from superficial description of emerging new lifestyles to attempts to penetrate more deeply into Japanese hearts. The former style of research was good for the early 1980s, when consumer needs were becoming more diverse and the news of new possibilities was enough to make reports interesting. Now HILL confronts the need to say something more profound, to penetrate Japanese selves more deeply. The difficulty is that new generations of Japanese no longer wear their hearts openly displayed in the costumes they don to play public roles. There has always been a separation of the true, inner (*honne*) and public (*tatemae*) self, but formerly people were more serious (*majime*), more innocent (*sunao*). Now everyone wears masks and keeps the inner self concealed. It is no longer just the foreigner who cannot understand what lies behind the mask. It is now a problem for everyone, including the Japanese themselves.

I find myself recalling the point, raised separately by both Shindō Kazuma and Shimamoto Tatsushi, that the New Breed's passion for using consumption as a way to create new identities has given way to snacking or grazing. Now, instead of searching for products that show the world who I really am, young Japanese consumers maintain a carefully 'neutral' distance from all of industry's offerings. Relationships with products resemble those with family and friends. Like air, products are there; like family, they are necessary. Neither should be allowed inside where the true me hides.

Consumers like these become more opaque to market researchers, who must then struggle to look more deeply and may feel very uncertain about just what it is they have found. Typologies give way to radar charts, and the figures in the center are question marks. Currents swirl around them, but predicting where they will move next becomes increasingly difficult.

To describe the Baby Boomer Juniors, Hakuhodo's arch rival Dentsu coined the label the 'dolphin generation' (iruka sedai). These young Japanese were, they said, highly sensitive to what is going on around them, tended to travel in packs, and were slippery and hard for marketers to get hold of. To describe Japan's children today, HILL researchers use the image of the water strider depicted in Figure 6.4. The marine mammal swimming in seas of information is replaced by an insect skittering here and there on the surface of the pools where it is found. To this reader, the implications are disturbing. The image is less human, more asocial, more alien. Members of this new generation of Japanese consumers seem wary but also vulnerable. How will they survive, I wonder, when storms break around them or monsters rise from the deep?

Changing, Yes, But How?

In the introduction to this book, I challenged a series of stereotypes which point to what are described as the essence of Japaneseness. They describe the Japanese as a uniquely group-oriented people who live in a vertical society. Dependent on superiors who act in loco parentis, they live severely regimented lives. They are so totally group-oriented that individual selves can hardly be said to exist.

These stereotypes are themselves the Scylla to the Charybdis of another, equally biased view that states in one way or another, 'The Japanese are just like us'. To the modernization theorists of the sixties, the Japanese were just like us, only a little less so. As they became more modern, they too would progress in the only conceivable direction, becoming more democratic, rational, and individualistic. In other words, they would cease to be traditional and become more modern, more like 'us', where 'us' meant the West, the United States of America and its European allies.

Today modernization theory may seem of merely historical interest. We now have rational-choice theory, which simply assumes that human beings everywhere are the same kind of economic animals. If the Japanese are human, they too must be creatures of the market and bound to respond as the market dictates. (For critical views of this proposition see Williams 1996 or Johnson 1995.)

Since, when looking back over the HILL research translated for this volume, what I find is an image of the Japanese which is neither totally alien nor yet totally 'just like us', I offer here a third perspective, summed up in three propositions.

- Japan is a modern nation affected by the same global trends, opportunities, and problems as other advanced industrial societies.
- Japanese responses to those trends and problems are constrained by material and institutional frameworks specific to Japan. These frameworks are not, however, uniquely Japanese, except perhaps for their coincidence in one geographically local place.
- There are, however, specifically Japanese ways of perceiving what has been going on in Japan. Here is where Japanese tradition and its transformations may have an important bearing on where Japan goes from here.

No one who reads this book and reviews the results of HILL research can escape the realization that Japan has been affected by the same sorts of social problems and processes encountered by all the advanced industrial nations. Like other OECD nations, Japan has made the late nineteenth to mid twentieth century transition from a traditional-agricultural to a modern-industrial form of economy. Now, like other nations, it is making a further transition to what many authors see as a postmodern economy. In Japan, as elsewhere, rampant consumerism and information technologies are driving a change in the sources of economic value, from hardware to software, from products to services, things to information, and, yes, from substance to style.

Jib Fowles writes about America, but virtually every word in the following description of industrialization applies with equal force to Japan.

> Over time, production and consumption became ever more sharply delineated spheres. The production and consumption which used to be commingled on the far separated into two discernible activities, signalled by their new and distinct loci in time and space. The day became exactingly sectioned into work and nonwork time; work took place apart from the home, in a building especially constructed to contain it. The autonomous factory, where no one lived by many worked, was virtually unknown before industrialisation but quickly became the standard.
>
> (Fowles 1996:31)

As David Harvey points out, the process of industrialization imposes new disciplines on the worker. The production of commodities by wage labor 'locates much of the knowledge, decisions as to technique, as well as disciplinary apparatus, outside the control of the person who actually does the work' (1990:123). Alluding to Jeremy Bentham's panopticon, a prison in which every cell is exposed to view from the guard tower in the centre, Zygmunt Bauman describes modern society as organized around two great panoptical institutions, industrial factories and conscript armies. Because of the centrality of these two institutions,

> Most male members of society could reasonably be expected to pass through their disciplining treadmill and acquire the habits that would guarantee their obedience to the order-constituting rules (and later to enforce those habits on the female members in their capacity of the 'heads of families').

> (Bauman 1999:22)

But now, he writes, the great majority of men and women are seduced instead of policed into accepting society's goals. Advertising has replaced indoctrination; need creation has begun to replace normative regulation.

> Most of us are socially and culturally trained and shaped as sensation-seekers and gatherers, rather than producers and soldiers. Constant openness to new sensations and greed for ever new experience, always stronger and deeper than before, is a condition sine qua non of being amenable to seduction.

> (Bauman 1999:24)

Here, however, the theorist's analysis begins to strain against the images that HILL research provides. There is something about that 'greed for ever new experience, always stronger and deeper than before' that clashes with images of water skippers skating nimbly over society's surfaces but never diving beneath them.

Perhaps in Ikari Tomohiko's generation, that 'burning' generation of now-graying corporate warriors, that greed was still strong. There was something of it still left in rebellious members of the New Breed who strove to construct new selves by creating new lifestyles. But the Boomers, who would never be heroes, the Juniors who prefer 'silent appeal', and now those water skippers: as in the case of modernization, once again theory imported from the West seems to miss something important in the Japanese experience.

Partly, I suspect, it's a matter of sheer intensity. When Sakaiya Taichi claims that what Japan became in the 1960s is the world's most perfect modern industrial society, the proposition is plausible precisely because Japan went further in pursuing modernization's ideals than its North American or European counterparts. Nowhere has the separation of work and home been more radical, with a workday so long that coming home to time with the family became an impossible dream for the men who found jobs as salarymen. Nowhere has the uniformity of education and the media been greater, with competition so thoroughly focused on internalizing the norms of industrial discipline.

Arguably it has been the radical depth of modernization that has shaped Japan's transition to a postmodern society where 'let me do my thing' has given way to 'love me but leave me alone'. The strongest case in point is relations between men and women. Clayton Naff captures it for us in an anecdote all the more poignant for being only slightly exaggerated.

> Off in the distance, skyscrapers reached for the clouds, defying the fatal logic of the quaking earth. All around me packs of young Japanese women promenaded in razor-edged, wasp-waisted jackets with epaulets and glinting brass buttons over miniskirts and knitted leg warmers. Some tottered on high heels that made their long, dark hair swing wide of their narrow hips as they walked. Others, with hair bobbed and curled like flappers, clopped along in high-fashion calfskin boots. Giggling, squealing, shrieking, thrusting glossy fingertips over neon-painted lips, they swarmed about in twos, threes, dozens.

> Clearly they were the ones out for a good time. The businessmen, ties askew, still in the suits they had worn to work, looked more like casualties than revelers as they stumbled homeward after a night of hard drinking. A small, red-faced man was vomiting wretchedly at the curbside not far from me. Two policemen emerged from their sidewalk police box to save him from pitching headlong into traffic.

> (Naff 1996:9–10)

It isn't hard to understand why younger Japanese women observing their older sisters' efforts to achieve successful business careers by emulating men have decided that a casual, take-it-or-leave-it approach is much to be preferred. Or, why many young men now favor feminized lifestyles that combine part-time work with absorption in personal appearance. It is hard to imagine a clearer case of consumerism transforming 'modern' ideals.

We must not forget, too, how different Japan's recent history has been from that of other advanced nations. How much does it matter, for example, that the troops who formed America's industrial armies in the 1950s returned home from a war they had won, while Japan's soldiers came home defeated and burning to win new battles on economic battlefields? How much difference does it make that virtually continuous growth in the sixties, seventies and eighties taught Japanese salarymen that going along with the organization would, indeed, have its rewards, while, in contrast, the Vietnam War and the Anti-War Movement left a generation of Americans profoundly disillusioned with the claims of organizations to sacrosanct authority? What has been the impact on organizational behavior of America's ethnic diversity compared to Japan's relative homogeneity? All are important questions that can only be raised here.

Thinking About Who We Are

In the 'Preface' to *Habits of the Heart*, Robert Bellah and his colleagues write,

How ought we to live? How do we think about how to live? Who are we as Americans? What is our character? These are questions we have asked our fellow citizens in many parts of the country. We engaged them in conversations about their lives and about what matters most to them, talked about their families and communities, their doubts and uncertainties, and their hopes and fears with respect to the larger society

(Bellah *et al.* 1985:iv).

In a very real sense, I think, HILL has done for Japan what Bellah and his colleagues have done for America. To raise moral questions and make them the subject of public debate has not, of course, been HILL researchers' primary aim. Their interest has been frankly commercial. Yet what they have done goes far beyond commerce. I would go even further and argue that, given the role of America, as conqueror, ally, trading partner, and model for late twentieth-century Japan, it is worth some effort to think through what these two sets of researchers wind up saying about their two countries.

Here we confront a serious question: No clichés are more tired than those which describe Americans as rugged individualists; and those which describe Japanese as so group-oriented that individual selves virtually cease to exist. What, then, are the alternatives?

In *The Organization Man*, William H. Whyte explicitly contrasts the organization man's group-orientation and need to belong with the rugged individualism he associates with the Protestant Ethic. Writing three decades later, Bellah and his colleagues offer a more nuanced view. Looking back at American history, they discover two classic varieties: they call them religious and republican. In both, individuals confront what they take to be ultimate objective realities: either God or the polity, the nation of which they are members. By the mid 1980s (when HILL was beginning its work in Japan), these two classic varieties of American individualism were being replaced by two new types, utilitarian and expressive.

Utilitarian individualists find success in efficient achievement of personal economic goals. Expressive individualists find success in persuasive, self-expression: the ability to understand and, thus, to stimulate change in others. The model for the one is the entrepreneur. The model for the other is the therapist. Both differ from classic individualists by pursuing self-selected goals whose value is defined subjectively.

Turning, then, to HILL research, we see none of the above. There is, to be sure, a classic quality about the Greying Corporate Warrior who sacrificed himself to achieve his society's and his company's goals. The same can be said of mothers whose self-immolation aimed to ensure their children's success. With the shift from producer to consumer that appears as early as descriptions of the Sneaker Middles' preference for selecting from a wide variety of choices over making something new for themselves, we see a parallel shift toward something that at first glance seems to resemble expressive individualism. Recall, however, the growing importance of 'silent appeal' and reports that describe Japanese children as increasingly 'neutral' in relation to both products and people. Rejection of anything pushy and a desire to live and let live are a world apart from the therapist/performer who seeks transformation in the client/audience.

Theorists discussing consumerism in the West have done much with the notion that 'Shopping is not merely the acquisition of things: it is the buying of an identity' (Clammer 1997:68). The HILL research collected in this volume persuades me that this is a time- and culture-bound idea. Applied to the New Breed, who consumed aggressively and saw in consumption a way to create selves distinct from those of older generations and of other subcultures among themselves, it appears to make sense. Applied to Baby Boomers who prefer multiple choices to making up new questions for themselves, to the young men and women in 'Living as One Thirty-Fourth' who reject the idea of becoming someone special, preferring instead a comfortably anonymous, arms-length relationship to the world, and most of all to the Amenbo Kids, those water striders who only 'snack' on the goods that industry offers, it seems to fit less well.

It is time to remember, perhaps, that aggressive consumerism is not the only alternative to selves submerged in groups and that Japanese tradition includes other paths to self-realization. In pulling together my thoughts about what HILL research tells us, I found myself drawn to the work of Japanese philosopher Yamazaki Masakazu. Yamazaki notes that Japanese have often been stereotyped.

> To make matters worse, Japanese themselves have begun to squeeze their own culture into a stereotyped framework, adamantly insisting that it is immutable. When economic issues arise, 'Japanese-style management' is proudly trotted out, with great emphasis laid on the group loyalties and cooperative spirit underlying it. Even less productively, friction over opening Japan's markets to foreign agricultural produce has been addressed with jingoistic sloganeering that touts rice as the symbol of Japanese culture and agriculture as the foundation of the nation.
>
> (Yamazaki 1994:4)

The stereotypes to which Yamazaki most strongly objects are those which see the essential Japan as permanently rooted either in agriculture or the collective identity and emotional warmth ascribed to the traditional Japanese household, the *ie*.

Yes, he agrees, it is true that 'land of vigorous rice plants' (*mizuho no kuni),* has been used as poetic metaphor to describe Japan since very ancient times. In the Edo period Japan's Tokugawa rulers did adopt the Confucian classification that ranks warrior above farmers, farmers above artisans, and artisans above merchants, positioning war and agriculture above the mechanical arts and trade. It is true to this day that many Japanese who live in cities are nostalgic for rural society and would like to see themselves as people with deep roots in the soil. 'Discursive essays on the decadence and callousness of urban life and the "insecurity of rootless grass" have even become a sort of journalistic style' (Yamazaki 1994:11).

Yamazaki points out that much of what we take to be 'typically Japanese' – tatami flooring, flower arranging, tea ceremony, Noh and Kabuki theater, for example – was invented in cities. Traditional arts embody 'a strongly urban tone, commercial and industrial spirit, and fairly high degree of individualism [that] makes them comparable to features that have characterized Western culture since the seventeenth century' (Yamazaki 1994:20).

Yamazaki is responding directly to theories epitomized by Murakami, Kumon, and Satō's *Ie Society as a Civilization* (*Bunmei toshite no Ie Shakai*, 1992). Setting up a stark contrast between Japan and other societies, proponents of these theories see the group harmony and close emotional ties ascribed to the *ie* as the polar opposite of Western individualism. The essence of Japanese social relations lies, they argue, in contextualism (*aidagara*). The Japanese individual is thus a 'relational self', with no independent grounding outside the group in which it appears.

To Yamazaki, however, the weight given to group harmony and close emotional ties in contemporary social thought is not essentially Japanese but instead a reaction to modernization and urbanization. Since the Meiji era, he writes,

> The father heading a household in the loneliness of the city, separated from the extended family of the village, had to strengthen the authoritarian side of his character to shore up the family's morale and fortify it for the struggle for survival. By the same token, the mother took on stronger features of family guardian. Both roles were products of temporary historical circumstances more than of tradition.
>
> (Yamazaki 1994:12)

But losing oneself in a pre-defined role is not the only possibility that Japanese tradition suggests.

According to Yamazaki, the shared aim of Japan's traditional arts is self-cultivation. This self-cultivation through the arts is not, however, that of modern individualism, which intrudes on others and regards them only as tools for self-expression. Neither is it groupism, 'a kind of collusion that is unconscious of others from the start'. It is, instead, 'a soft individualism that fears others even while placing them in close proximity and aims to realize the self within the context of other people's evaluation' (Yamazaki 1994:52). Neither an aggressive monad nor an emptiness submerged in a group, this Japanese self is conscious of its individuality but wary as well of what others think about it.

As I read Yamazaki, it seems to me that he and HILL are suggesting the same thing: Young Japanese are consummate consumers who prefer to enjoy their comforts while keeping others at a safe distance. They cultivate their connoisseur's skills of selecting things that suit individual tastes. Instead of public performances, the selves their habits construct are intensely private ones – and they want to keep it that way. The worker bees who labored to produce the Japanese miracle are becoming a nation of wary shoppers.

But that, we must never forget, is only this generation.

Conversation with Shōji Takashi, President and CEO of Hakuhodo Inc.

September 25, 1998

Shōji, 65, was born in 1933 in Yamagata Prefecture, where his family ran a small fermented bean paste (*miso*) business. He graduated from Tama Art University in Tokyo in 1957 and joined Hakuhodo as an art director in 1963. By 1981, he was serving on the Board of Directors and was one of the prime movers in the creation of HILL.

JLM: What was the concept behind the founding of HILL?

ST: To know the *seikatsusha*.

JLM: *Seikatsusha*? What does that mean?

ST: In Japan, it means the Japanese, but if you only understand the largest common denominator, you don't understand the Japanese. Even among the Japanese, each individual has his or her own way of life. We thought that if we looked more closely at individuals, we might see a new kind of Japanese.

JLM: In dictionaries, the word for consumer is *shōhisha*. How is a *seikatsusha* different from a *shōhisha*?

ST: A *shōhisha* is someone who consumes, in other words, someone who buys things. A *seikatsusha* is someone who has a life, even when they aren't buying things. In this respect, the concept is broader. It means 'a person with a life', who doesn't have to be buying things to be alive. In Japan we use *shōhisha* in expressions like car consumer (*kuruma no shōhisha*), food-products consumer (*shokuhin no shōhisha*), or electricity consumer (*denki no shōhisha*). In each case, people are seen from the point of view of the manufacturer who wants them to buy things.

From the electric company's point of view, a consumer of electricity is someone who buys electricity. But the consumer of electricity is also someone who takes naps or watches TV. She is the same person, but seen from a different perspective. So let's look at those connections, we thought. Let's look at the way these things fit together in an individual's life.

Or looked at another way, we wanted to look at people's lives from the inside *(uchi)* instead of the outside *(soto)*. If we look at food-products consumers, we see them from a food-products perspective. When we look at the same people as seikatsusha, we see them from an all-around perspective with them in the center. We see them from every direction, in a 360-degree view.

A man who buys a car, for example, may also want to go out with women. If we see him only as someone who buys a car, his wanting to go out with women seems beside the point. But from that individual's point of view, wanting to look good to women may have everything to do with his wanting a car in the first place. So we try to look at both at once.

JLM: You were the Director of HILL, when it was founded. How long did you hold that position?

ST: About ten years . . . . I was also on the Board of Directors of Hakuhodo. Kuramoto [who preceded Sekizawa] was in charge of day-to-day operations.

By then, Japan's economy had already experienced substantial growth; people's lives were becoming more affluent. That process had began around the Oil Shocks, yes, in the 1970s; getting by was no problem. As people became more affluent, their needs became more diverse, as is perfectly natural. During the rapid-growth period, what ordinary people wanted was very clear. With growing affluence, though, markets fragmented. They became much harder to understand. That is why we thought – as an advertising agency – that we needed a specialist unit to look into what was going on. That is why we founded HILL.

Advertising companies create links between businesses and consumers, and finding out what consumers think is part of our job. Advertising companies listen to businesses and think about how best to communicate their messages to consumers. When businesses change, they tell you what they are doing. But consumers don't; without doing research, you won't know what's going on with them. If you don't have specialists to do the studies, you won't know accurately how best to communicate with them. If you don't understand consumers, you can only perform half of an advertising company's role. To create ties between people, you need to know both sides.

When we set up HILL, we thought of ourselves as the company's intelligence service. HILL researchers would find out what was happening among consumers and feed back their discoveries to Hakuhodo. Hakuhodo would use what they found as a weapon, to communicate more effectively.

JLM: Was there some special reason for setting up HILL as a research institute independent of Hakuhodo?

ST: Partly it was because I didn't have much power back then. If HILL were a part of Hakuhodo, it would always have to give priority to Hakuhodo's needs. It would be asked to help out directly with on-going projects and become only another tool to increase profitability. I didn't want it prostituted like that. It was better to have it providing pure and uncontaminated feedback about what consumers were thinking. Only in that way could it really be useful. If HILL were only asking the questions that clients wanted asked, it wouldn't be performing its mission of understanding all aspects of Japanese lifestyles. Setting up a separate company, with a third-party point of view, kept it free of entanglements. It would thus be able to look at things objectively. It wouldn't be a matter of 'We're paying the bills, so shut up' (laughs).

JLM: Now you are president of Hakuhodo. Looking back at that original concept, do you think that HILL has been a success?

ST: Yes, I think it's been quite successful. Of course, as president, I wouldn't mind seeing the quality of HILL reports get even better (laughs). But the way that HILL is positioned is fine.

JLM: Changing the subject a bit, as you see it, how has Japanese society changed since HILL was founded in 1981?

ST: As society reaches a higher level, individual lifestyles become more diverse. That results in growing individualism. But while Japanese have become more individualistic, our individualism is more dependent (*amaete-iru*) than American or European individualism. Thus, if we can focus on the individuals who are making the biggest difference, we can see how society as a whole is changing.

Yes, individualism is the single biggest change. But taken as a whole, Japanese are very passive. We've become more individualistic without becoming more independent.

JLM: Are we talking about Professor Yamazaki's 'soft individualism'?

ST: His is a generous interpretation. What I am talking about is worthless individualism (*dame na kojinshugi*). It's merely doing whatever you like without taking responsibility.

JLM: Is that why I heard you say a few months ago, at the HILL retreat, that Japan needs to tear down its hothouse?

ST: Precisely. If companies would stop acting like hothouses, the way that Japanese have turned into hothouse plants would change. But most people still haven't noticed that. That is why they always say, 'Politics is to blame', 'Somebody else is to blame', anything but 'It's my own responsibility'.

JLM: There was that *Warning Bell from the Year 2020* series last year in the Nikkei. It seemed to be saying that the Greying Corporate Warrior generation had a mission and a real passion. They were going to overcome the West. As I see it, they succeeded. The problem is that later generations haven't found another goal, another vision.

ST: That is because of the hothouse. If they hadn't grown up in a hothouse, we would see something new by now. For the individual, living in a hothouse can be very comfortable. But new things are created only when people overcome difficulties, when they have to suffer a bit. Now people don't see themselves as confronted by problems that they themselves have to overcome. They expect someone else to solve those problems for them. That is why, as I said before, their individualism doesn't imply independence. It's too passive.

Recently, however, that passivity has begun to be shaken a little. If it's shaken a little more, Japanese will begin to work a bit harder again. Then we will see things start to happen. So I'm not too worried.

It wasn't very long ago, was it, that Americans seemed to be stuck. Things come and go in cycles. When things are too easy, people get lazy. When they get a little tougher, they start to work harder. At this point, the Japanese have lost that motivation. But if the environment changes, we can get moving again.

JLM: What about Sakaiya Taichi's idea that Japan, having radically transformed itself during the Meiji Restoration, can do it again?

ST: That would be very difficult. The urgency that people feel now is nothing like as intense as the urgency that drove the Meiji Restoration. That was at least a hundred times stronger. There was real fear that Japan was doomed. That is why so many strong figures emerged and made the Restoration happen. Whether the changes were good or bad, I can't say. Some of them led to war. In the same way, Japan changed after World War II. Japan had lost that war. Then, too, people felt their lives at risk and threw themselves into the struggle. But that was the Meiji Restoration and postwar recovery. The danger that people feel now is nothing like that. If things change now, they are going to change more slowly. They will, however, change.

REFERENCES

Allison, Anne (1994) *Nightwork: Sexuality, Pleasure, and Corporate Masculinity in a Tokyo Hostess Club*, Chicago: University of Chicago Press.

—— (1996) *Permitted & Prohibited Desires: Mothers, Comics, and Censorship in Japan*, Boulder, Colorado: Westview Press.

Asada Akira (1983) *Kōzō to Chikara: kigōron o koete* (Structure and Power: Beyond semiotics), Tokyo: Keizō Shobō.

Bachnik, Jane and Charles J. Quinn, Jr. (1994) *Situated Meaning: Inside and Outside in Japanese Self, Society, and Language,* Princeton: Princeton University Press.

Bauman, Zygmunt (1999), 'On postmodern uses of sex', *Theory, Culture and Society*, 15 (3–4) pp. 19–33.

Bellah, Robert N., et al. (1985) *Habits of the Heart: Individualism and Commitment in American Life,* New York: Harper & Row.

Benedict, Ruth (1946) *The Chrysanthemum and the Sword: Patterns of Japanese Culture*, New York: The World Publishing Company.

Bestor, Theodore C. (1989) *Neighborhood Tokyo,* Stanford: Stanford University Press.

Clammer, John (1997) *Contemporary Urban Japan: A Sociology of Consumption,* Oxford: Blackwell.

Douglas, Mike (1993) 'The "new" Tokyo story: restructuring space and the struggle for place in a world city', in K. Fujita and R.C. Hill (eds) *Japanese Cities in the World Economy,* Philadelphia: Temple University Press.

Drucker, Peter (1997) 'The future that has already happened', *Harvard Business Review,* September–October, pp. 20–24.

Fields, George (1989) *Gucci on the Ginza: Japan's new consumer generation*, Tokyo: Kodansha International.

Fowles, Jib (1996) *Advertising and Popular Culture*, Thousand Oaks: Sage.

Fujimura-Fanselow, Kumiko (1995) 'Introduction', in K. Fujimura-Fanselow and A. Kameda (eds) *Japanese Women: New Feminist Perspectives on the Past, Present, and Future,* New York: The Feminist Press, pp. xvii–xxxviii.

Fujimura-Fanselow, Kumiko, and Atsuko Kameda (eds) (1995) *Japanese Women: New Feminist Perspectives on the Past, Present, and Future,* New York: The Feminist Press.

Fujita Kuniko and Richard Child Hill (eds) (1993) *Japanese Cities in the World Economy,* Philadelphia: Temple University Press.

Garon, Sheldon (1997) *Molding Japanese Minds: The State in Everyday Life,* Princeton: Princeton University Press.

Geertz, Clifford (1973) *Interpretation of Cultures*, New York: Basic Books.

Gibson, William (1995) *Neuromancer,* New York: Ace Books.

269

REFERENCES

Hara Kimi (1995) 'Challenges to education for girls and women in modern Japan: past and present', in K. Fujimura-Fanselow and A. Kameda (eds) *Japanese Women: New Feminist Perspectives on the Past, Present, and Future*, New York: The Feminist Press, pp. 93–106.

Harada Yutaka (1998) *1970 Nen Taisei no Shūen* (The End of the 1970s System), Tokyo: Tōyō Keizai Shimpōsha.

Harvey, David (1990) *The Condition of Postmodernity*, Oxford: Blackwell.

Harvey, Paul A.S. (1995) 'Interpreting Oshin: war, history and women in modern Japan', in L. Skov and B. Moeran (eds) *Women, Media and Consumption in Japan*, Honolulu: University of Hawaii Press, pp. 75–110.

Helgesen, Sally (1998) *Everyday Revolutionaries: Working Women and the Transformation of American Life*, New York: Doubleday.

Hendry, Joy (1981) *Marriage in Changing Japan*, Tokyo: Charles E. Tuttle.

—— (1993) *Wrapping Culture: Politeness, Presentation, and Power in Japan and Other Societies*, Oxford: Clarendon Press.

HILL (1981) 'Mental maps', *Lifestyle Times* No. 7, January.

—— (1991) *Japanese Salariimen at the Crossroads: Changing Lifestyles in Japan 6*, Tokyo: Hakuhodo Institute of Life and Living.

—— (1994) *Gokan no Jidai* (The Age of the Five Senses), Tokyo: President.

Hosokawa, Shūhei (1997) Personal Communication.

Ivy, Marilyn (1989) 'Critical texts, mass artifacts: the consumption of knowledge in postmodern Japan', in M. Miyoshi and H.D. Harootunian (eds) *Postmodernism and Japan*, Durham: Duke University Press, pp. 21–46.

—— (1995) *Discourses of the Vanishing: Modernity, Phantasm, Japan*, Chicago: University of Chicago Press.

Jinnai Hidenobu (1995) *Tokyo: A Spatial Anthropology* (translated by Kimiko Nishimura), Berkeley: University of California Press.

Johnson, Chalmers (1995) *Japan: Who Governs? The Rise of the Developmental State*, New York: W.W. Norton.

Kaneko Sachiko (1995) 'The struggle for legal rights and reforms; a historical view', in K. Fujimura-Fanselow and A. Kameda (eds) *Japanese Women: New Feminist Perspectives on the Past, Present, and Future*, New York: The Feminist Press, pp. 3–14.

Katz, Richard (1998) *The System That Soured: The Rise and Fall of the Japanese Economic Miracle*, Armonk, NY: M.E. Sharpe.

Kawashima Yoko (1995) 'Female workers: an overview of past and current trends', in K. Fujimura-Fanselow and A. Kameda (eds) *Japanese Women: New Feminist Perspectives on the Past, Present, and Future*, New York: The Feminist Press, pp. 271–294.

Kelly, William W. (1992) 'Tractors, television, and telephones: reach out and touch someone in rural Japan', in J.J. Tobin (ed.) *Re-Made in Japan: Everyday Life and Consumer Taste in a Changing Society*, New Haven: Yale University Press, pp. 77–88.

Koestler, Arthur, and J.R. Smythies (1969) *Beyond Reductionism: New Perspectives in the Life Sciences*, London: Hutchinson.

Kondo, Dorinne K. (1990) *Crafting Selves: Power, Gender and Identity in a Japanese Workplace*, Chicago: Chicago University Press.

Kōseishō (1997) *Kōsei Hakusho* (Health and Welfare White Paper), Tokyo: Gyōsei.

Kusaka Kimondo (1997) *Kore Kara no 10 Nen* (The Next Ten Years), Tokyo: PHP.

Lynch, Kevin (1960) *The Image of the City*, Cambridge: The MIT Press.

McCracken, Grant (1990) *Culture & Consumption: New Approaches to the Symbolic Character of Consumer Goods and Activities*, Bloomington: Indiana University Press.

Miyoshi, Masao, and H.D. Harootunian (eds) (1989) *Postmodernism and Japan*, Durham: Duke University Press.

270

REFERENCES

Morikawa Hidemasa (1992) *Zaibatsu: The Rise and Fall of Family Enterprise Groups in Japan*, Tokyo: University of Tokyo Press.

Murakami Yoshiaki, et al. (1979) *Bunmei toshite no Ie Shakai* (*Ie* Society as a Civilization), Tokyo: Chūō Kōronsha.

Muramoto Kuniko (1997) *Shiawase Kazoku to iu Uso: Musume ga Chichi to Kotaru Toki* (The Lie Called a Happy Family: When a Daughter Talks with her Father), Osaka: Sōgensha.

Naff, Clayton (1996) *About Face: How I Stumbled onto Japan's Social Revolution*, Tokyo: Kodansha International.

Najita, Tetsuo (1989) 'On culture and technology in postmodern Japan', in M. Miyoshi and H.D. Harootunian (eds) *Postmodernism and Japan,* Durham: Duke University Press, pp. 3–20.

Nakamura Takafusa (1995) *The Postwar Japanese Economy: Its Development and Structure, 1937–1994*, Tokyo: University of Tokyo Press.

Nakane Chie (1970) *Japanese Society*, Berkeley: University of California Press.

Nihon Keizai Shimbunsha (ed.)1997 *2020 Nen Kara no Keishshō* (Warning Bell From the Year 2020), Tokyo: Nihon Keizai Shimbunsha.

Noguchi, Paul H. (1990) *Delayed Departures, Overdue Arrivals: Industrial Familialism and the Japanese National Railways,* Honolulu: University of Hawaii Press.

Noguchi, Yukio (1995) *1940 Nen Taisei* (The 1940s System), Tokyo: Tōyō Keizai Shinpōsha.

Ohmae, Kenichi (1997) *Jidai no Kōtai, Sedai no Kōtai* (Times Change, Generations Change), Tokyo: PHP.

Ōtomo, Atsushi (1996) *Nihon no Jinkō Idō* (Japanese Population Trends), Tokyo: Ōkurashō.

Painter, Andrew A. (1996) 'Japanese daytime television, popular culture and ideology', in J.W. Treat (ed.) *Contemporary Japan and Popular Culture,* Honolulu: University of Hawaii Press, pp. 197–234.

Pempel, T.J. (1998) *Regime Shift: Comparative Dynamics of the Japanese Political Economy,* Ithaca: Cornell University Press.

Plath, David W. (1980) *Long Engagements: Maturity in Modern Japan,* Stanford: Stanford University Press.

Prime Minister's Office (1996) *Seishōnen Hakusho* (Youth White Paper), Tokyo: Ministry of Finance Printing Bureau.

Sakaiya, Taichi (1997) *Tsugi wa Kō Naru* (What Comes Next), Tokyo: Kodansha.

—— (1998) *Arubeki Ashita* (The Tomorrow We Ought to Seek), Tokyo: PHP.

Sakurai Joji (1998) 'Tradition is no longer enough to prevent divorce', *Japan Times,* January 26.

Sampson, Anthony (1995) *Company Man: The Rise and Fall of Corporate Life,* New York: Random House.

Sekizawa Hidehiko, et al. (forthcoming) *Rōnen Bunka Ron* (Discourses on the Culture of the Aged), Tokyo: Iwanami Shoten.

Schilling, Mark (1997) *The Encyclopedia of Japanese Pop Culture,* New York: Weatherhill.

Sherry, John F., Jr. (1995) *Contemporary Marketing and Consumer Behavior: An Anthropological Sourcebook,* Thousand Oaks: Sage Publications.

Skov, Lise and Brian Moeran (1995) 'Introduction: hiding in the light: from Oshin to Yoshimoto Banana', in L. Skov and B. Moeran (eds) *Women, Media and Consumption in Japan,* Honolulu: University of Hawaii Press, pp. 1–74.

Smith, Robert J. (1983) *Japanese Society: Tradition, Self and the Social Order,* Cambridge: Cambridge University Press.

Tanaka Yasuo (1981) *Nantonaku, Kuristaru* (Something Crystal), Tokyo: Kawade Shobō.

REFERENCES

Tobin, Joseph J. (1992) *Re-Made in Japan: Everyday Life and Consumer Taste in a Changing Society,* New Haven: Yale University Press.

Tomiie Emiko and Ōzawa Hideko (1997) 'Koka no susumu kazoku to kazoku suru shōhi' (The individualizing family and family-making consumption), in *Brain,* 37 (6), pp. 5–12.

Treat, John Whittier (1996) 'Introduction', in J.W. Treat (ed.), *Contemporary Japan and Popular Culture,* Honolulu: University of Hawaii Press, pp. 1–14.

Tsuru Shigeto (1994) *Japanese Capitalism: Creative Defeat and Beyond,* Cambridge: Cambridge University Press.

Vogel, Ezra F. (1963) *Japan's New Middle Class: The Salary Man and His Family in a Tokyo Suburb,* Berkeley: University of California Press.

Whyte, William H. (1961) *The Organization Man,* London: Penguin Books.

Wilkie, William L. (1994) *Consumer Behavior,* New York: John Wiley & Sons.

Williams, David (1996) *Japan and the Enemies of Open Political Science,* London: Routledge.

Yamazaki Masakazu (1994) *Individualism and the Japanese: An Alternative Approach to Cultural Comparison,* Tokyo: Japan Echo.

Zimmerman, Mark (1985) *How to Do Business with the Japanese: A Strategy for Success,* Tokyo: Charles E. Tuttle.

Zora, Marion (1981) *All the Great Ones Are Married,* New York: Times Books.

INDEX